SEND IT

Canada's Snipers at War in Afghanistan

Library and Archives Canada Cataloguing in Publication
Cullen, Gordon, author
Nisbet, Barry C., author
Bahmanyar, Mir, author
Send It/Gordon Cullen, Barry C. Nisbet & Mir Bahmanyar

Issued in print and electronic formats.

ISBN: 978-1-998501-57-1 (paperback)
ISBN: 978-1-998501-58-8 (ebook)

Cover Design: Axel Peralta
Interior Design: Richa Bargotra

Double Dagger Books
Toronto, Ontario, Canada
www.doubledagger.ca

SEND IT

Canada's Snipers at War in Afghanistan

By

Gordon Cullen & Barry C Nisbet with
Mir Bahmanyar

"There is no hunting like the hunting of man, and those who have hunted armed men long enough and liked it, never care for anything else thereafter."

– Ernest Hemingway

Glossary

2IC	second-in-command
ANA	Afghan National Army
AO	area of operations
AOR	area of responsibility
ATB	appears to be
ATV	all-terrain vehicle
BG	battle group
blue on blue	friendly fire incident
CADPAT	Canadian Disruptive Pattern
CAF	Canadian Armed Forces
CCB	clean cold bore
CFB	Canadian Forces Base
CO	commanding officer
COA	courses of action
COP	combat outpost
CP	command post
CSM	Company Sergeant-Major
CSOR	Canadian Special Operations Regiment
CSS	combat service support

DAGR	Defense Advanced GPS Receiver
DD	determining distance
det	detachment
DOPE	data on previous engagements
ELR	extreme/ extended long range
en	enemy
EW	Electronic Warfare
FAM	fighting-age male
FFP	final firing position
FML	fuck my life
HLTA	Home Leave Travel Assistance
HME	homemade explosive
IED	improvised explosive device
IFF	identification friend or foe
IMP	individual meal pack
INS	insurgent/s
IOT	in order to
IPSC	International Peacekeeping and Security Center
IR	infrared
ISTAR	intelligence surveillance target acquisition and reconnaissance
IVCP	illegal vehicle control point
JDAM	Joint Direct Attack Munition
JTAC	Joint Terminal Attack Controller
KAF	Kandahar Airfield
KLA	Kosovo Liberation Army

LAV	light armoured vehicle
LMG/ GPMG	light/ general-purpose machine gun
LRSWS	Long-Range Sniper Weapon System
LZ	landing zone
MCpl	Master Corporal
MRSWS	Medium-Range Sniper Rifle System
MSR	main supply route
NATO	North Atlantic Treaty Organization
NOD	night optical device
NVG	night vision goggles
O group	orders group
OC	officer commanding
ODA	Operational Detachment-A (Green Berets)
OOM	order of movement
OP	observation post
OPP	Ontario Provincial Police
ORV	objective rendezvous
PB	patrol base
PID	positive identification
PLO	Platoon Warrant Officer
POL	pattern of life
POO	point of origin
PPCLI	Princess Patricia's Canadian Light Infantry
PRR	Personal Role Radio
PRS	Precision Rifle Series
PWT	Personal Weapons Test

QRF	quick reaction force
R22eR	Royal 22nd Regiment
RCD	Royal Canadian Dragoons
RCMP	Royal Canadian Mounted Police
RCR	Royal Canadian Regiment
RI	Ranger Instructor
RIP	relief in place
RTU	return to unit
SA	situational awareness
SD	standard deviation
SLR (camera)	single-lens reflex (camera)
SOF	Special Operations Forces
SOFLAM	Special Operations Forces Laser Acquisition Marker
SOP	standard operating procedure
TBI	traumatic brain injury
TI	Tactical Infrastructure
TIC	troops in contact
TOC	tactical operations centre
TOW	Tube-launched, Optically tracked, Wire-guided
UAV	unmanned aerial vehicle (drone)
UMS	Unit Master Sniper
VCP	vehicle control point
W/O	Warrant Officer

Preface

Send It: Canada's Snipers at War in Afghanistan was not written by a ghostwriter or a novelist to glorify or aggrandize a mission or two. Instead, it was primarily written by a few snipers about their training as world-class shooters and applications of their skills in real-world scenarios. In Afghanistan, Canadian snipers earned an outstanding reputation and have worked closely with JTF 2, Canada's premier special operations unit, American Green Berets and JTACs, the U.S. Air Force's joint terminal attack controllers, and others.

The idea for the book started many years ago. Unit Master Sniper (UMS) Gordon Cullen was recommended to me by a former Navy SEAL. Gord, later the Sniper Program Manager for Special Operations, and I stayed in touch throughout the long, arduous journey of getting *Send It* done. He introduced me to other snipers and also asked me to watch some Canuck spec ops guy's parachute. Thanks Gord. Along the way I made good friends.

After receiving permission from the green machine in 2016, I visited with the Royal Canadian Regiment snipers under Unit Master Snipers (UMS) Rick Burnette, Greg Lightle and Curtis Allaby, as well as MCpl J.K.M. Hogan at Garrison Petawawa in Ontario. The original intent was to author those experiences, but it became clear I was not qualified to do so accurately. Therefore, I asked a few of the veterans if they wanted to write their own stories and fortunately some did. The book is superior because of it. It is limited to the RCR but hopefully it translates well to the experiences shared with their sniper peers in the armed forces. I apologize to the young snipers for not writing about them as was originally intended.

I want to thank all the authors, and the snipers who did not write a chapter, for their time and patience. Some preferred privacy or were subsumed by life. In the end we have a very special book on Canada's snipers in training and at war in Afghanistan. *Send It* is part technical manual, including theories of sniping and tools of the trade, and part practical real-world applications on the battlefield. We also witness the transition from peacekeeping in Eastern Europe to warfighting. It chronicles the changes of the sniper program as it adapted to the new, mostly urban, recruits. An appendix with several after-action reports and other records is included. It is a unique look into the theory and practice of Canadian snipers. It is also a tribute.

—Mir Bahmanyar

Salawat Ghar, Afghanistan 2010

It was now up to Dee. His breathing was slow and deep, waiting to be two-thirds exhaled—then he'd squeeze the trigger. It would be a bit of a surprise when it went off.

"Stand by," Dee whispered as he ex-haled.

Nisbet focused in on the soon-to-be-dead man. "Send it." This was their language. They had uttered it thousands of times during their sniper training. It was instinctual. If there was a better phrase in the English language, Nisbet had yet to hear it.

Three pounds of pressure exerted on the trigger was all it took. The firing pin snapped forward, indenting the primer, igniting the precisely measured powder in the cartridge and starting the 250-grain 338 calibre bullet in motion. The right-hand twist of the lands and grooves of the barrel turning the bullet as it sped its way down the barrel. The spin added to the bullet's stability, accuracy and penetration. The gases from the ignition of the powder were trapped by the baffles within the suppressor as the bullet exited. The bullet was now free of its cage and had only to defeat the grip of gravity as it hurtled towards the man in blue. The right-hand twist of the round produced a slight amount of spin drift to the right at 600 metres. The fall of the round was minimal as it cut through the morning air at over 3,000 feet per second. It was over in less than half a second.

Introduction

Warrant Officer Gordon Cullen

I have always had a passion for sniping; that doesn't mean I was any good at it, but every aspect of it intrigued me and motivated me to learn more and expand my understanding of it. I will preface all this by first saying that my experiences and opportunities were not common: my path was particularly lucky, and I was fortunate to have had the timing that I did. I completed the Basic Sniper Course in 1999. I was extremely fortunate to have had a staff of very competent snipers but, more important, craftsmen who wanted to pass on the torch of their trade. All too often we see "badge protectors", members qualified in the trade, who think it is up to their judgment and not the abilities of the candidate to decide who passes or fails. These badge protectors are usually the reason we get stuck in dogmatic practices and feel the pinch of the low manning within our communities. I'll give a quick shoutout to my mentors, Len, Joe, Dave, Bruce and Mike. Your examples of how to guide and enable a candidate stuck with me my entire career. Upon graduation, I moved from Recce Platoon into the Sniper Group. My first UMS was Bruce, a very intense and accomplished individual on loan from Joint Task Force 2 (JTF 2). He would lay the foundation for me and provide the example of how to train, lead and mentor snipers. During this era in my growth, I had the opportunity to work with JTF 2 snipers, attend the FBI Observer and Sniper in Service Course (another shoutout to Special Agent Glen S., great instructor), and attend the Canadian Forces Small Arms Competition (CFSAC) and Canadian International Sniper Concentration (CISC). I gleaned as much as I could from every encounter, regardless of whether it was police snipers, Rangers, Irish Defence Force, our brothers from R22eR (Royal 22nd Regiment), PPCLI (Princess Patricia's Canadian Light Infantry) or OPP (Ontario Provincial Police). We all did some things the same, but the things we didn't intrigued me, and I tried to exploit every opportunity to ensure my understanding of sniper operations was holistic.

The two biggest learning events of this timeframe were the riots in Mitrovica, Kosovo, where we had the opportunity to work with the Royal Green Jackets from the UK and the French Marines, and my deployment exercise to Camp Lejeune where we had the opportunity to work with the Marine Scout Snipers. At each evolution I learned more and became more invested. I attended more competitions, taught on several Basic Sniper courses and deployed on my first tour to Afghanistan in 2003. Post-Roto 0 my eyes were opened to war. I had completed the Sniper Detachment Command Course and became more practised in understanding sniper operations. While teaching on a Basic Sniper Course in 2004, one of the candidates committed suicide—he was in line to top the course. His reasons were personal not professional, and I will respect him as a warrior by not expanding more. Due to this, we ended up restarting the course in Fort Benning, running our Canadian course out of the U.S. Army Sniper School. During my two months there

I was able to learn a lot from the guys there. They ran a more condensed course but a quality program none the less. For some of the U.S. units the schoolhouse provided the steppingstone to more advanced or unit-specific sniper training. Upon our return, I was moved into the position of Master Sniper and attended the Advance Sniper Course with Jody and Jim. I genuinely enjoyed all that the course offered with regards to planning training but, more important, planning sniper operations. I was able to finish as the top candidate amongst a very accomplished group of seasoned snipers.

From here, 2006, I deployed to Afghanistan as the UMS, returned and conducted more training and more courses. Due to the "importance" of our capability in that theatre, the powers that be decided that the position of the UMS should be upgraded from sergeant to warrant officer. Luckily—I told you timing—I had just finished my DP3B (Infantry Warrant Course), was promoted and left in the position of UMS for the tour in 2010. Those years seem like a blur of training, getting better, qualifying more snipers, training, getting better and deploying. During those tours I had the opportunity to work with our JTF 2 snipers again, two Operational Detachment-A (ODA, i.e., Green Berets) teams, members from what we called the Trident Group and Canadian Special Operations Regiment (CSOR) snipers, some of whom I put through their basic course much like the U.S. Army Sniper School before conducting Special Operations Forces (SOF) sniper training.

Although I occupied several operations positions after my 2010 deployment, I never lost interest or focus on the Canadian Sniper Program. I attended the writing board to update the training pam (pamphlet) and qualification standard for the

Detachment Commander and Advance Sniper Course, getting to put some personal input on "the duties of a Master Sniper". While on a two-year posting to Thunder Bay with the Lake Superior Scottish, a truly great Primary Reserve Unit, I also had the opportunity to work with the North West Ontario OPP ERT (Emergency Response Team) team, providing information and assistance with camouflage and concealment in Urban and Rural Operations. This timeframe also saw the completion and release of *Hyena Road*, a project I had the opportunity to work with Paul Gross, providing the sniper content to his production.

In 2016 I was asked by a good friend to help rewrite the CSOR Sniper Training Manual. It was this interaction that set the conditions for my latter employment, in a support role, as the CSOR Sniper Program Manager. I had the opportunity to be the first in the role, looking at new weapons systems, capabilities, assisting with the first CSOR Sniper Course and watching their program take massive leaps into excellence. I am super-partial to Canadian snipers, the top of their trade and masters of the craft, but the guys in the CSOR Sniper Group were rock stars. This was the only time during my career I felt a little, well, old. It is probably why I chose at this point in my career to retire. That torch had been passed; as a matter of fact, a sprinter ran past me grabbing it, almost extinguishing it, until I saw it again burning brighter than ever in someone else's hands.

So, like I said, my journey was not a common path. I taught on seven Basic Sniper courses and two CSOR Sniper courses. I assisted with change and evolution with both regular and SOF sniper training. I had the opportunity to work with the world's greatest from Canada and internationally, deployed four times as a sniper, three of those to Afghanistan and two as the UMS.

Specific to my sniper employment I received a JTF Afghanistan Commendation, Commander CEFCOM Commendation, Commander-in-Chief Commendation as part of Operation *Medusa* and a Meritorious Service Medal (MSM). I passed my final exam while cutting my teeth in Afghanistan; I don't believe there is a spectrum a sniper could be exposed to that I haven't experienced. All in all, I spent almost 20 years with snipers. The evolution of technology, ballistics, weapons systems and tactics is staggering. I know where it is going, and I am proud to know that it is in the most capable of hands.

When first introduced to the idea of *Send It*, I was hesitant. Canadian snipers are a close bunch, and we have a strong history of excellence that we surprisingly don't tend to boast about. Let the records speak for themselves, yes, but perhaps it was time to have a conversation about it. Perhaps we are at a time where being proud of our accomplishments, stories and history is required. Talking with Mir and learning about his literary lineage was critical to building the confidence to open up and talk freely about my experiences and introduce him to the culture. His dedication to history and, most important, ensuring the legitimacy of his pages provided the confidence to be open about my story as a Canadian sniper. Mir has a strong background in military operations and was able to provide incredible guidance and friendship throughout the process.

Aside from all this, there are several personal reasons why I wanted to share what I had experienced in my military career as a soldier and sniper. In the early stages of writing, I found the words hard to find, many of them buried deep in what I will later refer to as my compartmentalized mind. I had organized them into depths of experience and comprehension that I liked to draw on in good times and bad. Voluntarily pulling some of these experiences from this place brought a lot of emotion and judgment that I had not subjected myself to in quite a number of years. I'm not going to paint it as a freeing experience. There were times when I just wanted to stop; I was conflicted. Like many of us I thought I had dealt with the overwhelming emotions that were tied to some memories. Putting words down for someone else's scrutiny made me a bit defensive and sometimes argumentative, the latter more with myself than Mir. However, as the process moved forward, I found the sharing or storytelling therapeutic. It gave me an avenue to share without really impacting anyone else's day.

Another motivation for participating in this venture was to try and reinvigorate the pride that I felt as a sniper in the Canadian Armed Forces. Perhaps one or two young readers will get something out of the pages in this book and find the motivation to want to be a Canadian sniper, show up at the recruiting office and state, "I want to be a sniper in the Canadian Armed Forces." Honestly, don't do that, the recruiter will probably just let you know about the obstacles that lay in front of you. No fault of their own, they just don't know. Perhaps one or two of them will read these passages too and give a "Fuck ya, let's do it." I unfortunately was asked if I liked camping. Perhaps one or two of the young soldiers doing locker security in the lines will read this and want a bit more, to see what is out there. Regardless, perhaps sharing my highs and lows will invigorate the curiosity of Canadians to want to learn more. We do what we do as professional soldiers for Canada and Canadians. Our successes are yours and our accomplishments should be shared by all in support of a strong Canada.

In these pages you will find events that went really well and others that went really wrong. They happened to real people. They have elements of humour, intensity and sadness. The words throughout are mine, my opinions based on my knowledge and experiences. They aren't for everyone, but you won't know until you get to the end. In several places, you will find where descriptions or explanations are left open ended. I hope these instances cause you to want more and continue to research on your own, further expanding your knowledge on snipers and their craft.

We as former and serving military can be incredibly critical of what we do when described by other people. My hope is that you can relate or recollect experiences that shaped you as soldiers as some of these were critical in my growth and understanding.

One of the topics that I did not bring up in this book is family. I am fortunate to have had two families: the military and my wife and kids. In some instances, I feel like I gave to one while taking from the other. Sacrifice, not an easy topic, is one that I will keep in that brain of mine. I gave everything I could to my military family while deployed: I would put myself in harm's way, I would be that sounding board when shit needed to be said, I would lead when it was time and follow when that was more important. My wife and kids felt sacrifice by allowing me the support I needed, to be the person who could lead and make difficult decisions, in some cases with other people's lives. They are brave and stronger than anyone else I know. Who on a normal day gets a phone call from their husband on a Sat phone in Afghanistan telling them, in veiled speech, that he doesn't know if he is getting out of this one. Who does that and carries on caring for two young children, goes off to work and supports their husband's career? Who does this time after time, deployment after deployment? Heroes, that's who, the bravest and most resilient people I know. They have heard all my stories; they know the good and the bad. For them I hope they see how amazing they are and how I could only be here to write these words because they know sacrifice and resilience. It would be ridiculous to say that the military brought me home—they provided the transportation—but it was my family that gave me the strength.

I hope that everyone gets something out of these pages, even if it only creates discussion.

To all, I hope you can find your calm, that space inside where you can operate, to provide clarity but not detachment, focus without being overwhelmed, an understanding without emotion … stillness.

PART ONE

Becoming

1

The Journey

Corporal Gordon Cullen
1st Battalion, Royal Canadian Regiment
CFB Petawawa

Arriving at the battalion, having just completed a fairly challenging Basic and Battle School, I still had really no idea what it meant to be in an infantry unit. All the things I knew were like reading an outline to a field manual. I was in the Duke's Company of 1RCR (Royal Canadian Regiment), the right of the line for the regiment, formationally speaking. Also contained within our lines were Bravo, Charlie, Echo and Foxtrot companies. Bravo and Charlie were just like us, mechanized infantry companies with undermanned platoons working at breakneck pace for no real obvious purpose. Echo contained all the enablers: mortars, pioneers, anti-armour, and recce platoons. These groupings would be a mystery to me for a couple years to come. Foxtrot held all the support elements, primarily focused on the battalion's ability to move and maintain its equipment.

Working in the Duke's Company as a private soldier was very basic. Show up on time, in the right dress, ready to do whatever was going to be asked of you. Stay fit and focused and your life was easy. Operating in this mindset was very easy, but not always rewarding. This is when I started looking down the breezeway and wondered what all those other doors held behind them. So, I started asking my supervisors questions. What does Mortar Platoon do? What does Anti-Armour or TOW (Tube-launched, Optically tracked, Wire-guided) Platoon do? What is a pioneer and what does a platoon of them do? What does Recce mean and what do they do? After getting a basic breakdown of each, my interest was piqued. Now the biggest hurdle was how to get chosen for one of these courses, so I'd have a chance of getting picked for one of these platoons. I was fortunate to have a section commander who was a former member of TOW Platoon. I expressed my interest in Recce and TOW, to which he replied, "Forget about Recce, you are too junior." Too junior? I am 25 years old; having joined later than most, I was already older than most privates in the company. "You don't have enough time in the unit to be considered for the Recce Course."

Not satisfied but understanding my place in the pecking order of the company I accepted my place. So, after a tour to Bosnia in '95, I requested to be placed on the TOW course. Success. I was course-loaded and finished second. This strong performance secured a position in the TOW Platoon and a foot in the door of Echo Company. Now I would to be able to see behind those doors. TOW Platoon focused on tank hunting. This aspect of closing with and destroying armour in small, well-meshed detachments was very appealing.

But the question remained: what do the other platoons do? Pioneers seemed interesting: big burly infanteers (infantryman) who filled the combat engineer role in the battalion. From my still-very-junior viewpoint, these bearded monsters had built things that helped the battalion get across obstacles and blew up things that blocked the battalion from getting places. Mortar Platoon provided the battalion with an imbedded indirect fire support group. They launched mortar bombs on the objective to allow the rifle companies to advance onto the position or covered their withdrawal. Recce Platoon provided the battalion with a reconnaissance ability. They defined objectives, led units onto attack positions, laid up in OPs (observation posts) and were masters of fieldcraft.

Of course, after a year and another tour to Bosnia with TOW, I would have a more in-depth view of each and expand upon my first impressions of Echo Company. While deployed in Bosnia, I had the opportunity to interact with one of the Recce Platoon detachment commanders. His knowledge and understanding of all things infantry impressed me and drew me to the conclusion that I needed to be in Recce Platoon. I wanted to be in a detachment of highly skilled infanteers who could project further into the bad guys' area and get closer to them than any other enabler, who could move undetected through any terrain and provide in-depth information on the bad guys using some of the unit's most advanced kit. Upon returning from deployment, I petitioned my Platoon Warrant Officer to get a position on the next recce course. Luckily, I had performed well in TOW Platoon, and he was being posted over to Recce as the Platoon Warrant. He told me that the course wasn't going to be easy and that it was going to be very competitive. Recce

Platoon only ever took the best. Now I finally understood why I had been too junior before: I'd had no understanding of what the role of a rifle company was in a mechanized or light role, nor did I know what other enabler roles were in the battalion and how they contributed to the fight. Having been on several exercises and deployments, I now had a much stronger understanding of what all of this meant.

The Platoon Warrant was right: the course was balls. We ran faster, rucked further and pushed past levels of exhaustion that I didn't know existed. We navigated across unimaginably shitty terrain under very strict timelines, evaded dogs, set up observation posts that were undetectable to the human eye and lived in them for extended periods. We understood and were tested on all the operations a battalion undertook in all phases of war and understood what the role of a recce platoon was throughout it. After a gruelling two months, I managed to top the course and was successful in gaining a position in the platoon. Now I was at the top of the trade, a reconnaissance soldier.

Nope.

On my first battalion-level exercise with Recce Platoon, I was introduced to the top of the trade. We were at a rendezvous (RV) point waiting to move forward into a vantage point to gain info on the enemy when out of the woods appeared two silent and focused individuals in capes of leaves, which I would later learn were ghillie suits. *Who or what are these guys*, I questioned? They are the snipers; they have been out here for two days getting eyes on the enemy. They had a bolt-action rifle with high-powered optics and other specialty equipment I hadn't seen before. They slithered into our RV, disseminated some info with the detachment commanders and silently disappeared back into the woods. During my very brief time in Recce, I hadn't noticed these individual before, and now had many questions. When I asked the Platoon Warrant how I could become a sniper, he laughed. He explained it was one of the hardest courses in the military with a fail rate of about 80 percent. Challenge accepted, I set my sights on learning everything I could about what they did, their equipment and how I could get a position on the course.

One year later my opportunity would present itself. There was a call for volunteers to put their names in for the Basic Sniper Course. It was explained that to be considered for the course you had to volunteer for the training, be screened by the Unit Master Sniper (UMS), be recommended by your chain of command and approved by the commanding officer. I really didn't think anything of it at the time, just knew that this is what I wanted to do.

So, what is a sniper? The Canadian *Sniping Publication* defines a sniper as:

> *The sniper is a highly skilled infantryman who can select and occupy an advantageous position, stay there for extended periods of time under difficult conditions, and kill selected enemy or destroy critical equipment at long ranges with rifle fire.*

Their role is then further defined as:

> *The role of the sniper is to defeat the enemy by delivering long range precise rifle fire by day and night, in all weather conditions, and in all operations of war, systematically destroying the enemy and reducing his will to fight. A*

secondary role of the sniper is to gather combat intelligence and acquire targets, and/or designate them, for engagement by supporting arms.

To be precise, the following requirements and suitable traits are taken directly out of the *Sniping Publication*:

GENERAL

Candidates for sniper training must be carefully screened. The rigorous training program and the great personal risk in combat requires high motivation and the ability to learn a variety of skills. The unit Master Sniper must determine and assess the potential aptitude of aspiring snipers.

REQUIREMENTS

Candidates shall be qualified Basic Reconnaissance Patrolman and meet the following prerequisites prior to acceptance into the sniper program:

    a. **Marksmanship**. *A high standard of marksmanship is essential since other skills associated with snipers are such that they demand a large proportion of the training time. Sniper students must be [a] qualified Marksman on the service rifle Personal Weapon Test (PWT) within six months prior to the start of the course. Experience as a competitive marksman will often assist the potential sniper during training.*

    b. **Physical Condition**. *The sniper, often employed in extended operations with very little sleep, food, or water, must be in outstanding physical condition.*

Good health means good reflexes, good muscular control, and good stamina. Self-confidence and self-control, which come from participation in athletics, especially team sports, are definite assets for a sniper. Snipers should also have no record of drug or alcohol abuse.

c. **Emotional Balance and Mental Condition.** An infantryman in the heat of battle kills an enemy emotionally and instinctively, as a matter of survival. However, a sniper must kill calmly and deliberately, shooting carefully selected targets. He must not be susceptible to feelings of anxiety or remorse. A candidate whose sole motivation towards sniper training rests mainly in the desire for prestige from performing a unique function may not be capable of the cold rational thought which the sniper's job requires. A proper mental condition cannot be taught or instilled by training. An emotionally stable personal life, combined with patience, attentiveness and perseverance, will greatly assist the sniper in functioning effectively under stress.

d. **Intelligence.** A sniper's duties require a wide variety of skills. He must learn, for example, ballistics, ammunition types and capabilities, adjustment of optical devices, radio operation and procedures, observation and adjustment of artillery fire, map and compass reading, and military intelligence collecting and reporting. In sniper operations involving prolonged independent employment, the *sniper must display decisiveness, self-reliance, good judgement, and common sense. Applicants must possess the ability to make situational assessments and mental calculations rapidly and accurately.*

e. **Fieldcraft.** *The sniper must be familiar with and comfortable in any field environment. An extensive background in the outdoors, such as experience as a hunter or woodsman, and knowledge of natural occurrences in the outdoors, will assist the sniper in many of his tasks. Furthermore, the potential sniper must possess the ability to work closely with another individual in confined spaces or to work alone for extended periods*

PREFERRED QUALITIES

Preferred personal characteristics include the following:

a. **Glasses/Contact Lenses.** *Eyesight is the sniper's prime tool, and he can be rendered helpless by losing or damaging glasses or contact lenses. Glasses are a liability to a sniper. Although many expert riflemen wear them, glasses reflecting light can betray a sniper's position. Contact lenses are potentially unsuitable for sniper operations as they require daily hygienic maintenance, which would seldom be possible due to the poor sanitary conditions often experienced by a sniper during operations.*

b. **Smoking.** *A sniper should be a non-smoker. Smoke or an unsuppressed smoker's cough can betray the sniper's position, and even though he may not smoke* *while on a mission, abstention may cause nervousness and irritability which lowers efficiency.*

c. **Left-handedness.** *Unless highly qualified, a sniper should not be a left-handed rifle shot. [The sniper rifles at the time were not ambidextrous: a left-handed shooter may have had difficulty chambering subsequent shots or manipulating the weapon to the same precision as a righty.]*

Critical Personnel Selection Notes:

a. *Candidates should not be apprised of their status during selection.*
b. *Non-volunteers should not be considered.*
c. *The best qualified candidates should be selected for training. Alternate and future candidates must also be identified.*

Throughout my screening I was kept in the dark about everything. I had a very laid-back chat/interview with the Unit Master Sniper, something I wasn't quite used to, having adhered to very strict military deportment up to this point. He addressed me as Gord, not Corporal Cullen. He was interested in my hobbies and what my life experiences were. He asked questions that related to my decision-making and problem-solving skills and experiences that tested my patience and judgment. Not at all what I was expecting. He didn't take any notes—just listened and interacted. I was prepared to talk about my skills on the range and standing on previous courses. I thought he would want to know if I was a hunter or had killed an animal before.

The next stage at this point was the administrative side. Did I meet the physical standards, and did I have the required training to proceed? I suspect that some of my answers with the UMS must have impressed him as he signed off on my file, even though I wear contact lenses and have a degree of colour blindness. I am also not a hunter. I shoot well but was not outstanding at it. Given the weight that a UMS pulls in the battalion, something I would later experience for myself, the CO signed off on my suitability and I was course-loaded.

In its truest form the Sniper Course is meant to put little induced stress on the candidate. But in reality, it is the most stressful course most candidates will experience in the green army (regular army). This phenomenon isn't due to the instructors, it isn't due to the length of the course (two months), and it isn't due to the difficulty in learning new skills. It is solely due to the type of candidate who has been selected for sniper training. He is an A-type personality who is driven to succeed and be a top performer. He is physically fit and focused and will not stop until success is achieved. He is a team player but can also operate with the same intensity as an individual. Not everyone can be a sniper. There is a certain intuitiveness that comes with being able to operate as a sniper. Now watch what happens when someone who has been good at just about everything in their career, is at the peak of their physical and mental conditioning and able to leap tall buildings with a single bound and tell them that they failed. Then see what happens when most of the other candidates fail something—stress. The instructors will tell you it will happen. They will tell you where most people have difficulty on the course—stalking. They will always be there to assist and provide you with the knowledge they have gained through years of experience, but that doesn't mean squat to the candidate signing his final warning notice, knowing that he has only one last kick at passing one section of the course. He has seen the light. He knows snipers are the pinnacle of the battalion, getting the best training and opportunities along with the best kit available at the time. Placing the possibility of failure in a warrior's mind is unsettling and takes even more strength to push through it. In most cases this is where the individual who wants to pass the course so he can say he is a sniper, and the sniper are separated.

So, what is involved in training a highly effective infanteer to be a sniper? Simply put, it is shooting, spotting, determining distance to a target, observation skills, stalking, operating tactically and operating as a member of a sniper detachment. Oh, and all these are assessed, and failure of any one is enough to be removed from training. Digging a little deeper, we can explore each one.

Shooting: the sniper candidate is instructed and tested on three systems. First, the Sniper Training Rifle: this is currently the C3 Parker-Hale .308 with a Mauser action, employing anything from a dated Unertl 10x power fixed-magnification scope to a 3–12 variable-power Schmidt & Bender scope. The ammo is normally a 168-grain Norma match round, hollow point boat tail, but may be a 175-grain IVI due to training/budget requirements. During my training, the Parker-Hale was the primary sniper rifle and only employed the Unertl 10x power scope. Regardless of the generation of equipment or effectiveness of the ammo, the .308 is an excellent platform to learn how to shoot. It has good ballistic qualities that will challenge the candidate and spotter at short (300 metres) and intermediate (600 metres) ranges. It is affected by the candidate's ability to set up, which means his ability to naturally align with the target, successfully press the trigger without disturbing the sight alignment and control the recoil so that the natural jump and recoil of the rifle allow the shot to be released on target. It is also light enough and travelling at sufficient feet per second that it can achieve a sub-minute of angle grouping and be affected by wind.

During the initial portion of the shooting package, the candidates are instructed on ballistics, fall of shot (spotting), basic and advanced shooting techniques, marksmanship, the theory of small arms and how to maintain a precision rifle. They are also instructed on how to employ some of the equipment that will aid them in shooting, primarily the spotting scope. Other aids are introduced later in training that most wish they had during the initial phases. These would include anemometers (measuring wind speed and direction), ballistic calculators, laser range finders and a better understanding of ballistics.

Before moving onto the next weapon system in the toolbox, let's introduce spotting. Sniper teams work in pairs, and dets (detachments) that are normally two teams of two. The number one in the two-man team is the shooter. In the Sniper Group or platoon, the number ones are normally the newer or less-experienced snipers. The number two is the spotter. As expected in the group or platoon the number two is the more experienced sniper. He is required to communicate target information to the shooter, develop a priority of targets based on the situation, communicate on the radio to apprise several possible levels of command on the situation, track any developing situations on the net or in the battle space and, finally, be able to spot the round and give corrections immediately. Not to undersell the number one, he is responsible for getting on the target given to him, applying the appropriate sight settings given to him, and engaging the target to the best of his skill level. The team is not an arbitrary grouping, and snipers they must be able to operate with any of the snipers in the platoon. All efforts are made to match teams based on skill and experience to set them up for success. Now when I was first told that I was going to watch a very small projectile go downrange through a high-powered optic, I was a bit skeptical, perhaps based on voodoo and sorcery. In essence, without delving into ballistics and atmospherics, the projectile passing through the air, when viewed through optics, is like watching someone drag their finger across the top of water in a bathtub. It has a point and causes a ripple behind it that is affected by wind and trajectory. The first time I recognized it in the spotting scope was the first of many "Aha" moments during the course. Talking with many successful sniper candidates you find that during each phase of training came an "Aha" moment. This was when that part of the training made sense and the ability to apply it became achievable. Like shooting, spotting is a skill that must be learned, applied and trained on. It isn't simply seeing the projectile fly directly into the target. In fact, that scenario is rare. Many snipers will refer to this as "seeing the BB" (a reference to a BB gun round). This is achievable in most cases when the sun is behind you at a low level and you are actually able to pick up the base of the round. If this happens on test day, hallelujah. Normally, what you see is the projectile launch at a rapid rate (calibre specific) and disappear at its culminating point, or the highest point in its trajectory. It is then up to the spotter with his understanding of small-arms fire, external ballistics and atmospherics to predict where the impact is. At shorter range this is easier due to the high-powered optics—you will see a quick disturbance of air just above or on the point of impact. As the range to the target grows, so does the height above the impact point grow where you see the disturbance or swirl. So, as you can imagine, when shooting a .308 168-grain bullet at 600 metres, the swirl is most likely well above the point of impact on the target. This is then exacerbated by the wind blowing the round in whatever direction it pleases. Now the spotter is looking at swirl high right of the target in a right-to-left wind engagement at 600 metres trying to predict were that round will impact: voodoo. By the end of the training-rifle part of the shooting package, the successful candidate will have learned to effectively engage a target, proper sight settings and marksmanship principles. And then on the command "Change around", spot his partner's rounds in the same applications and provide him with the right corrections required to hit the target.

After successfully passing the Personal Weapons Test (PWT) with the training rifle the candidates move to the Medium-Range Sniper Rifle System (MRSWS). This is currently a .338 platform firing a 250-or-more-grain bullet with a 5–25 variable-power scope. I don't want to get too specific about what the platform looks like because by the time you read this it will have most likely evolved in one aspect or another. The .338 is the workhorse of the sniper's arsenal. It is ridiculously effective between 100 and 1,200 metres and, given the right atmospherics, beyond. The 250-grain Lapua Magnum round has strong ballistic properties allowing it to be relatively unaffected by wind out to 600 metres. The larger projectile also affords the spotter a greater opportunity to pick up the swirl. Given the weight and velocity of the round, it also packs a good punch at range. There have been several overseas engagements that have only required one round to neutralize the threat. The theory of progressive training during the sniper course enables the candidate to normally experience a smooth progression from training rifle to MRSWS. All the hard lessons learned with the lighter calibre are now easily employed to the .338.

Again, after passing the MRSWS PWT, the candidate moves onto the last system taught on the basic course, the Long-Range Sniper Weapon System (LRSWS). Currently the army uses the McMillan Firearms .50-cal bolt action rifle with a 5–25 variable-power scope. The current round of choice is the Sniper Elite .50 709-grain round. This round is available in a couple of different configurations to support various desired target effects. The .50 was originally introduced to address the anti-material role that snipers were finding themselves in during an evolving period of conflict from 1999 to 2001. Chronologically, the .50 came into service approximately four years before the .338. It was also responsible for crushing Carlos Hathcock's long-range sniper kill of 2,286 metres in 2001/2 during Operation *Athena* in Afghanistan. During this engagement the snipers were employing the Raufoss Mk. 211 multipurpose, anti-material, high-explosive incendiary, armour-piercing projectile made by Nammo, vice the Sniper Elite which came into use later. The loan from the U.S. during the operation contributed to the success of the engagement and future R&D. For the spotter, the .50 is obvious. It is often referred to as a garbage can lid going down range. The swirl is enormous. Although the .50 cal is a beast downrange, it does not have the extended range you would expect, tapping out at around 1,500 metres. However, the energy maintained by the projectile given its weight and velocity, has a devastating effect on personnel and light armoured targets. One of the major drawbacks from the .50-cal program is the effect on the shooter. The recoil and overpressure caused from releasing the round has led to concerns and a study on traumatic brain injury (TBI) from firing the system. My preference, when it could be achieved operationally, was to fire the .50 unsuppressed. This allowed the brake on the barrel to divert the gases rearward as the projectile exited the barrel, lessening the felt recoil of the weapon. When suppressed, you received almost 100 percent of felt recoil. Years after it was introduced a 20-round cap was put on rounds fired during a training event—to reduce the risk of retinal separation not TBI.

Upon successful completion of the LRSWS PWT, the shooting package is complete, and you have one piece of the pie under your belt. The hardest part for many new shooters isn't necessarily learning how to effectively engage a target with a precision rifle system—it is effectively spotting for your sniper partner. During the unknown-distance part of the PWT for each of the systems, the spotter can make or break the shooter. Ultimately, if the shooter employs all the marksmanship principles, applies proven DOPE (data on previous engagements) and makes a solid initial wind call, the rest is on the spotter's shoulders. Once the spotter can no longer see physical hits on the target, he has to use his newly acquired knowledge of spotting swirl to ensure round placement is optimal. If he makes a bad estimation on wind or elevation, the shooter could fail the test. This routinely happens during the practice tests and ranges—stress. The shooter is doing all the right things, but the spotter has a bad day, and you fail. During my time as an instructor there were many occasions where either the spotter or the shooter would approach me and say they didn't want to either spot for or have someone spot for them. Unfortunately, in most of the cases, this is a poor decision. I would always recommend staying together as a team: they have built a rapport, they know how each other operates and each can tell when the other has a bad shot, regardless of if they called it. I would normally lay on the mound with the team and spot with them. Most of the time the calls were correct and having someone else there was the confidence boost they needed to keep making the calls. It is way too easy to say "Shot not observed" than taking responsibility for a bad call. I believe earlier on in this chapter we discussed stress, and this is the effect. Test day is now, and you have to put your success in someone else's hands and if you fail, they are going to have to swallow it and do better next time or watch you turn in your gear. Stress.

Determining distance (DD) to a target and observation are core skills that are usually met with a great deal of success. When DD'ing a target, you are taught to use all the tools at your disposal: you are taught how to bracket, use known distances like telephone poles running down the side of a road, taking a group average, using your map and known features on the ground and using the reticle in your scope. The most accurate was to use the reticle in your scope to "mil" the target. This involves looking at a target for which you have the approximate size and place it in your reticle. You then take the number of mils (mm), either height or width, and apply it to the WoRm formula: 1 mil in the scope equals 1 metre at 1,000 metres. For example, you know the average size of a man is 1.82 metres and he appears to take up 3.6 mils in your reticle. The equation is therefore 1.82 x 1,000 ÷ 3.6 = 506 metres. Where the skill comes in is being able to cut your mils with precise accuracy. Is the man 3.6 or 3.4 mils, a difference of 5 metres at short range? But the same .2 mil error at longer range could be 200 metres. Most sniper candidates grasp this knowledge well and are able to apply it immediately. The biggest gripe is why they can't use laser range finders on the course since they are issued to the sniper dets. The unfortunate and dogmatic response is batteries fail but snipers don't. Although I still believe that all snipers must be able to "do it old school", I think not training them on equipment they are going to use in the dets is an oversight.

Observation sounds very simple but can be troublesome to a candidate. The whole purpose behind observation exercises is to teach the candidate how to methodically search ground. They practise looking from right to left, dividing and searching the ground into near, middle and far ground. They look for the identifiers, shape, shine, colour, texture, and so on. Then they are tested on their ability to identify a number of objects in a small exercise area that the instructors have taken the time to blend into the surroundings. Rarely do we ever see anyone fail this. Most of the time if someone is having issues it is due to their use of time on the line, and they aren't using their aids to search the ground properly. First, look with your eye and see what stands out, investigate with your binoculars and confirm with your spotting scope if necessary. Identify and "burn" the likely areas where an object might be placed or hidden. And if all else fails because the instructors have been overly creative in placing the objects, deliberately scan in detail from right to left with your optics until you find them all.

This is the only exercise where my colour blindness was an issue. There were some instances where I had a really hard time drawing the objects out of the background and had to rely on the shape, shine or texture to really attract my eye. The benefits of this type of exercise were not truly realized until I started deploying. It became second nature when setting up to scan the ground in this fashion. You would identify all the suspect places where IEDs (improvised explosive devices) or bad guys might be hiding. You would look for the indicators on the ground and confirm with your optics. You'd take painstaking efforts to burn the area to the point of tears to make sure you were not missing anything. An untrained observation of the area would miss the disturbed earth or out-of-place stone. It won't see the triangle shape of a bipod camouflaged in the grape rows or the slight movement of a branch going opposite to the wind direction.

This brings us to the "maneater" (candidate removal exercise) and most debated skill of a sniper, stalking. Stalking is the ability to apply all the skills learned up to this point in one go. The candidate needs to be able to identify and move to within 300 metres of an enemy OP undetected and engage with no more than two rounds a target that is actively scouring the area where he is operating. During the Basic Sniper Course, the candidates are put through several stalks and must then pass a set number, currently two. This standard has changed several times, and it is difficult to rationalize why, other than saying it's hard. Ultimately, the candidates are given a six-figure grid reference of an enemy OP, a start point and boundaries they must remain in during the exercise. This will identify the area of interest; then using their maps, aerial photos and other aids, they will try to determine where precisely the OP is, possible routes, obstacles and danger areas and possible final firing positions (FFPs). They will be given a three-hour time limit to identify the OP, ideally from as close to the start point as possible, plot a route that will keep them undetected within the boundaries and establish an FFP within 300 metres of the OP, from which they will fire a live or blank round. Prior to this phase, they will have been instructed on tactical movement, camouflage and concealment, FFP development, and refreshed on navigation. One of the complementary exercises is concealment. This quick field exercise sees the candidates walk out from the OP into an area within 300 metres of it and quickly develop an FFP. This allows the candidates to see the ground that the OP is observing from their perspective and then choose a suitable location while not being observed. After a set time limit the OP will turn around and begin looking for the candidates. OP personnel can only use issued binos and are not allowed to support their arms. We use folding chairs in the OP. Badge protectors, as I like to refer to instructors who do not like graduate candidates, would turn the chairs around to stabilize their arms on the back of the chairs. This gives them the advantage of keeping steady and not exerting energy to scan the ground with the binos. The usual standard adhered to is to sit normally in the chair, using muscle and skill to hold the binos to scan the ground, forcing the snipers in the OP to be more professional—scan the ground with the naked eye, identify oddities or movement, scan again with the binos to confirm what they have seen and then maintain contact while talking a walker onto the possible sniper candidate. Much harder.

In support of both the candidates and the OP are walkers who have radios in contact with the OP. They will not disturb the candidates' positions unless they physically walk on to them, but they will do everything the OP tells them to do. For example, the OP might tell the walker to yell "Freeze." The walker then screams "Freeze," and all the candidates must now remain in the exact position that they were in when they heard "Freeze". This can be precarious at times. The OP must then talk the walker onto whatever it was they saw.

For example, "Walker, turn to your left [or right], and walk. Stop. Turn to your right. Walk two paces forward. Walk one pace to your right. Place your right arm out to the side. Bend your knees and go all the way down. Your right hand is touching a sniper."

If so, the walker would say "Correct," and the busted sniper would get a quick but detailed debrief over the radio as to why he had been seen in the context of shape, shine, colour, contrast, shape, texture and movement. Normally movement is the giveaway. If the walker's hand was not touching a sniper, the walker would simply say no or negative. The OP would have one more chance to home in on what they were seeing. If unsuccessful twice in a row, the walker would walk away, and the exercise would continue. Doing this first in the context of a concealment exercise, focusing mainly on the FFP, ensured that the candidates had practice in setting up their firing position, camouflaging their gear, creating a loophole if needed and employing depth to conceal their position. Depth is always the key. Blend into your foreground and background equally with a clear path for your bullet to pass through. If not for the concealment exercises, some candidates would never know what an FFP was.

Knowing this is the "maneater" of the course and the final hard check before the final exercise, tensions are always high. On my basic course, upon arrival at a stalk that several people needed to pass to remain on course, when the back door of the troop slammed open, one of the candidates puked out the back of the truck. This was one of the guys you'd see in the lines and hear people talking about how checked out he was, a warrior in all senses, truly respected. Nobody in the truck judged that guy. This was not only acceptable but rejoiced over. There are more nervous stomachs, bladders and shits than I care to count on stalk days. Do what you gotta do, empty the bladder, clear the pipes or lighten the load. Whatever it was, it was okay as long as you kept moving forward.

Once in the admin area, which normally doubles as the start point, the walkers will confirm the grid of the enemy OP. They will then very intently watch the candidates apply or confirm directions with their compasses. (It was sometimes humorous for the staff to put a back bearing on your own compass, put it up and align it. This normally only worked once, but the look on the candidates' faces when the staff was pointing in the exact opposite direction was priceless.) The candidates would then be given a period to camouflage up. This would entail taking natural cam and adding it to your ghillie suit to blend in with your surroundings. This needed to be done several times along your route to ensure you continually matched your ever-changing surroundings.

The candidates are then instructed that they are under observation. This is the cue that—most likely but not always— as soon as they move away from the admin area towards the OP they could be seen. This means you must try and identify the OP from the admin area or as soon as possible. This also means that you need to very careful of how you move across the ground until you find the OP. This is the most stressful part of the stalk. You know in what direction they are; you know approximately how far away they are, but you can't see them. They could be in a depression, behind a tree in the middle ground but from your vantage point is blocked or blends in with their background too well. Regardless, you are moving blind and that is never good. The most common response to this is get on your stomach and crawl like a snail across the ground. Having been that snail a couple times, I know the feeling of desperation that goes along with it. Then comes the "Aha" moment again. You find the OP and can plan your route into the box (150 metres wide x 300 metres deep) using depth and tactical movement, stopping along the way to refresh your cam and confirm your direction. It's that simple—locate, move, set up and engage. Had someone said that to me on my basic course, I would have punched them in their throat. It's not that simple when everything you do is being evaluated and walkers are yelling freeze every two minutes because people are getting busted all around you. Or worse, you did something stupid because for one second you weren't paying 100 percent attention to how fast your body was moving and what foliage it was disturbing or for a moment you stepped out of line with the bush you were using to block the OP's view of you and now the walker is coming straight for you. You can hear the directions on the radio: "Walker, stop, turn to your left, put your left arm out, all the way to the ground, you are touching a sniper ... Negative, okay, walk away." That's it, that's your one freebie. Now refocus and get back on line. This is where most of the candidates fail. They either can't ID the OP soon enough or don't pay enough attention to what they are doing. This usually means they get caught "turkey necking" (bringing their heads over or around the cover that was concealing them instead of trying to "burn" through the leaves or trees) or moving in the open. There have been candidates who never find the OP during their time on course. They let their nerves get the better of them and try and push forward blindly. There are also some rare candidates who never find the OP until they are in the box. This is usually identified by three quick "fuck, fuck, fucks" followed by a very slow and methodical reconnection with the ground. Most internally tell themselves that *I am good here* and immediately go into developing their FFP.

Normally, if you make it into your FFP you will be successful. Keep it slow, only trim what you need to trim, cam your position, confirm your target, set your range and make a wind call of "Sniper ready to fire". This is a war cry for the OP: someone has made it into the box and set up an FFP under their watchful eye. Once declared, the walker will announce over the radio that he has a sniper ready to fire. The OP is then given two minutes to thoroughly scan the box for the trespasser on their land. If nothing looks out of place, the OP will give the walker the prompt to carry on. The walker will then move to within 20 metres of the candidate, which could be in any direction as long as he isn't standing between the OP and candidate. The candidate will then identify the OP. Normally the walker will ask, "Who do you want and where?" The candidate will either indicate the left or right member in the OP or by name and indicate head or chest. Head or chest refers to where his crosshairs are on the OP member. For example, "Man on the right in the head". The OP then has two minutes to scan again. If nothing is detected the OP will give "Stand by" over the radio and then hold up a head-shaped target where the candidate indicated. The target will have an S, N, I, P, E or R on it. The candidate must correctly identify the letter. Once identified, the walker will move to within five metres of the candidate, and if nothing is observed by the OP over the next two minutes, the candidate is good to go. He will remain there until it is time to take the live shot on target. Of course, at any point if the OP does see something during the sequence, they will talk the walker in and crush any hopes of the candidate moving forward.

I really feel we should revisit induced stress mentioned at the beginning of this chapter. The candidate, through no other reason but pure desire to be successful, has most likely crawled 1,000 metres across thorn-packed ground with his asshole firmly puckered for the last three hours and knows that he will have to do it again tomorrow if he wants a position in the platoon. Once the time limit is up, the live portion of the stalk commences. The observation post guys are replaced by two steel gongs in the shape of a standard kill-zone target. They then move to the closest declared sniper and issue him two rounds. This provides positive safety, working from the closest sniper to the farthest. The candidate then engages the same target that he declared on, hoping to hear the *thwak* of the copper meeting the steel. If not, he has five seconds to re-engage. Most of the candidates are successful at this point. If they are truly crafty, they will have ensured that no branches or obstructions in front of their barrel are going to send the round astray. Although sight settings and wind calls are important, given the range to the target and the ballistics of the round, it is doubtful that they would miss that size of target due to a .2 error in estimation.

Normally at the completion of the stalking phase of the course, you are looking at your successful candidates. The optimal course load for the Basic Sniper is 18 candidates. In the past this phase of the course has seen anything from one to sixteen. I think it would be fair to say that most of the time you see half the candidates removed from training due to failure of a phase or injury.

The last piece to the pie is the final exercise. This is approximately five days long with little to no real rest for the duration. This is the candidates' opportunity to operate and conduct missions in a sniper detachment, and the Sniper Platoon's opportunity to see "who's who" among the successful candidates. There are candidates who have had the will and knowledge to be successful in all the phases, but when put into a group with pressure applied, they aren't able to perform to the desired level. Candidates are evaluated on their abilities to react and maintain focus, demonstrating their ability to support sniper operations under difficult conditions while confirming all the new knowledge gained throughout the course. Over the years this phase of the training has been pared down to reflect the candidate's understanding of his knowledge and ability to function in a team environment under duress. Again, in the past the final exercise has seen gruelling insertions over kilometres of ground, evading dogs and tracking teams to get into the target area, set up an OP, provide real-time commentary on the enemy position and culminating with a live shot on the target area. We have also seen candidates injured during this phase of training, resulting in a medical RTU (return to unit)/failure. Checks and balances, train the men, give them the tools to be successful, test their abilities and provide them with the opportunities to develop from within the platoon. Not cull the herd and break the survivors.

Why are Canadian snipers respected around the world? In my opinion there are three key reasons:

1. The Canadian Sniper Program has evolved and devolved only to reinvent itself again and again, which is why it produces the world's best army snipers. It isn't stuck in dogmatic practices. It adapts not only to evolving threats but evolving candidates. Gone are the days when the

Infantry is populated by hunters and farmers who grew up in the woods shooting guns. The majority of snipers in the modern era are city dwellers with little or no experience outside the concrete jungle. The ability of a program that can react to developments in technology and threats while keeping stride with the capabilities of its baseline candidates is proven and will continue to succeed.

2. We show up. Every major conflict in the world has seen Canadian snipers succeed. We as a country aren't risk averse. We want to get out there and showcase our abilities as snipers and demonstrate how well we can operate with other nations against the threat at hand.

3. We are the sheepdogs of the battlefield. Our focus isn't on body counts or prestige. Our success is measured in the success of others. When we deploy, we become the experts on the pattern of life (POL) in our area of operation (AO), so we know what is out of place. We are experts with our systems and ruthless in their employment to ensure the safety of the soldiers around us.

One of my most cherished memories of being a sniper is from my third tour in Afghanistan. I was co-located with Bravo Company, 1RCR, in Shoja. This area had seen a great deal of insurgent activity in the form of ambushes and IEDs. As I was the UMS at the time, I normally stuck to the Tactical Infrastructure (TI) or with the OCs (officers commanding) of the AOs. During my time in Shoja I had routinely gone up to the observation tower with the McMillan TAC-50 and relieved the member up there on sentry. This allowed me to give the young soldiers a bit of a break and further my understanding of the AO through development of the pattern of life. Over time I was able to identify an insurgent VCP, a vehicle control point. In this case it was a crew of bad guys shaking down the locals to affirm their hold on the surrounding villages—to be totally accurate it was an IVCP, an illegal VCP—north of the camp, interdict insurgent activity east of the camp and provide commentary to patrols who were within observation of my optics. On one occasion a patrol departed from the camp and was moving north. Having spent time getting to know the area, I was able to immediately identify an insurgent observer and cause the early initiation of an ambush through interdiction. Fortunately, the surprise caused the insurgents to think they were under effective fire and reveal themselves while friendly forces were well out of effective range and had solid cover. Bad day for insurgents. So, the best and most memorable part of all of this was when a private sat down with me at dinner and asked if I would be up in the tower tomorrow. He was part of a patrol departing at 1300 and they were heading east (can't remember the town). I said I would be unless something went sideways. His section commander came over, a good friend, and apologized for intruding. He said having a sniper in the tower while they were out had given them a boost in confidence, knowing someone had their back.

The reality is that just because you passed the course doesn't mean you will be able to press the trigger on a human being. Some snipers are never put in a position where they need to kill someone, and that is okay too. Snipers who have been put in a position where they had to kill another human being have expressed mixed emotions and some inner conflict, but what is common to all is their description of being able to find that moment of stillness, the moment in all the chaos and violence where your brain is says, *Okay, now press the trigger.* During an engagement you have a million thoughts running through your mind: *What if I miss? Is that really an AK-47? Is there anyone behind him that I might kill if the bullet passes through? How fast is he walking, will he stop, why is he doing this?* And then the noise goes away. *Yes, that is an AK, and he is going to hurt one of the good guys, I have a clean shot well within my capabilities. Squeeze the trigger.* A Canadian sniper is trained to dissect a situation and act upon it; we push past the who and focus on the what. Sniping isn't a shirt and coin affair. Sniping begins after the course is over—that's when the real work begins. How do you know who will be a good sniper? There is no gauge to measure that head space. All you can do is provide the sniper the tools to do the job, the training to become a master of his craft and the reinforcement to succeed. He will find that moment of stillness or the noise will overpower him.

2

Is There Anyone Out There ... Detection

Warrant Officer Gordon Cullen, Unit Master Sniper
1st Battalion, Royal Canadian Regiment
CFB Petawawa

Sniping, from its very inception in warfare and subsequent carryover into law enforcement and civilian culture, is an art. There will always be those who consider themselves snipers because they employ a long-barrelled weapon with some degree of proficiency, but those who truly embrace the dedication to the art will be known as snipers.

As alluded to, basic sniper training focuses on mastering the fundamentals of the infantry, regardless of agency or country. Shoot, move and communicate have been the framework of the infantry for generations. The sniper is a master of these fundamentals and executes them to the highest degree. Shoot: the sniper is a master of all his weapons. They understand their functions, operations and limitations. They understand where to employ them and how to get the maximum effect from each. Move: they can move undetected through any environment using tactical considerations and camouflage. They can hide in plain sight as easily as they can blend into the surrounding foliage, urban and rural. Communicate: they are trained observers, intelligence gatherers and, most important, able to read a situation as it develops and relay it to whoever needs it. So, where the infantryman focuses on closing with the enemy by employing these three principles, the sniper through his mastery of them can operate amongst the enemy. Their small team structure, when employed to its fullest potential, can genuinely alter the outcome of battle.

This execution has held true since the Revolutionary War in North America where citizen soldiers with strong hunting backgrounds influenced the battlefield to modern-day snipers operating in current conflicts. As less and less farmers and hunters populated the ranks of the infantry, the sniping program had to adjust. The lessons learned from generations of accomplished hunters and shooters needed to be taught to a more predominant generation of urban dwellers whose lineage may have been rooted in industrial or professional backgrounds. Using my own experience as an example, I am the son of an RCMP officer who grew up on a farm in Alberta and a mother whose early childhood was shaped by the bombings of Gosport, England, during World War II. After moving around the country for a short while, our final posting was to Whitehorse, Yukon. Arriving there when I was 9, I had transitioned through Manitoba, Newfoundland and Ontario. All the activities I enjoyed in the Yukon involved being out in the woods. I had exposure to guns and animals and felt very comfortable in that environment. After joining the military and earning a spot on the Basic Sniper Course, it was very evident that this background was the common denominator with everyone who successfully passed the course. All the candidates were comfortable in the woods, knew how to navigate and conceal themselves to a basic level; each had varied experience with guns and ammo, but all had some. As such, the course instruction was more of a refining of an already intuitive skill.

Teaching on several courses after mine, Canada generally relies on battalions or brigades to run their basic sniper serials vice sending them to a schoolhouse; the instructors are active snipers from the battalions, ensuring that the knowledge presented is current and relevant. We started encountering a very high failure rate, with only three successful candidates out of 20 for two serials in a row. What had changed? The candidates who were being selected for the course were no longer the same. They came from cities and concrete environments. We now needed to change the way in which we delivered the training. The focus was still the same—mastering the core skills of the infantry—but more emphasis had to be placed on teaching what was previously intuitive. Camouflage, stalking, tactical movement and shooting were now broken down to the roots and built up over concealment exercises, stalking lanes and unknown distance ranges. We spent a great deal of time breaking everything down. The marksmanship principles that someone coming from rural Canada would already be employing needed to be broken down into principles that could be reinforced through dry and live practice. Position and hold, alignment, shot release breathing and trigger press all need to be dissected. We also started taking cues from civilian shooting culture, using visualization and breathing techniques to mentally tune the prospective sniper.

Another challenge that we encountered was stalking—being able to close with the enemy undetected over any terrain. The modern-day candidate was familiar with urban structures and cityscapes but struggled with land navigation, camouflage and tactical movement. Because stalking can be applied to any environment and the principles behind planning and executing the movement make up the foundation of many additional skills, stalking had to be mastered. This was still the maneater of the course. Many talented shooters and truly gifted candidates were still being removed from training due to their failure of stalking. Unable to add more time to the course, the only solution was to run pre-sniper training. With a maximum course load of 18, the pre-course would be overloaded with 25–30 mentally screened, physically fit, proven soldiers who had volunteered for the opportunity to become a sniper. The pre-sniper focused on mostly fieldcraft. Cam and concealment, judging distance and observation skills were introduced, ghillie construction and tactical movement practised. Normally one or two range days focusing on the in-service carbine qualification standard as marksman was a pre-requisite of the course. Most of the ten-day course was stalking, normally two stalks a day, each followed by a detailed debrief from a qualified sniper. This now produced a candidate with the baseline exposure and understanding to embark on the two-month sniper course. By taking a more detailed and instructional approach to training, we were now able to see success in our modern-day candidates. Courses of 18 now saw eight or more successful candidates. To this day, the success of the Canadian Sniper Program, both green army and SOF, is the ability to remain flexible and adapt to the demographics.

With the evolution in candidates also came the advancements in technology. As we move forward into what the current and future sniper looks like, I would like to plant a seed. The driving force behind advancement in sniping is detection. The baseline requirements for the sniper—shoot, move and communicate—have not changed. How they conduct business has, however, and where many people will automatically focus on the advancements in precision shooting and extreme long-range (ELR) shooting as the focal point, I want to explore the real driving force: detection.

My first deployment as a sniper was to Kosovo in 1999. We were coming to RIP (relief in place) with the PPCLI Battalion (Princess Patricia's Canadian Light Infantry—the Patricias) that had survived in-post NATO bombing and Yugoslav force withdrawal. We were operating in two-man sniper teams, a traditional grouping at the time and employed the C-3 which was our in-service .308 sniper rifle. We were sporting basic optics for observation: binos, spotting scopes of different designs and a 10x fixed Unertl scope on the sniper rifle. Our night vision consisted of NVGs (night-vision goggles), Kite and Maxi Kite sights. Our primary radio was large and heavy with equally large and heavy batteries. Our focus was the activities of the KLA, the Kosovo Liberation Army, the mainly Albanian group supporting the separation of Kosovo and designated a terrorist group. Due to their lack of night vision and observation equipment, we were able to move quite handily across the terrain of urban and rural Kosovo. We would occupy positions at night to identify and report on KLA activities. This involved occupying rooms in buildings that housed businesses, getting eyes on police stations from abandoned shops and infiltrating across kilometres of farmland that might have been mined or littered with unexploded ordnance from the NATO bombings.

On one occasion, my sniper partner and I were tasked to get eyes on a KLA rally that was to take place in a farmer's field. The landscape in this area was very picturesque. The rolling hills and low mountains opened onto sweeping fields delineated by stone walls and hedgerows. We were dropped off at the base of a re-entrant approximately five kilometres from the target area. Knowing that the area was still being used for farming, and many of the goat trails were in fact still being used by goats, allowed us to move with some confidence up the mountainside and onto the open fields. We had planned to be out for three days which would allow us time to identify the area, report on the pattern of life and be set to observe the KLA activities. At the time reliable reporting wasn't as it as today. The intelligence we based our planning on was a bit vague, but we knew the area and approximate size of the group that would be attending. It was up to our observations of the target area to decide what field would be the gathering place and what OP location would allow us the best vantage point. Everyone makes mistakes … based on the access roads in the area, what fields had cows in them, where the farmers worked and the size of each plot, we set up in a hedgerow that overlooked two east–west-running fields that could hold the 200 or 300 hundred KLA members and families being called for. Our task was solely to identify and report on KLA members: how many wore uniform, what markings they had, did they have weapons, what type and kind, who looked like they were in charge, was there a structure or rank system, et cetera. So, there we were tucked nicely away in our ghillie suits, completely hidden from observation or detection by the naked eye. We were away from grazing areas that animals frequented or, more important, where the shepherds would hang out. We did not have to worry about detection from the air nor were we concerned about the employment of thermal devices trying to detect us. We judged the range to the centre of the target area to be 450 metres, well within our .308's capability, plus we also had carbines for personal protection. We were good to go.

You know that sinking feeling when you were in school and got caught looking at someone else's paper—ya, we all did it. At approximately 1400, we were enjoying the heat of the day and the calmness of the area. Our OP was on the southern side of the second field as we'd assessed that the rally would most likely take place on the lower or northern of the two equally sized fields. But no, we started seeing men with KLA uniforms meandering in the field directly in front of us. Most were unarmed but there was a good number of AKs amongst the initial group. Then woman and children and more uniformed members of the KLA with more guns. Fuck. No big deal, we started reporting, confident we were well concealed. We informed our QRF (quick reaction force) of the situation who then moved from their holding area to just shy of our pick-up point—all good. We had solid numbers, identification and were starting to make a solid assessment on leadership, when off to our right, about 15 feet from our OP, I heard a couple twigs snap loudly. I glanced at Dave and his eyes were the same size as the soccer ball that just crashed into the woods where we were sitting. We looked to the crowd moving across our frontage and saw a young girl scanning the hedgerow. She was holding hands with her mom, most likely trying to pull away to see where her ball went. Dave and I had about 30 seconds to make a decision: do we try to move laterally away from the ball while still remaining concealed and continue observation? Do we put on our rucks and slowly move out of the area and call for pick-up? … Too late, just as we were putting our arms through the shoulder straps of our rucks, the little girl broke away from mom and was now screaming like only a 5-year-old can because two prehistoric animals were trying to steal her ball. I suspect that's what she saw anyway. This of course drew the attention of everyone in the vicinity. Both courses of action that we had quickly discussed were now off the table: we were busted. This is where having a good understanding of culture and capability comes in. We knew that snipers were feared by the locals due to their effectiveness and ruthlessness during the conflict. We knew that the area was littered with woman and children and the chance of getting into a gunfight was very low, even though we were horribly outgunned. So, we called in to the QRF that we were moving to our extraction point due to being compromised in location. We then stood up, walked directly out of the hedgerow, maintaining spacing of course, and walked east out of the field and out of sight. The whole thing is a blur to be honest. I remember hearing people yelling and I remember focusing on scanning my immediate arcs but not raising my carbine into the shoulder. I remember hearing Dave or perhaps it was me murmur, "Fuck, fuck, fuck" a few times and I remember effortlessly hopping over a stone wall due to the amount of adrenaline pumping through my system, taking a knee, and looking back at the crowd. Total confusion: some of the men were slowly moving towards us but with no real conviction. Some women were holding back their husbands and sons, children were flipping us off, but no one really wanted to commit to an action. That damn little girl with her stupid soccer ball was crying on her mother's shoulder, holding the ball like a long-lost teddy bear. We quickly navigated through the hedgerow to our pick-up point making best possible speed. No one attempted to pursue. Ultimately, I think the boldness of action created enough confusion that the transitioning crowd had no recourse but to continue to the rally. Fortunately, we had gathered some info and were able to relay that to the intelligence people so that they could further define the KLA and its structure.

There were a couple more close calls that included the riots in Mitrovica but our ability to conduct operations was never impeded. In 1999 we relied heavily on our ability to move at night due to the lack of night-vision capability of the bad guys and knew that we could remain in location for days without being detected.

Fast-forward to June 2010. I am on my fourth tour as a sniper, third tour to Afghanistan and second tour as the Unit Master Sniper. I could probably make this all a little less confusing:

- 1999 Kosovo – Sniper
- 2003 Kabul, Afghanistan – Sniper
- 2006 Kandahar, Afghanistan – Master Sniper
- 2010 Kandahar, Afghanistan – Master Sniper

Detection

We now operated in four-man groups at a minimum. We employed a semi-automatic AR-10 accurized .308, .338 Timberwolf and .50-cal McMillan. What had changed over the years—the bad guys didn't get bigger or farther away—was the threat of detection due to increased capability of the bad guys and the need to engage sensors or anti-material targets. We no longer moved with impunity across the battle space. The bad guys now had the ability to observe and engage us at longer ranges with heavier weapons. This also increased the level of technology that we employed as a group. We now had laser range finders that we hooked up to a GPS that would give us the grid and firing solution for artillery. Our radios were lighter and more compact with better range. We could use satellite radios and encrypted satellite phones to communicate. We could range targets within an error of two metres, we employed thermal binoculars, and could call on balloon-mounted sensors, drones or aircraft to identify and target the bad guys. We were on the verge of turning night into day.

The ability to detect the bad guys at long range by day and night drove advancements in sniping. We could now employ large-calibre rifles like the .338 to engage targets out to 1,200 metres, and we could interdict bad guys, teams or components out to 1,800 metres or more with the .50 cal. Our increased ability to discriminate non-combatant from bad guys at long range allowed us to increase our stand-off and security.

It is important to note though that the basics of sniping never changed. Even though we could sit back at longer ranges and affect the battle space didn't change how we got there. We still used the mastery of tactical movement and concealment, still used the contours of the ground, and still gathered, reported on and actioned intelligence to dominate the ground. I recall an evening in 2006, post-*Medusa*. The entire group was at Sperwan Ghar supporting the Green Beret ODA and their efforts west. The two dets had pushed out on a couple occasions with them and supported their movement through the villages; we had also supported them from the top of the *ghar* (mountain) multiple times as they cleared around the camp. We had become very comfortable working together. The ODA JTAC had left his SOFLAM (Special Operations Forces Laser Acquisition Marker), and thermal sight mounted on a tripod at the top of the ghar where we had bedded down. He had gone back to Kandahar for a couple days on rest and refit. He had given us some of the basics on it and left the training code entered in the SOFLAM. It was a good thermal sight, and we used it in conjunction with our optics to observe and to call for fire. The bad guys had been quiet for a week or so and we left the surveillance of the surrounding area to the sensors mounted on the Coyotes, a recce vehicle employed by the Royal Canadian Dragoons (RCD) in Recce Troop. At approximately 0200 we got a call on the land line that had been run up the hill. The CP (command post) wanted us to look to the south and see if we could identify a fighting-age male (FAM) digging on a road next to a grape hut. It was in dead ground and the sensors mounted on the Coyotes masts couldn't get the elevation to see. Really not expecting it to be a legit target and, to be honest, with a bit of complacency, I threw on my flip flops and went up to the OP. I turned on the thermal and SOFLAM and waited for them to prep. I also turned on the hand-held Sophie thermal binos, which cooled down pretty quick and used them until the SOFLAM was ready to go. Lo and behold! there was a lone fighting-age male digging behind a wall on the roadway. He had what appeared to be small jugs next to him and appeared to be burying them in the ground. I called it in to the CP. Fortunately, there was an F15 on station and the company CP was able to get him to come over and have a look as well and confirm the activity. I used the range finder in the SOFLAM to get a distance to the IED emplacer—1600 metres, way out of our capability at night. We currently only had the Simrad sight available to conduct night engagements and the Piggyback II system—the Piggyback image-intensifier night-vision scope sits on top of your normal sniper scope, maxed out between 600 and 800 metres depending on the ambient light. The IED threat around Sper had already claimed several lives, military and civilian.

The CP was requesting we engage the bad guy. I informed them that it was outside of our capability but did add that we had the ODA equipment up with us. I honestly didn't think they would go for it but the next thing I heard was the pilot, who had dropped down to our net, asking for the code. It was very odd, and I still have a hard time believing it happened but there I was holding the targeting laser on the wall where the bad guy was digging and hearing the roar of the F15 as he climbed out of his attack run. I watched as a 500lb bomb landed slightly right of the bad guy— "Good hit, good hit" was my response to the jet. I had heard the JTAC say it a hundred times and it seemed appropriate. He orbited a couple times conducting his own BDA (battle or bomb damage assessment) with his sensors and we concluded that the IED layer, the HME (homemade explosive) he was placing in the ground and a significant chunk of road and wall was gone. I scanned the area for additional interest; no one came around for about a half hour, so I let the CP know I was off the optics and going to ground. Later that morning while eating a breakfast ration, I remember being a bit overwhelmed by what had happened, shaking my head and saying, "Fucking technology."

Now, March 2022, just recently retired from the military as the first Canadian Special Operations Regiment (CSOR) Sniper Program Manager I look back at our equipment in Afghanistan as borderline bush league. The advancement in technology relating to observation and target acquisition is staggering. The sniper now has choices in sight technology to define and engage the bad guys, each with its own capability and of course user preference. We see a family of UNS (Universal Night Sight), MUNS (Magnum Universal Night Sight) and DUNS (Dual Band Universal Night Sight). The DUNS is the most popular as it blends thermal and image intensification plus thermal grouping of HISS and HISS-XLR, and thermal range-finding binos like the JIM-LR and the Mosqui TI. The game isn't changing but the technology behind it is.

In addition to the increase in ability to locate the enemy, there has also been a massive increase in the ability to engage the enemy. We are now looking at calibres like the .375 and .408 employing monolithic bullets and once again discussing base bleed technology (a system that reduces base drag of a projectile to increase range) to propel our projectiles farther with more stability across supersonic, transonic and subsonic flight. Our engagement range has pushed well past what we thought was long range into what we now know as extended or extreme long range (ELR).

Further, our enemy isn't just sitting in OPs anymore: they are launching drones and employing detection devices that will use your well-placed round to locate you and immediately launch a volley of hate onto your position. And if that isn't enough, the bad guys can now use a laser to detect optics across its frontage and if detected fire another laser to burn out the eye of the poor soul looking through that optic.

The good news is the basic sniper tactics of using the ground to move and conceal their location still trumps this massive amount of technology. Be a master of the ground and your chances of success are exponentially increased.

Globally, military forces are facing a growing reality of peer and near-peer threats. Future conflicts will be operating in a heavily congested and contested technological overmatch. This evolution in the threat landscape is forcing militaries to re-examine their tactics.

In a high-tech world of joystick operators engaging in push-button warfare, the sniper of the future may very well prove that the world's most dangerous weapon is the human mind, especially the one that knows how to weaponize science and math to calculate long-distance ballistics.

3

Rifles and Optics and Radios, Oh My "Geardo"

Warrant Officer Gordon Cullen, Unit Master Sniper
1st Battalion, Royal Canadian Regiment
CFB Petawawa

Over the past 20 years sniper equipment has evolved at least that many times, times ten. Much of this is due to addressing the capabilities of evolving threats, but a good deal is also due to the "geardo", the equipment groupie. If you can imagine it and address the gap in capability that it will bridge, industry will build it. When I first started out in Sniper Platoon and embarked on my first deployment as a sniper to Kosovo, the mission essential kit was nowhere near as diverse as it is now. Don't get me wrong, snipers have always adhered to the idea of tools in the toolbox or clubs in the bag, but post-1999 the technology and capability advancement boomed. I vividly remember packing my kit with my sniper partner, ensuring each of us had the required equipment based on our role (number one or two) and whatever needed to be double banked was. For weapons we had the C3, the primary and only sniper rifle in our arsenal. It was a Parker-Hale bolt-action rifle with a Mauser action and free-floating barrel. It employed a fixed 10x power Unertl scope and newly added Harris bipod. We were firing .308 168-grain match-grade bullets, stacked in a five-round mag. The scope employed a mildot reticle made of wax dots on wire. As you can imagine this was problematic. If you left your scope unprotected from the sun, your mildots would melt off the wire or become misshapen, both outcomes wreaking havoc on your ability to range a target or engage a mover. Small man-portable laser rangefinders weren't as common as you might have expected back then. As an aside, you can always spot the old or perhaps dated sniper: he will never walk away from his rifle without laying his hat on the scope. In addition to the C3 we were armed with C8 short-barrelled carbine chambered in 5.56, and the 9mm Browning pistol. For optics we had the 20x power Bushnell spotting scope and standard issue binoculars with a decent reticle, able to assist in ranging targets. We also had newly purchased Swarovski 60 x power spotting scope that could be married up to a fairly decent SLR camera. These greatly enhanced our ability to observe and report on bad guy activity.

Night vision consisted of a Simrad sight which piggybacked on top of the Unertl, allowing us to employ the C3 at night out to about 400 metres, a monocular night vision goggle and a small family of Kite sights for observation/detection. To assist in night engagements, we also had laser pointer and IR illuminators that could be held on a target by the number two, allowing the number one to place the crosshairs of the C3 through the Simrad sight on the dot. The number one on many occasions would not have the target definition so the number two would only really be identifying the dot. Communications gear was pretty basic. We employed a man-packable VHF radio, roughly 25lb with batteries and a field-expedient antenna. To round out the load, throw in map, compass, GPS, note-taking material, reports and returns, some form of IFF (identification friend or foe), extra batteries of all types, ammo of all nature to include frag(mentation) grenades, smoke grenades, trip flares and finally enough food and water to last 72 hours. As an example, the basics:

Number 1 (Shooter)	Number 2 (Spotter)
C3	M203 – mission specific
C8 carbine with Paq-style laser aiming device	C8 carbine with Paq-style laser aiming device
9mm pistol	9mm pistol
Simrad sight	Bushnell spotting scope and tripod
night vision goggles	night vision goggles
spare radio batteries	VHF radio and EIS
NVD – Kite/Maxi Kite	spare batteries (AA)
spare batteries (AA)	GPS with spare batteries
map	map
compass	compass
sketching material	reports and returns
shooting sock	small sheers
first aid equipment	first aid equipment
shooting sticks	binoculars
frag grenade x 2	frag grenade x 2
smoke grenade – 1 LZ marking	smoke grenade – 1 LZ marking
ammo 5.56 front line x 150 rounds	ammo 5.56 front line x 150 rounds

Number 1 (Shooter)	Number 2 (Spotter)
ammo .308 front line x 60 rounds	ammo .308 spare x 20 rounds
ammo 9mm front line x 30 rounds	ammo 9mm front line x 30 rounds
machete	ammo 40mm M203 x 8 bombs (mission specific)
IFF – strobe/glow sticks	IFF – strobe/glow sticks
rations for 72 hours	rations for 72 hours
water for 72 hours (6 litres)	water for 72 hours (6 litres)

Fast-forward ten years with vested interest in Iraq, Afghanistan and associated nations. Things had changed somewhat. The semi-permissive partner nation/post-genocidal states where NATO was operating had evolved into semi- or non-permissive theatres ruled by sophisticated terror groups, amplified by warlord states trying to assert their rule post-extremist occupation.

The success the Coalition special forces had in Iraq with anti-material neutralization quickly translated into a new capability that was directly transferable to sniper organizations. This introduction to long-range precision rifle fire coupled with an environment suitable to reinforce its need gave direction to the purchase and implementation of the .50-cal sniper rifle, later referred to as the Long-Range Sniper Weapon System (LRSWS). Initially bought as an interim weapon, the McMillan bolt action suppressed .50-cal sniper rifle was brought in to meet the needs of Canadian snipers. It provided a robust platform that could deliver a 700+-grain round downrange with enough energy to cause lethal damage to material and humans alike. It is important to clarify that material neutralization does not mean hunting tanks. A well-placed round could defeat a component of the system but was not intended to penetrate hardened armour. It had great success against missile systems, early warning components and power-generating units as well as human targets. This was further amplified during Operation *Apollo* and the success of the Canadian snipers working with Coalition forces to root out Taliban fighters in the mountains. With this gained interest and knowledge in long-range ballistics and success at long-range interdiction, a medium-calibre system was sought. The C3 was very effective out to 600 metres and could produce effective harassing fire out to 800 metres. The .50-cal Big Mac, as it was later termed, was able to reach out to 1,500 metres with good impunity but was way more gun than required at shorter ranges. This identified the requirement for a medium-range sniper rifle system (MRSWS), which saw the fielding of a .338-cal suppressed sniper rifle system capable of excellent accuracy out to 1,200 metres, bridging the gap between .308 and .50 cal. The platform was to be a local brand in the Prairie Gun Works (PGW) Timberwolf. PGW would later become PGWDTI, adding the Defence Technologies Inc. The Timberwolf fired a Lapua Magnum round downrange with impressive accuracy, in some circumstances reaching out past 1,600 metres with the aid of the 3–12 variable-power Schmidt & Bender scope with a mil dot reticle. The 3–12 would be replaced by the 5–25 Schmidt & Bender providing better target definition at long range. The .338 was lighter and easier to fire than the .50 cal and was more accurate than the C3 at short and intermediate range. This made it the go-to system in the toolbox. Nothing has come close to replacing the lethality of the .50 cal, but in most instances in Afghanistan, the .338 proved to be a more than sufficient. As the battles in Afghanistan and Iraq grew in intensity, frequently moving from rural to urban, the requirement for a more rapid firing accurized weapon system that could be employed by snipers was identified. This capability would allow the sniper detachment to make rapid short-range engagements with sufficient stopping power to affect the battle space. The Canadian army's response to this was yet again another interim buy, this time in the form of the ArmaLite AR-10. The AR-10 is a semi-automatic .308 with a free-floating barrel and variable-power Leopold scope and suppressor. It comes with several different mag capacities to include 5, 10 and 20 rounds. These new additions now added up to four sniper rifle systems in the toolbox instead of just the C3, which was destined to become the training rifle for the army.

With the advancements in sniper rifles and ammo also came advancements in the understanding of ballistics. Snipers now needed to understand the effects of the atmosphere outside that of wind and spin drift in order to place precision fire on small targets at long range. Ballistics programs spanning from Xbal to Applied Ballistics Analytics became common knowledge and applied regularly in the battle space. By 2010, most snipers could easily navigate the programs and be confident speaking about point-blank zero and vertical dispersion, employing anemometers and knowing what to do with all the outputs.

Along with the new capabilities of the smart sniper came the need to not only see further by day and night but also to communicate better. This saw the introduction of the Harris 117F, multiband radio. It provided a robust system capable of VHF/UHF and satellite communications. This system would meet the detachment level requirements to reach back to whatever

HQ needed. Within the det the old PRR (Personal Role Radio), which had huge line-of-sight, battery and crypto dumping issues was replaced by the MBITR (Multiband Intra/Inter Team Radios), a hand-held, software-defined radio. Another lesson learned from our U.S. counterparts was that the MBITR was carried by each member of the det, providing a secure inter-det communications capability and provided for double banking of comms. Now that we could see further by day and night, shoot with more accuracy in multiple range bands and communicate better, we had to revisit our tactics.

Operating in a semi- to non-permissive environment meant drastic changes to our force laydown and our expected survivability. Prior to Afghanistan, Canadian snipers were proficient in conducting operations in two-man detachments over a 72-hour period. There was no way that this would work in Afghanistan. First and foremost, the bad guys were capable. They had some level of training, access to all sorts of munitions and employed communications to varying levels of command and proficiency. They knew the terrain like the back of their hands. If a rock moved on the side of the mountain, they spotted it right away and, in some instances, would launch mortar rounds onto it just to see what happened. They would move in groups and use the terrain to their advantage. They emplaced IEDs at critical points of navigation and had a really good idea where all the legacy mines from previous fights were laid. To us, this meant changing from a two- to a four-man det as a minimum. In some cases, up to six snipers would go out on missions depending on the assessed threat.

This also meant that the duration of our operations was reduced. It was poor judgement to believe you could occupy an

OP for more than 48 hours. Either the bad guys would discover you and try and light you up or the locals would come upon you and tell the bad guys who would then light you up.

Another hard lesson learned was how much kit at a minimum you needed to get the job done. In the early deployments it seemed we kept relearning the same lesson. Pack all the stuff into your ruck and carry it all. By mid-tour that would change to what do I really need to be effective? Radios, weapons, ammo, water, batteries, optics, more batteries and perhaps a bit of high-protein food compressed as small as possible would usually round out the load. Get all this stuff spread across the det into as small a bag as possible so that you retained your agility when out doing the business.

Roads, pathways, gaps in walls and *wadis* (gullies or dry riverbeds) were not options. We had to navigate across grape fields and over walls. Choose the shittiest ground and be able to navigate it stealthily, fully aware of your surroundings and be prepared to fight at any moment … at night. This is what gave us our security. By the latter tours we had this down pat. We were light and agile and were able to bring a sizable fight to whatever we had been directed at.

Now the det load out is broken into two groupings, the det and its toolbox. There are items common to all to include the sniper's personal preferences on gear and load carriage, as well as basic mission necessities. Based on the threat, mission duration and required capability, the toolbox can be drawn from to meet the needs of the team to include additional snipers or enablers. Below are examples of the det configuration and toolbox, this is only an example and will vary between units and mandates.

Equipment Common to All

Sniper Detachment Commander	Sniper Detachment 2IC	Sniper	Sniper
MBITR/ AN/ PRC 163	MBITR/ AN/ PRC 163	MBITR/ AN/ PRC 163	MBITR/ AN/ PRC 163
AN/ PRC 117F Harris Radio			
Pistol (Sig 320/ Sig 226/ Browning HP)	Sig 320/ Sig 226/ Browning HP	Sig 320/ Sig 226/ Browning HP	Sig 320/ Sig 226/ Browning HP
First Aid Kit	First Aid Kit	First Aid Kit	First Aid Kit
Watch (Garmin/ Suunto Watch)	Watch (Garmin/ Suunto Watch)	Watch (Garmin/ Suunto Watch)	Watch (Garmin/ Suunto Watch)
Individual Night Vision Goggles	Individual Night Vision Goggles	Individual Night Vision Goggles	Individual Night Vision Goggles
Batteries	Batteries	Batteries	Batteries
Rations	Rations	Rations	Rations
Water	Water	Water	Water
IFF Marker	IFF Marker	IFF Marker	IFF Marker
Compass	Compass	Compass	Compass
Map	Map	Map	Map
Personal Gear	Personal Gear	Personal Gear	Personal Gear
Ammo of required natures	Ammo of required natures	Ammo of required natures	Ammo of required natures

Frag Grenade	Frag Grenade	Frag Grenade	Frag Grenade
Smoke Grenade	Smoke Grenade	Smoke Grenade	Smoke Grenade
Distraction Device (DD)	Distraction Device (DD)	Distraction Device (DD)	Distraction Device (DD)

The Toolbox

Weapons	Optics	Night Vision	Special Equipment
C8 Heavy Barrel Supressed	Vector LRF/ PLRF	Simrad KN 203	PEQ 15/ PEQ 2A/ PAQ 4
AR-10/ Sig 716/ Colt C20	Leupold Spotting Scope with external equipment rails	UNS/ MUNS/ DUNS	Hog Saddle
C9 Machine Gun	Individual Binos	Thermal Weapon Site (Light/ Medium/ Heavy)	RRS Tripod and Ball Head
C6 Machine Gun	Night Force ATACR 7-35 Rifle Scope	SOPHIE Thermal Binos	Shooting Sock
Remington Shotgun	Schmidt & Bender 5-25 Rifle Scope	JIM LR	Shooting Bag
M203	Red Dot/ Variable Power/ Individual Sight	Jim Compact	Kestrel 5700

.338 MRSWS Supressed		Thermal Clip-on with Magnifier	Peltors
.50 LRSWS Supressed			CF-19 Computer
ESSO System (in development)			Panasonic Toughpad
.375 Cheytac Supressed (in development)			Samsung Tablet with ATAK
300 Norma Mag Supressed (in development)			Dagger GPS
			Garmin Fortrex
			1tb Hard Drive
			Night Force Prism
			Charlie Tarac Prism

The biggest area of influence compared to previous years is the crossover of information from the civilian shooters to the snipers. I suspect the advances made in war and information that was passed to the civilian shooting groups caused unprecedented success in their competitions. They were able to take the initial applications and capabilities and grow them in their garages, much like Steve Jobs. Hand loading ammo with performance scales, the likes of which never seen before, could produce SDs of 4 across an entire batch of ammo (SD = standard deviation).

In many cases the issued sniper ammunition has a higher SD like 12. This indicates that there is a significant difference in muzzle velocity due to ammunition inconsistency. An SD of 4 means that every round is almost perfect, though there may be a small change in muzzle velocity from shot to shot.

Some of the developments include:

o Cracking the nut on internal and external ballistics and providing the formulas to replicate effects.

o Changing the shape of the projectile to more reflect a penetrator than a typical G7 hollow point boat tail bullet.

o Temperature-stable powder measured to the 1,000th of a grain.

o Developing new and innovative reticles to be placed on the first focal plane of crystal-clear sights.

o Breaking further through long-range barriers by employing these rounds in precision weapons with specific twist barrels to ensure stability in supersonic and transonic ranges. The list goes on.

o Employing Doppler radar to determine the exact drag curve of a specific round fired from its matched rifle.

PRS, Precision Rifle Series, was now pushing the capabilities of the sniper world. Sniping is now seen as a market and industry has taken notice. Weapons platforms, ammo, tripods, shooting socks, night vision, target detection—all things sniper is now a commodity. It is only a matter of time before range doesn't matter: "Mortar team at 4,500 metres, stand by." The good news is there will always be a need for snipers to dominate the battle space through observation and fire. Although the equipment and technology will continue to break boundaries, the sniper in his purest form will be able to develop the pattern of life, identify a target, engage or report on it with equal lethality, all without the reliance on loiter time or the fuel of UAVs (unmanned aerial vehicles, or drones). He will close with and without warning or remorse, dispatch his target.

4

The Stalk

Master Corporal Barry Nisbet, Sniper Candidate
1st Battalion, Royal Canadian Regiment
CFB Petawawa, 2005

I can always remember the ride out to the stalk, in the back of the ML, the big six-wheeled diesel monster we were crammed into, with the rickety wooden bench seats, the tarp down and tight, locked in the darkness with a few rays of light shining in through the rips and tears in the heavy tarp that hid us from the outside. The first few minutes of the ride were filled with the normal back and forth, the bullshit, the bravado. But it would soon turn into silence, the smell of the diesel exhaust wafting in and engulfing us, the low rumble as we sped towards our next iteration, our test; it was physically challenging, but that could not compare to the self-induced stress that I would put on myself, that most of us felt. This was different, failure was the norm for the majority … passing a minority.

The odd smoke would get lit in the back of the ML, the flash of the lighter casting a dull light on us. In that brief few seconds of light you would see faces of anxiety, hope and sometimes despair, like portraits hanging on a wall, only to be extinguished in an instant. I knew that on the way out to the next stalk some of those faces would no longer be illuminated. If you were on the bubble, it meant if you failed this one you would be turning in your gear, heading back to whatever rifle company you came from, defeated, rejected, a failure. I wasn't on the bubble this time but there were some waiting for theirs to burst, their portrait's taken down from the dimly lit gallery.

We had been trained well, given all the tools to pass, but employing those were on the individual soldier. This was as far from being in a team as you could be in the green army. This was dog eat dog or more like snake eat snake as we spent most of the time slithering around. I never failed in the army; if I said I wanted to do it, I did it. My mind always raced. *What if I fail, then what?* I don't fail and as much as I wished I could say that I said something cool to myself like, *Then don't fail,* I did not. Fear is a great motivator if channelled properly. I was not scared of getting hurt or anything like that, I was simply afraid to fail although the odds were stacked against me, against all of us.

Stalking is a maneater. It did not care what you did, where you came from, your rank, overseas deployments, it simply did not care and in the mid-2000s there was a certain amount of badge protecting that seemed to take place. The instructors, all qualified snipers, wanted to keep the club small, elite; it was the pointy end of the spear as far as the regular army went. Stay on their good side or they could make it worse. Having later been on the instructing side of the house, I could see just how easy it could be to fuck someone over if you actually wanted to. Dream crusher, maneater.

The ML began to slow. We stopped and the tarp was thrown upward, blasting us with light. Eyes half shut, we offloaded, silent by choice. We lined up in single file and removed our C3A1s from our drag bags. We slid the bolt to the rear and held out our two empty magazines for inspection, no live rounds, the instructor walking behind yelling "Clear" as he checked the last rifle. We numbered from right to left and the instructor recorded this. We use this number to identify on the stalk, no names are used. The instructor nodded to the ML driver who slowly drove away and out of sight. We watched it leave as an instructor said, "I wonder who's gonna get into the truck first today?" No one answered. The back of the ML was the graveyard—you failed, you went to the truck.

It began the moment you got off the truck, that feeling, the doubt; it was almost always silent, that's how I remember it. I would look around and although I knew where we were from our pre-stalk brief the day before, this was the first opportunity to see the ground, the colour of the foliage, the beginning of three hours that I would equate to a non-stop rollercoaster ride in slow motion. *Is there wind, what direction, where is the sun now, going to be in a few hours, which way will the shadows fall when I'm in my FFP, if I get to one that is?*

On the stalk we were always accompanied by two "walkers". They were both qualified snipers whose job was to give us a final brief before we started and, most important, they communicated with the two snipers who were sitting in the OP: we referred to this as the "chair" or just OP as they always sat in two metal chairs spaced about two feet apart; this was what/who we were trying to get close enough to "kill". One walker would always stay with the lead or front group of snipers and the other would stay in the vicinity of the rear group as the stalk progressed. Each sniper or chair in the OP controlled one of the walkers via a radio, giving them specific commands of how and where to move to. The walkers were an extension of the chair: they moved and only did what the chair told them to do. When the OP/chair called the walker on the radio they followed their direction to a T, or at least they were supposed to.

The two walkers gave us the stalk brief, confirming the six-figure grid of the OP/chair, the four corners of the box. The box is the area every sniper must get into to set up their final fire position. It's usually about 150–200 metres wide and the back of the box is 300 metres to the OP/chair and the front line of the box, which you can't go beyond, is 150 metres from the OP/chair. You have to get into this area from the back of the box, not in through the side, no exceptions. The stalk started anywhere from 1,500–1,200 metres from the OP/chair, so minimum distance to get into the box was about 900 metres straight line. Seems easy enough, not even a kilometre. But get on your hands and knees and try it. We were given ten minutes to "prep": check maps, bearings to the OP/chair, and cam up our ghillie suits.

Our ghillie suits were all handmade, by our own hands. We had been provided with an old set of olive drab combat uniforms, top and bottom, which would be the base of our suit. We were also given thick canvas to reinforce the knees, elbows and chest. Padding would be added to the knees and elbows. Knees took a beating, and it was normal for them to be rubbed raw halfway through a stalk, though elbows seemed to last a bit longer. Netting would be sewn and glued onto the back of the shirt, up over the shoulders and partly down your chest, and down the outside portion of your arms. Some guys would do this to the back of their pants, but I opted not to. Once this base was established, the arduous task of peeling the scrim or hessian began. Long rolls of different-coloured hessian, each about three inches wide would be cut and stripped down to single stands. Once you had a considerable amount, about a garbage bag full (probably about six hours to do) you would grab 10 to 15 strands about 10–14 inches long in a bunch and tie them into the netting using a basic overhand knot. This would be repeated ad nauseam over the entire net area until it had a nice "flow" to it. You didn't want it to be uniform. The idea of the ghillie suit is to break up the body's natural outline, to soften the sharp angles of your shoulders and arms, to aid you in blending in with your natural surroundings. Natural camouflage was important. Long pieces of green 550/para cord would be tied all through the netting, which allowed you to tie in natural camouflage as required, and it usually was. Once you had a sufficient amount of scrim/hessian covering your suit, you would lay it down in the grass and look for holes or areas that needed a little bit more. A clean ghillie suit stuck out like a sore thumb and the instructors took care to ensure this did not happen. Your ghillie suit aided you in adapting to your surroundings, matching as best you could the colours and materials that you were laying in to *try* to remain undetected. Natural cam dies and wilts as soon as you cut or tear it from the ground; knowing that if we added live greens early on, they would inevitably wilt and discolour the longer they stayed on your suit. Forget to change it when in your FFP and more than likely you get caught; have a leaf flipped over and exposing the lighter underside and you get caught; rise above your surroundings aka turkey necking and you get caught;

moving the foliage silently around you on a windless day and … I think you get the picture.

This exercise was repeated for the hat, which came in all shapes and sizes. Lots of guys used baseball hats, a favourite team for luck, while others used various military-style hats. I used a standard CADPAT (Canadian Disruptive Pattern) bush hat. I cut the wide brim down about an inch and then attached a piece of the netting to the hat, which had a long veil about 18 inches hanging off the back but following the shape of the hat on the sides and front. Hessian, or scrim, and 550 cord was painstakingly attached all over the netting. I always remember being told by the instructors that when on a stalk, it was much easier to make your colour darker if required but very hard to make it look lighter, so with that in mind I mostly used light browns and greens throughout my suit and hat, with a splash of dark brown here and there. With 550 cord all over the netting on the hat, these tie-downs would allow me to add natural camouflage to my head, a part of the body that risked the most exposure when setting up a final fire position. The long veil was crucial to me, almost a security blanket. During the stalk you could spin your hat around, so it was at the front and drape it over your binoculars when you were looking out, or "glassing", an area ahead. When in your final fire position, I would spin my hat around and drop the long veil over my rifle and scope.

Our basic load out on the stalk consisted of our trusty Parker-Hale C3A1 bolt-action rifle weighing in at 7.52kg. Fitted on top was an Unertl fixed 10x BDC (bullet drop compensator) scope; it was ancient, the reticle inside was thin wire and the dots, mil dots, inside were actually made of wax, and they had a tendency to "warp" when they got too hot and resembled an oval more than an actual circular dot.

How you carried your rifle on a stalk was personal choice. We had all been issued a drag bag. It was a soft case that held the rifle inside securely with straps and unzipped the length of the bag. At the barrel end of the bag was a heavy-duty loop that you could fit your hand in and literally drag the bag beside you as you crawled. I opted for this method. Others took their gun out of the bag and carried it with them in their arms. Others would tie about a 4–6-foot cord to the hand loop and then secure the other end to their belt at the back and then drag the bag behind them as they crawled. It really came down to personal choice. I liked the drag bag as I could fit other things inside it as well. We all had some sort of shooting sticks or modified camera tripod that we used, which allowed us to rest the rifle on top of it if we needed to gain some elevation when setting up our FFP. This added height always came with consequences of being higher than the foliage around you, which resulted in the dreaded turkey necking. This sent many a hopeful back to the waiting ML, including me, some never to return again.

Inside my drag bag was also my shooting sock, a large tan sock filled with either plastic beads or in my case popcorn kernels. This was placed under the butt of the rifle when you were preparing to shoot: if you squeezed the bag with your hand, the butt would raise ever so slightly, lowering your barrel and conversely your reticle. Lessen your grip and the opposite occurred, slightly raising your barrel and reticle. This allowed minute changes in your point of aim.

My map was in my right cargo pant pocket, because I usually laid on my left side. It was a 1:50,000 scale of the training area and it had the start point, OP/chair, and four corners of the box that I'd marked on it. The scale didn't really give great detail, but it was crucial. My compass lived in a small pocket that I'd sewed to the outside of my left sleeve of my ghillie suit; it was tied to the pocket by its lanyard. The compass and map were indispensable items on the stalk, and as I would find out about a year later, indispensable when calling in artillery and air strikes during Operation *Medusa* against dug-in Taliban in Panjwai.

My binoculars hung from my neck. I would tuck them under my shirt when not in use. They were old and heavy but had good-quality glass in them and were as important as the rifle on a stalk. I also carried a pair of pruning shears in my drag bag, to cut natural camouflage like grass and other foliage that I would use to tie into my ghillie suit and also to build my FFP. A small canteen, some cam paint, bug juice, an energy bar and my wind chart would usually fill out my drag bag. This was our basic load out; we all had variations on this but the key items we all carried.

As our ten-minute prep time ticked away, we would put the final touches to our ghillie suits, adding cam paint to any exposed areas, checking and rechecking our "rough bearing" on our compass pointing in the general direction of the OP/chair. Stomachs tightened, and the odd nervous shit was taken.

The walkers were doing their final comms checks with the OP/snipers in the chair, we strained to hear the response so we could figure out who was in the chair. It could make a huge difference. A calm, familiar voice chirped on one radio, "Yep. We're good to go." Great, it's Gord—his eagle eyes could pick off many of us from 1,000 metres away. I felt my stomach tighten.

What the chair had to do was direct their walker step by step to where they saw, or thought they saw, a sniper. Then direct him to move his hand to be able to touch any part of the sniper or his equipment. The walker would only do what the chair told him. This was initiated by the chair telling the walker to yell "Freeze" and every sniper needed to freeze in place while the chair directed the walker. The freezes were agonizing. You had nightmares that began and ended with that word being yelled out.

The minutes crept by. We were about to be launched out of a slow speed cannon, but no fuse would disperse us. It was five words every sniper would always remember: "YOU ARE NOW UNDER OBSERVATION." With those words we have 2 hours and 50 minutes to get into the box and declare sniper ready to fire without getting busted. As hot as the summer air was, you could guarantee to freeze more than once.

Getting caught, or busted, on a stalk where you thought you were doing everything right was demoralizing. You wondered, *Who the fuck are these assholes in the chair and how the hell did they see me?* The guys in the chair and the walkers were all instructors on the course; they had all been through what we were going through, but still our animosity to them built over time. Some would be smoking and joking after the stalk, talking about how many "kills" (candidates they busted) they got after a stock. Some did it in earshot—they wanted us to hear. At times stalks became us versus them; it could get personal, very personal. We always wanted to know who was in the chair trying to locate us. Today Gord was one of them, and although he was eagle-eyed in the chair, he was always fair, uncompromising. The candidates always had respect for him; he wanted us to succeed and when Gord busted you, you knew you were getting busted by one of the best. Some instructors wanted us to fail, and they made no effort to hide this, badge protecting: if they let someone into their club, eventually someone would be let out, so no one in = no one out. So, suffice to say, the odds are stacked up favouring failure and the numbers of successful candidates did not lie. Now that being said, there were other knowledgeable instructors, solid guys who saw new blood as a way of making the Sniper Platoon a better place. They knew some of the old dogs had to go and with Afghanistan looming on the horizon and our unit poised to deploy, there was no doubt that success on the course granted you access to the club. This would allow you to see Afghanistan in a manner only few ever have, through a high-power scope attached to a high-power rifle, putting everything you have learned to the test, a hunter of man, to feel fear of death, to feel the loss of comrades in battle, to feel victory and to feel defeat, to put it all on the line in ways the normal person can't even fathom. Three of 18 would pass this course and eventually we would see Afghanistan and slither along its unforgiving terrain.

Our ten minutes of prep was about to expire, the walkers did a time check and advised us we had 2 hours and 50 minutes to declare "Sniper ready to fire". I always found those words hard to say—clearly, I was not a sniper—but if you got that far and were ultimately successful that day, it brought you that much closer to being one, on paper anyways.

"YOU ARE NOW UNDER OBSERVATION!" the walker yells out.

I start my stopwatch, The OP/chair is now binos up, watching, waiting for a mistake, a turkey neck, a flash of the sun on your binos, a ghillie suit too dark for its surroundings or vice versa. Movement always draws the eyes the fastest: they look right to left as we had been taught in our observation exercises, opposite of what the eye is used to doing when reading, to catch something you would not normally see. *So many mistakes to make and Gord in the chair. FML [fuck my life]*, I said to myself jokingly. The first few steps into the unknown waiting for the first heart-stopping "FREEZE" to bellow out.

Find the fucking OP. You can't stalk unless you can see what you're stalking. I think that is pretty self-explanatory. This stalk started off 1,400 metres from the OP, so a quick bit of math and I have 1,100 metres to get to the back of the box; that's fuck all, walk that in ten minutes or so. I always stalked slow, I stop, and I watch, we have a six-figure coordinate for the OP/chair that's accurate to 100 metres so that narrows it down slightly. Sometimes they put a small flag at the back of the box which can help orientate you. Okay, breathe, in and out. I can feel my pulse racing. Two hours and 50 minutes to declare, to call out "Sniper ready to fire", seems like a long time to cover 1,100 metres but for me it was never long enough. Remember to STOP LOOK LISTEN PLAN.

In a stalk, minutes sometimes feel like seconds and ten metres crawling on your stomach can seem like ten miles. Breathe, look. Okay, so this stalk started on low ground, sparse trees, seems like easy movement to begin. I have opted to carry my 7.52kg rifle in my drag bag. With all my other gear I am dragging around 25lb of dead weight behind me, while wearing a fur coat in full sun with half a litre of water—we all volunteered for this. Life is good and misery loves company.

"FREEZE" is yelled out minutes later.

Shit, it's me, they've seen me from a kilometre away. What the fuck? I'm so stupid. Freeze means freeze, hard to do, a sore point on my course and many others I have taught on; it takes integrity to not move a hair knowing they may be walking on you, mindful it might just be two inches of your hat protruding above your cover. The thing is the walkers are always watching us, taking notes; they know who sinks, who moves when supposedly frozen, they get to know each candidate by the colour and shape of their ghillie suit, how they carry their rifle. And if you get to stick around long enough, even how you crawl and where you like to set up inside the box.

A freeze followed by the *crunch, crunch, crunch* of boots means one thing: a walker is near you and if he is walking with a sense of purpose he is being directed by the chair: *crunch, crunch, crunch*. Most walkers, the good ones anyways, were helpful to a certain extent and of course this went hand in hand with what I said above: freeze = integrity = the odd hint, a comment in the form of a question— "You gonna go across that?" or "I would think twice about that." *Crunch, crunch, crunch. Don't fucking move, Nisbet. You're good. He's not on you* and onward he marches, the *crunch, crunch, crunch* of his boots fading away in the dry grass and I'm only left with the *thump, thump, thump* of my heart ready to beat out of my chest. Not freezing makes you a target: a sinking sniper is a marked man, and the OP/chair will put extra effort into your area—they take it personally as well, as they should.

Time continues to tick by as I am on all fours frozen, drag bag in my right hand, sweat running down my face mixing in with my cam paint and bug juice running into my eyes, stinging and burning.

"CARRY ON!" the walkers scream out.

I am released from my statuesque pose. I drive my body hard down into the dirt, my left cheek strikes the ground with vigour. I inhale through my nose, drawing in the freshly disturbed earth.

I taste it in the back of my throat. I feel safe now, invisible, I can breathe again. *Fuck. I still haven't found the OP, but they can see us. What the fuck.* I check my watch: 22 minutes have passed, and I've gone about 100 metres. *Fuck, fuck, fuck.* 1,000 metres or so to the back of the box.

We are taught different movement techniques on the course: The walk (popular but rarely used), the monkey run, the leopard crawl, the stomach crawl and so on. You can use your imagination to figure those out. They get more painful and slower as you go down the list. The most interesting I always found was what I called the worm crawl or simply fucking the ground. You lay flat on the ground, cheek to the dirt, ankles splayed out and arms extended; you drive your pelvis into the ground to keep your ass down. To move you flex your ankle, pulling your toes towards your knees, dig them into the ground and push back, all the while keeping your ankles pressed into the ground. Simultaneously, you extend your fingers outwards and pull the ground toward you, moving about three or four inches, each time scraping your cheek across the ground. You want to keep as much of your body in contact with the ground as possible This is used as the terrain and your cover dictates. It is slow, deliberate, and at times what you need to do. This can also be the "oh fuck" position, the "I'm fucked" position, the "this is useless" position, the "why did I volunteer for this" position, and so on. I remember being told that if you think you could be crawling on all fours, then get one level lower and you should be good. Words I lived by ... most of the time.

As you progress on a stalk, the vegetation/ground/foliage starts to become more sporadic; it makes you get lower and lower, it slows your movements. There are usually no trees in the box, maybe some clumps of small bushes and always a lot of tall grass and rolling ground.

I slowly rise to a low crawl, on all fours, I spot a small dip in the ground with a clump of bushes about 20 metres ahead and to my right. That's my next move. My movements are slow and planned, head up just enough to see where I am going. My compass tells me the OP/chair is in this general direction. At this point I'm stalking the bush; it doesn't see me coming and I stop about five feet behind it and slowly drop down, sweat continuing to pour down my face and mixing with the cam paint and bug juice. My ghillie suit smells like a mixture of perspiration, mud, grass and panic. It gets worse every stalk and I want it to smell worse.

I've got some bushes in front of me, some trees behind me. I can "burn" through bushes with my binos (when looking through something close with binos, they tend to blur out the closer object and you are able to see or burn through it). The colour of my ghillie is good. I turn my hat around and drape the long veil over my binos as I bring them up to my eyes. I rise ever so slowly, elbows out wide. As I bring them in closer, I get a touch higher. I feel so exposed. I burn through the bush ahead of me. I am still well below it, up a little more, scan right to left, up a little more, scan right to left.

"FREEZE!" echoes in my right ear, and the inevitable *crunch, crunch, crunch* as the walker's boots rise and fall in the tall, spindly grass. The sound grows louder and louder. He's on me, it's me, I'm too high, shit, all I can do is not move, not a muscle. I move and they will for sure know they have me and stop at nothing until they get me. So, I hold as still as I can, binos up to my face, looking towards a future I may never actually realize. The walker is behind me now and I hear "Stop" on the walker's radio. He's so close, I can feel the minutes ticking by.

"Take ten steps to your right," the radio spews.

He's going away from me, mild relief,

"Back five … left two … right two … back five … left two."

They are bracketing for depth, trying to put the walker in front of what he sees and then behind. Then within those five to ten steps there is a sniper. As this plays out, we are all still frozen, precious minutes continue to tick by. Although relived it's not me, I have no choice but to wait it out.

The radio crackles, "Right arm out and down to the ground; you are touching a sniper."

The walker responds with "Roger." The sniper gives the walker his number that was assigned to him at the beginning of the stalk, so the OP/chair does not know the name of whom they have just caught. The busted sniper is given short debrief. He stands up, removes his hat and begins to walk out of the stalk lane and to the waiting truck, pissed off, alone, with no one to blame for getting caught but himself.

It is usually a short but memorable walk; there is nothing shameful in it, but with each walk you make to the truck the self-imposed stress is compounded. I've made that walk plenty of times, teeth clenched, asking myself how I could have been so stupid. I always remembered why I got caught, what the walker told me and what the OP/chair said to me on the radio, vowing, sometimes unsuccessfully, never to make the same mistake twice. In my day we did eight stalks. You accumulated points as you progressed during the stalk: 10 was a perfect score, that being you stalked into the box, observed the OP/chair and hit your target; 8 points if you missed but that was still considered a pass. You also accumulated points for getting into the box and identifying the OP/chair … every point counted. You needed 48 points from four stalks passed to carry on. Much easier said than done.

"CARRY ON!" the walker yells out.

I remain motionless for another minute. I raise my head ever so slightly, almost turkey necking. I catch a flash of movement in my binos: it's a head, wait it's two heads. I can just see them from the nose up. It's the OP/, the chair, I've found them. I need to landmark them now, note what's behind them … the tree line … what sticks out … okay, that large tree … one finger left is the OP/chair. I can see that tree from most places, I think. Compass out, I shoot a bearing to the OP. Slowly I lower myself back to the ground, chin in the dirt, map out, look at the ground, plot the bearing on the map, double-check it, confirm I can see the tree that I landmarked just above the OP/chair.

Now I have no excuse, now I need to employ all the fieldcraft—the movement, observation, concealment—with just a little bit or a lot of luck. I need to plan my next bound, I need to move, need to keep crawling forward, 45 minutes gone, 800 metres to the back of the box.

The sun beats down on me. My ghillie suit is soaked and gets heavier with every ounce of sweat. My movements are as calculated as they can be. I crawl and drag, crawl and drag, sweat dripping and stinging my eyes. It's amazing how you can lose your bearings when trying to navigate from your stomach or crawling on all fours It's also amazing how the tiniest bush or rise in the ground can hide you from the all-seeing OP/chair. I am making decent progress now. I'm continually orientating myself to the OP/chair. I landmark my tall tree; one finger left is the enemy. The ground has a way of funnelling you, of gently and mischievously guiding you into its folds, into what you think is low ground but ends up being an exposed position. It has a way of giving you a false sense of security, of anonymity when that is exactly what you want but don't actually have. I remember the words spoken to me about the ghillie suit: "It is not a cloaking device; it does not make you disappear." The ghillie suit softens the harsh angles of your body, disrupts the symmetry of your head. It has to be employed properly to work; you need to know its limitations and you need to constantly update and change the natural cam you have tied into it to match what is around you, especially when you are setting up your FFP. Check your foreground and background, you need to be in the middle, you need to master the use of depth, hiding in the open, hiding in plain sight. It's a hard concept to master, let alone even accept on the course as they cram so much information down your neck. But once you understand it and can employ it with some degree of success, you can do just that: disappear in the open. "DEPTH, DEPTH, DEPTH," I can remember Gord telling us all the time. I remember him telling us how he did a stalk in our regimental T-shirt, which is sky blue. He did it using depth.

I cover the next 200 metres rather quickly, in about 20 minutes. I slide up the right side in a good bit of dead ground, hidden from the OP/chair as long as I stay low. I crawl towards a low bush; I see the sole of a boot. Shit, someone is already there … we are forbidden to talk to other candidates while on a stalk: it is an individually assessed event.

He hears me behind him and says, "Hey, where the fuck is the OP?"

In my mind I think, *How the fuck did you make it this far?* But that's how it goes sometimes; some guys go head down balls to the wall and go with *If I can't see them, they can't see me*, which usually ends in the hatless walk.

Crunch, crunch, crunch, the walkers always know. They have been in our boots. They see when we get near to each other, and they hear everything.

"You two need to separate," he says. Quietly.

The good walkers can walk and talk to us without giving the slightest hint to the OP/chair that anyone is around. We both acknowledge and I slowly slide to the right and around to another small shrub about ten metres away. I pull out my compass and shoot another bearing to the OP/chair to check my line. I just start to slide my left boot in towards my body when I hear "Freeze! Don't you fucking move." The voice is directed at me.

My left boot is hanging out to the side of the shrub. I'm about four feet behind it, using depth. My colour is good. *I'm low fuck, fuck, fuck, I'm so close to the box now.* CRUNCH, CRUNCH, CRUNCH. It's deafening, the boots are near me now.

I hear the radio *beep*, and the OP/chair tells the walker to "Face me … now turn around … now walk … STOP!" crackles from the radio. The walker stops, he moves only as told by the OP/chair. He is an extension of him out there, and so begins the bracket: *crunch, crunch, crunch*; he walks mere feet to my right.

The radio beeps, "Stop … two steps to your right."

He's directly in front of me now. I can feel the adrenaline surge through me. My heart is pounding. I feel it reverberate through my body.

"Turn around," the OP/chair tells the walker, and he does.

I hear the walker say, "Don't move. He won't get you for depth." *Crunch, crunch, crunch.* He walks within a foot of my boot and back about 20 steps.

The radio crackles, "Tell those guys we're on them."

I heed the warning.

"Carry on" is called and I drop my left ankle to the ground and slowly draw it in line with my body, cheek into the dirt. I am in my happy place, fucking the ground, knowing that could have ended differently but happy it did not. Sometimes that's all it takes, a heel not flat on the ground, a drag bag slightly off line. And sometimes guys have been busted looking 90 degrees away from the OP/chair, disoriented and lost.

This stalk box is marked with two small yellows flags on a six-foot picket driven into the ground; they are usually very hard to see until you are within about ten metres of them. This is the back of the box. Get through that imaginary line and you can start to look for and set up your FFP. Just getting into the box gives you two much-needed points. The box will have a minimum of two positions for each sniper on the stalk. The areas or "lanes" we stalk in have usually been used on past courses and have been successfully stalked by qualified snipers to prove they are attainable.

I must keep moving. My muscles are starting to ache, my knees and elbows are raw from the constant rubbing of my ghillie suit and dragging along the ground; my throat is dry, my water is gone, my drag bag seems to have doubled in weight, the sun lashes out at me, drenches me in its rays, there is no shade other than that of my hat which is soaked with sweat, my cam paint has almost all worn off, flies gather around as the smell of my suit signifies to them that something is near death. I check my watch: 1 hour 15 minutes to declare, I must be near the back of the box now. STOP LOOK LISTEN PLAN.

To my right the ground dips behind a low rise; the low ground leads off left in the direction of the OP/chair. I know I can't go straight to it. I have to go back; fuck, I hate going backwards. As if crawling on your guts forward isn't bad enough, backwards is the fucking worst. You have to go straight backwards to stay in line with the cover you're using to block out or hide from the OP/chair. If you simply turned around and started crawling, you would get off line and out of your cover. So, I start the arduous task of crawling backwards. My pant legs ride up, the stirrup straps I built in out of elastic both snap under the weight and strain as my knees press into the ground; they ride up and I can feel the dirt and debris building up, slowing my progress even more. The bottom of my shirt acts as scoop, seeing how much of the ground it can jam into my stomach and eventually down my pants; my drag bags seem to immobilize my right hand as I try to draw it back. I crawl back about five metres and it seems to take ten minutes. My lower legs and abdomen itch after being dragged and scraped through the tall grass, my shoulders burn, as does my throat. Every breath I draw in dust and debris. But I made it ... no "freeze". I slowly move to my right, head always towards the OP/chair. I need to stay in line, a couple more feet and I'm good. I push the drag bag to my right and then ease myself over until I push up against it. One more slide to the right.

"Freeze" gets yelled of to my right. The walker nearest me tells me I'm good and can keep moving. he disappears, *crunch, crunch, crunch* ...

I crawl forward on a slightly different line. I have no bush in front of me but I'm staying a level lower than the grass and the low rise about 30 metres to my front. I dig in with my elbows, legs are flat to the ground, knee up and out at about a 45. I push and pull for every inch of ground. Friction is not your friend: every inch of ground taken comes at a cost, precious energy is expelled and when you get tired, you start to make mistakes, you get lazy, take risks, and those get you busted. *Not this time*, I tell myself. *I have to make it.* Push and pull, push and pull. I press on, keeping to the low ground and I follow it to the left and forward. I glance to my right, and I can see the yellow flag. It flutters quietly in the wind—I note about 3 kph from the 10 o'clock position, the OP/chair being 12 o'clock. Nothing to worry about as far as the shot is concerned but good to know. The wind gently blows the grass all around me, helping to conceal my movements as I draw ever closer to box, closer to my always-suspecting prey.

I infiltrate deeper into the enemy-held ground, staying low and sticking to the dead ground. They know it's there, they are watching it, they are looking for me, as I am looking for them, hunting. I am almost parallel to the flag now. I'm so close to the box but now I can see that my low ground is not so low anymore; it begins to rise just at the back of the box, as if they set it up that way. *Those fuckers! Why would they do that? Why would they crush me like that?* I am momentarily demoralized. I curse the ground beneath me but then remind myself how I got here and why I am here.

Straight ahead is no longer an option. Do I go left or right? More room to the left, more box, more people, more movement. Do I go right and run out of ground, out of time, out of luck? I quickly pull out my map; the 1:50,000 scale does little to aid me in my decision. This one is not life or death. Those will come later and much further away.

MAN IN THE BOX

I decide to go right. I crawl closer and closer to the flag. *Crunch, crunch, crunch*, I hear. "Getting pretty close to the flag, aren't you?" the walker says. It's not a question, it's a warning. He meanders away. I know he's watching me.

About five metres ahead of the flag I see a small scrubby bush sitting about three feet high, it's in the box. I crawl up, set up and shoot, or so I think. *This is it ... it has paid off ... I've got this.* I slowly crawl towards it, checking my bearing on the OP/chair. I'm in line. I landmark my tree. I'm good to go. I crawl and crawl and crawl. I can taste it. I can feel the recoil of my C3A1 as I send my round downrange to disintegrate against the metal kill zone gong that will be hanging in place of the OP/chair, hearing that sound of a muffled bell as it strikes. I'm at the bush, about three feet back. I spin my ghillie hat around and drape its long tail over my binos. I raise them to my face. I bring my elbows in and rise upwards, exposing a little more of myself with every inch, I can't see them. I can't see shit here. *Wait, where's my tree? It's right there on the horizon, one finger left and OP ... nope ... FML.* The ground is barren in front of me and another low ridge runs across the ground. I'm blocked out completely. If I go any higher, I will silhouette myself ... it's no good.

Now what?

I check my watch. I've got 45 minutes to declare; my mind starts to spin. *Do I have enough time? Where the fuck is everybody else? No one came this way because it sucks! Because there is a huge-ass ridge blocking the OP.* I'm hot, sweaty and tired, my calf muscles flirt with seizing up. I rest my chin on the ground, inhaling the mixture of dirt and bits of grass that I have crushed from moving around; they stick to the back of my throat, my knees and elbows ache from over a 1,000 metres of crawling and zigzagging, blood trickles down the left side of my face from a thornbush I dragged myself through ... and I embrace it: the discomfort, the sweat stinging my eyes, the smell seeping from my every pore, the freedom to do what I want and to go where I want, no one telling me what to do. I decide my actions—I alone am responsible for them; it is a freedom you seldom feel in the regular army. I love the solitude of the stalk and although it is interrupted often, it is mostly silent. I'm flying solo, surrounded by the smells of the grass, dirt and my ghillie suit.

"Sniper ready to fire" is called out off to my left. Someone is in, ready to fire. It's a good feeling even though it's not me. We aren't competing against each other: it's us against them. Fuck them.

Okay, I've had my moment. It's time to get on with it, to move, to stalk. I crawl low on my knees and elbows, barely 12 inches off the ground. I move forward into the low ground while keeping an eye on my compass bearing, stopping to landmark the OP/chair. That rise that blocked me before now starts to tail off to my left and as it does, I can start to see the ground behind it. I am now facing the OP/chair head on, or at least where I think it is. My head is up, I see my landmark as I slowly edge to the left, the tall grass keeps me hidden. I lower my body, chest on the ground. I can feel my pulse start to race. I know I'm close now, about 250 metres from the OP/chair. I slowly ease myself to the left, inch by inch, that ridge to my front continuing to drop, exposing more and more of the ground it had hidden from me before. About ten metres to my left there is another scraggly-looking bush; you can see right through it, but it might help.

I continue my slow, methodically panicked movement to my left, elbows and knees stinging as they press firmly into the hard earth, chin in the dirt. I pull my drag bag towards my body and stop. I pull my binos out from under my shirt and slowly raise them to my face. My adrenaline is pumping, my body wants to go fast but I need to breathe, control, go slow. I can see over the ridge in front of me. I keep the binos to my face and ever so slightly ease to the left, willing my body to stretch out and see what lies just beyond that ridge to the right … a little more, a little more …

I always get that "oh fuck" feeling when I see the OP/chair once in the box. Through magnification they look so close. I can see who it is, can pick up their mannerisms. I can just see the head of the man on the left as I look at the OP/chair, the binos up to his face, radio in his right hand waiting to call the freeze. If I can see him then, technically, he can see me. I know who it is, but I don't care anymore. His partner is still blocked off by that ridge to my front which is always an advantage. I slink back down and a few feet to my right. I am safe behind the ridge, but I still need to keep low. I start to look for a good position to set up my FFP. I take a look behind and try to picture what the OP/chair sees and what my background will be. I need to blend with my foreground and background. I need to stay lower than my cover and blend in. After a few minutes I decide to move backwards and utilize the low ground behind me to see if I can incorporate that scraggly bush into my eventual FFP. I get back to it quickly, knowing I am hidden by the ridge to my front.

CAMOUFLAGE IS AN ART

I stop safely behind cover and take the pruning shears from my drag bag. I cut a bunch of grass around me. I take my hat off and begin to carefully tie the grass into the netting, mixing it with the scrim. I make sure I cut the roots off as those are a dead giveaway—roots tend to not grow in the air. I make sure the grass is running in the same direction on my hat and will make sense when looked at from the OP/chair. I quickly take off my ghillie jacket and tie more grass onto the shoulder and arms, any areas that will be exposed to the OP/chair while I am in my FFP and behind the gun. I cut a little extra and stuff it into my drag bag. My thought is to keep moving to the left enough to block out the left-hand man I originally saw from that scraggly bush while using the ridge to block the right-hand man from the chin down.

If I get the right angle, I think it should work. In my head it's perfect. I continue moving left, inch by inch. *I need to go slow, I need to be deliberate, I need to …*

"FREEZE!" gets yelled off on the left flank.

I'm not as concerned as I was. The walker nearest me softly says, "Carry on." I don't see him but know he's near. I continue trying to calculate the angle in my head that I need … a little further, a little further … I feel the ground rising slightly. Not good. I move backwards, conscious of the ticking clock. I check my watch: 17 minutes to declare. As I back up, I also continue to creep left. That scraggly bush is now right in front of me. I'm low in the grass; it sways with the wind. I precariously raise my head to see my landmark tree—one finger left should be the OP/chair. I pull my binos out from under my shirt, hat turned around, elbows flat as the binos meet with my eyes, elbows in, a little higher, a little higher. Just off the right edge of the bush I catch movement of an arm from the OP/chair. Okay, I'm blocked but so are they for now.

"Fifteen minutes to declare!" calls out the walker,

Lots of time. I slide inches to the left, the scraggly bush about seven feet to my front. It provides some good depth when used in unison with the tall grass around me. It doesn't look as scraggly from the OP's perspective, or so I hope. I slowly pull my C3 from the drag bag. I estimate my range to be about 230–250 metres. I set my elevation dial on my Unerlt to 2 and up 1, winds are still coming from the 10 o'clock at about 10 kph now. I take a quick glance at my wind chart and decide on ½ a minute to the left. I double-check my cam and add some grass to an elastic around my barrel to break up its straight line and disrupt its black colour. With my rifle now cradled in my arms, I slowly move back to the spot where I could last see the arm of the OP/chair, my drag bag laying between my legs. The ground rises, giving me some much-needed elevation, dipping behind me and then gently rising again. A uniform sea of grass is what I hope the OP/chair can see. The bush is a likely firing position, but I think I have offset enough from it not to be busted should the OP/chair try to send the walker in.

I am in position. I extend my rifle out in front of me. She is old but beautiful, grey green stock supporting the heavy, free-floating barrel. 78G are the last three characters of the serial number. She is well used, and I am hoping to use her again today. Click by click I compress the Parker-Hale bipod to its lowest configuration. I double-check the elevation setting and confirm my wind call. I drape the veil of my hat over the scope. In my veil is a small ring of 550 cord that I loop around the end of the scope … I am now connected to my rifle. We move as one.

The scope or scope ring is something that has busted many snipers, the black ring of death. You can be looking from the OP/chair and see nothing but a field of grass and then this perfect black circle appears, and it only means one thing, it is unmistakable. They have shown us this and harped on it in training. It goes to show that you can hide a six-foot man with a sniper rifle perfectly but not a 1½- inch black circle. Camouflage is an art … I need to remind myself to slow down, slow my movements and my thoughts and not to get ahead of myself. I have practised this set-up dozens of times—it is always different but the same. I am relieved that I can set up in the prone position. It does not always go this way, and I am happy to leave my rickety jerry-rigged tripod in the drag bag. My FFP needs to be an invisible masterpiece that to the OP/chair looks unchanged. From my perspective I must see them and will ultimately deliver a 168-grain 7.62mm projectile into the hardened-steel kill zone.

I drape scrim left and right of the scope ring, leaving only a narrow slit about ¼-inch wide. The scope has an amazing ability to gather light and still allow you to see when it is partly covered. I remember in training they would have you behind your rifle looking through your scope, and then set a loonie (dollar coin) against the front lens and you could still see everything. Sniper black magic, I suppose, but a valuable lesson.

I triple-check the cam on my hat, arms and shoulders. This is it. I know the clock is running dangerously low. I exhale and slowly rotate the rifle off its side and to the right and into my shoulder, my right hand resting effortlessly on the grip of the stock. My right index finger is perched above the trigger as my left hand slowly moves to the butt. I raise the butt ever so slightly and slide my popcorn kernel-filled shooting sock underneath and slowly lower it until it settles in. The rifle will stand on its own at this point with minimal input from me. My cheek finds its home on the pad of the butt, the foam soaking up my cam-paint-bug-juice-sweat medley as I rest my head and stare through the scope.

I am intimate with this position from thousands of rounds on the range. I can do it all by feel. I push lightly forward with my toes to get my eye relief set just right. I look through the scope and begin to orientate myself with this much higher magnification view. At this point it is so easy to "lose" the OP/chair and not even be able to find it at all. The narrow field of view and 10 x magnification of the Unertl scope makes everything look gigantic and I see blurry grass blowing back and forth. I slow my breathing, in/out/in/out, everything needs to be methodical, no movement without purpose. I scan low to start and move the rifle butt millimetres from left to right then back to the left. I relax my grip on the shooting sock to allow the butt to lower and my scope to rise; right to left I scan slowly. I see the arm again. It's so colossal in the scope, I feel I can reach out and touch it, it seems too close. I scooch slightly to my right. Shit, I can see more of him than I like, from about upper chest to head. I watch his head to make sure I can clearly make it out, make sure it's the right-hand man as I look at it. It is. I am set up; I am ready to fire.

I exhale slowly, my heart is racing, adrenaline stores have been replenished, and I need to just slow down and breathe. I close my eyes and revel in the darkness and silence. I need to make sure I can reacquire the target. My eye opens, my hold is true, my target remains. I will shoot through the tall grass that conceals me; it will not affect the round's trajectory. If I used the bush to hide behind, I would have to line the rifle up on the target, remove the bolt to allow me to see straight down the barrel and make sure there were no sticks to the front that the round would hit, aka a stick shot, that would deflect my round off target—been there, done that. STOP LOOK LISTEN PLAN.

"SNIPER READY TO FIRE!" I yell out, fearful that the OP/chair can hear me from this range. The wind will help dissipate my call, my war cry. This time the *crunch, crunch, crunch* of the walker's boots is a welcomed and soothing sound, a feeling that will not last long as he asks for my number.

"Six," I reply.

He informs the OP/chair he has a sniper ready to fire. They now have two minutes to search the area all around the walker. They are two uneventful minutes.

"Who and where?" the OP/chair asks.

"Right-hand man in the head, white on black." This info is relayed to the OP/chair. I have called a head shot, white on black meaning the right-hand man will hold up a Hun's head or Figure 12 with a letter on it. It will be a letter from the word SNIPER; the letter will be white on a black background. He will hold it up for five seconds then I will have to correctly identify it.

The radio squawks, "Tell him to stand by for indication."

It sounds easy enough. You have a stable position and it's going to be one of six letters, but it is amazing how you can second-guess yourself. The OP/chair can be pretty selective with the letter they use. R and P have a very similar shape. Add in blowing grass, sun, sweat, and that P is an R or is the R a P or is the P actually a P? Five seconds to look. I can ask for another indication but that seldom helps as it is usually the same letter again. I get it wrong, and my day is done. I don't think I've ever seen an N on a stalk. Too easy. P and R are the staples, and the others are used sparingly. It is part of the self-induced stress that you can put on yourself, the second-guessing. The OP/chair must stay seated, but they can twist their upper body to look left and right; however, when they hold the letter up, they sit perfectly straight, facing the direction in which the chair was set up, but sometimes adding some angle to the letter, depending on where you set up. This is my case as I am fairly off to the right, or the OP's left.

The Figure 12 Hun's head goes up. *Is it an R or a P ... shit the mind fuck. Just add the "I" and we have ... well, how I feel right about now: RIP.* Get this wrong and I will be doing exactly that—laying, resting, but in anything but peace. It's a test of my position, of my ability to set up an effective FFP, to be able to clearly identify the enemy and if required to kill them. They are teaching us to take a life, to kill, but I just want to pass. Sometimes the realities of what we are being trained to do are lost on us. We are learning to kill, plain but not simple, we are learning to hide and seek out an enemy and to kill them.

The letter drops down in a swirl of black and white. I catch a glimpse of what I think is the 45-degree part of the R. I replay it in my head, but it happened so fast.

"So, what's it going to be?" asks the walker calmly?

It's an R. I'm 90 percent, so I try to confidently say "Romeo", although there is a hint of reluctance in my voice. I've declared now. I wait. The wind sways the grass around me. The OP/chair knows this is torture, they know I'm waiting, they have been here yet still they wait. I've done all that I can do. I wait. The longer the pause the more I start to second-guess myself. *Was it a P, was it Papa?* Tick tock, tick tock.

The radio crackles, "Sniper is correct."

I begin to breathe again. Only my chest moves, everything else in me is frozen, but my chest must move. I need to breathe.

That was the easy part I feel a weight lift from me. "Fucking R," I mumble.

The walker now moves within ten metres of me, but not to my front. I can hear him move but I cannot see him, I am motionless, I am frozen, locked onto my target. He then indicates with his arm my general direction and the OP/chair begins another methodical two-minute search of the ground, looking for anything out of the ordinary. Shape colour, texture, spacing, movement, the list goes on and on. All the while I am locked in a gaze with him. I can see his binos up to his face, radio in his right hand. He is thinking about where he would be hiding, and he scours the ground. Seconds are minutes now. I feel the wind pick up and the grass all around me bends dangerously earthbound— something my body can't do. I am fixed in place, I am part of the ground, motionless other than the slow rise and fall of my chest. I feel nothing but the coolness of the metal that my right index finger sits on, perched just above the trigger. Breathe in, breathe out.

After an eternity the radio chirps, "Okay, move within five metres and indicate direction."

The walker moves to within five metres of me, so close he's in my peripheral just to the right of me. I don't hear the crunch of his boots in the grass anymore. It no longer matters. Moving is not an option. I see his left arm shoot out. It seems to be pointing directly at me now. He tells the OP/chair he's within five and indicating direction. They know the drill, they know what's happening, they've been where I've been.

The radio squawks, "Take five steps to your left."

The walker complies robotically, and I feel his boots pass dangerously close to mine.

"Face the OP ... left arm out to your side and down to the ground ... you are touching a sniper."

"Negative" the walker says.

"Stand up," the radio barks with some agitation in the OP's voice. "Take one step to your left ... take five steps forward." The non-choreographed dance ensues. "Take one step to your right." Back and forth he goes.

The walker smirks and mumbles under his breath, "I don't think he has you."

The words cast an uneasiness in my head and bounce around. I want to believe them but am unable to. My scope is locked on my target the OP/chair has his binos up, seemingly staring right at me. The wind blows the grass around me with silent fever, yet I remain still. I blink and I breathe.

"Take a step to your right ... back to your left ... one step back ... take a quarter step right ... right arm out and down to the ground."

I've lost track of the walker. I know he is close and behind me. Then my eyes widen and the scope blurs; my mind is asking, *Where is my drag bag?* My kit is an extension of me: touch it and you are touching me. At that moment I feel my drag bag as I move my right leg a fraction of an inch inwards. I feel the rough material kiss my leg; it is as flat as a pancake between my legs. The OP/chair is burning through the bush to my left, the obvious spot. They see something and I don't care what it is because it is not me.

"You are touching a sniper," the radio crackles.

"Negative," answers the walker who is so close to me I hear every word as if the OP/chair is sitting in a chair next to me and holding the radio to my ear. I become oblivious to any other sounds around me. I am so focused on the few feet around me that all other sounds simply blend into one another and fade away. I hear the buzz of the radio like a bee in my ear, the menacing sound of the walker's boots as they draw ever closer. I am surrounded by grass, laying on the hard earth and the slightest touch of the walker's hand can turn it into a tomb.

Today I live. The walker comes over to me and the OP/chair asks him to put his hand on my head. They want to see where I am. He does, like an emphatic pat on the head, an attaboy of sorts. The OP/chair gives me a short debrief over the radio while the walker holds it to my ear. I am elated but reserved. I know there is more to come. This is a live-fire stalk. I still need to shoot, to kill. The walker marks the position of my bipod legs and checks my elevation setting, that I can't change—if I'm off I must adjust in my head. The windage I can change when it is my turn to shoot. I slide out from under my hat and leave it in place, providing shade to my scope to protect it from the hot sun. I slide beyond the cover of my hat and, once clear, I drop my head to the ground. I feel the grass press against my forehead as the wind begins to send a chill through my sweat-soaked body. I raise myself to my knees and look around. The OP/chair is so close. They are busy moving the walker onto another sniper. To the right sits the ML, the collector. A few guys mill about and a couple more are laying out in the sun on the hood. I feel a slight bit of guilt that they are there, and I am here, but I've been there a few times too, watching from the sidelines. I've felt the ground reject my attempts to cross it stealthily. Each time you make that hatless walk to the ML, it's one more chance you have squandered, one less opportunity to roll the dice. But not today, today I did it right, with some luck, and soon it will culminate with a light trigger squeeze followed by a dull *gong* and the walker calling a hit.

In the last three hours I have dragged, crawled and clawed my way over 1,200 metres, or 1.2 kilometres, while dragging all my gear with me. I have only seen a couple other people and have been a little too acquainted with the walker for my liking. I stand up after over three hours and a stretch feels good. Everything looks so different now. It all looks so easy.

Once time is up and all snipers have declared, the OP/chair is replaced by two steel frames, from which will hang the steel "kill zone" gong, the head measuring 15cm x15cm attached to the 33cm x 38cm body, with the kill zone freshly spray-painted in white. They are meant to sit in the exact position as the snipers in the chairs, but it does not always work out like that. After a quick range-safety brief, everyone gathers behind the first shooter, who is usually the closest to the OP/chair and from there we work our way back. We all know the effort it took to get to this point and busted or not we are there to support each other. We gather around the first person to shoot. We all want to hear that gong sound as the 7.62x51mm 168-grain round strikes at over 2,700 feet per second. We all want to hear that sound. No sound and the walker calls out, "Miss." He will start to count down from five. Before he hits zero, you must cycle another round, make an adjustment and fire again—it is hurried and feels like time moves at double speed. Miss with your second round and that's it. We are all silent as we will that round onto its target. That sound is forever locked into a sniper's mind. As is the silence of a miss.

THE SOUNDS

The group gathers behind my position and the walker gives me my two live rounds. I roll them in my hand to agitate the powder inside to ensure an even burn. The brass casings clink together in my hands as the sun shines on them. This will be a CCB shot, CLEAN COLD BORE. Each rifle acts differently when the first round is fired through it. The barrel is clean, and the metal is cold. We meticulously record this first shot every time we fire it, noting the variations that occur compared to when the rifle has "warmed up".

I drop to my knees behind my rifle, the pain gone for now. I stare at the gong hanging in the frame and it seems to be moving away from me.

"Don't fucking miss," the group mumbles. The words barely register, it is in jest, it is kind at heart and is usually followed up with, "Don't worry, you got this and even Black [or Brown] could hit it from here."

I must get my breathing under control. Slow in and slow out, watch the wind at the gun and the wind at the target. I lower myself to the ground. If I was religious there would be a short prayer, but at this point I believe in trajectory, gravity, wind speed and direction, shot release and follow through and hopefully terminal ballistics. I lower my chest to the ground, my elbows digging in. There is no pain anymore—it has subsided. I lower my head and put my hat on. My cheek instinctively finds its place on the butt of the rifle, my right-hand glances against the metal of the trigger guard, and my trigger finger seeks out its usual perch on the cool metal below the chamber. My left hand grasps the shooting sock as the butt stock nestles ever so lightly into my shoulder—too much pressure creates a "pulse". As much as I can, I let the gun sit and steady itself on its own. Breathe in, breathe out, in and out. I find the target in my crosshairs; it has a slight angle to it, but I can clearly make it out from about mid-chest up. I made a head indication for my letter, but a hit anywhere on the gong is a pass. You should shoot what you call and although the thought of an epic head shot fills my brain, the fear of missing takes a stronger hold. A kill is a kill. I insert the magazine into the rifle and the metallic click signifies it is seated. The bolt is fully to the rear and I top-load the second round, placing it on top of the magazine and pushing the round forward slightly with my finger to ensure it is picked up by the bolt. I guide the bolt forward, chambering the round. The second round is in the magazine should I need it. I rotate the bolt downward, locking it in place. My hand falls to the stock, my thumb wrapping around the grip. Breathe in, breathe out, breathe in, breathe out.

I have done this over a thousand times on the range, at triple the distance, but nothing can emulate the feeling of a live stalk. I've worked so hard to get here today—if you've done it, you know. I place my crosshairs about three inches below where the head meets the body, my finger has dropped onto the trigger. My body is autonomous as I inhale and exhale. Silence surrounds me. The walker is set up behind me with a spotting scope fixed to my target. He is on my side, now acting as my spotter but he will only call miss or hit. I don't need him for that: the target will tell me before the words can escape his mouth. I will either hear the dull *gong* of the round impacting the steel, or the silence.

I inhale. My crosshairs are motionless on the target. I can feel the vertical grooves of the trigger on the pad of my finger as I apply the slightest amount of pressure. My heart beats low and slow.

"Stand by," I say to the walker, making my intentions to fire known.

I am immune to any sounds except him saying "Send it" back to me, giving me the authority to fire.

I exhale and before the walker can say "it", I double the pressure on the trigger to 2.27kg … the firing pin snaps forward, igniting the primer at the base of the round. The powder ignites and a sharp *crack* echoes, sending the round into the barrel where it's gently hugged by the lands and groves which begin its slow rotation to the right, adding stability to the round as it cuts supersonically through the air. It exits the barrel followed by the expansive gases that belch out. The recoil presses the rifle gingerly into my shoulder. This all falls on deaf ears—my mind is only waiting to hear one sound … and in an instant I hear that dull metallic thud, like a distant bell has been rung. *Gong.*

In less than a second, it's over. There is no pain in my knees or elbows anymore; it has been erased just as the round disintegrated as it slammed into the hardened steel gong.

"Hit neck," the spotter calls out. "Thought you called head."

I slowly ease the bolt back as the empty casing angles out of the chamber and is gripped between my fingers. I rest my forehead on the butt off the rifle and allow myself a private smile. I remove the mag, and walker inspects and clears my gun.

"Good job," he says and on to the next one.

Was there ever any doubt? I say to myself, knowing the answer is yes.

We continue with the remaining snipers, many hits and few misses with the agonizing five seconds that follow, the onlookers hoping the next round will hit. Some do and some don't. That's just how it goes. As the last round is fired and the distant bell is rung, a collective cheer rings out. We have finished on a high note and as we pack up and walk back to the ML, each of us is doing the math in our heads, adding our points up and thinking about the next one. For some it will be do or die as that self-induced pressure builds. We load up on the ML and embark on the long ride back to base. The rear tarp stays open now, spewing a mix of dust and diesel fumes into the back but allows us to see each other. We talk about the stalk, and we hear about the guys who got busted and the how's and why's. Eventually silence falls on us; the gallery is fully lit and the portraits hang ominously. The clean fresh canvas that was dimly lit on the ride out has been replaced with dirty, tired, cam paint-smeared faces. Eyes are closed, heads bob with the bumps. There are no priceless masterpieces. We are soldiers. The stalk is over, history.

We graduated three out of eighteen on my course and two of us would be sent to Afghanistan as part of the Sniper Platoon. We would put these new skills we had learned and many more to ultimate test, against a prepared, combat-hardened foe. They taught me to kill. But I also learned how to fail because we all do on that course. And failures have a way of teaching more than the successes. Now we're just waiting on a war, more history to be made, remembered by the living and forgotten by the dead.

PART TWO

Afghanistan 2006-2007
Task Force 3-06

5

To the Sand ...

Master Corporal Barry Nisbet, Sniper Candidate
1st Battalion, Royal Canadian Regiment
CFB Petawawa
2005

Crack. The bullet rips downrange and snaps through the paper target. The recoil from the 7.62x51mm 168-grain hollow point boat tail projectile pushes purposely into my right shoulder and reverberates down my body, exiting through my toes. The bullet flies through the paper Figure 11 target unknowingly, small flakes of paper drifting to the ground from the new hole. My target looks like a soldier advancing towards me; I will kill and wound him thousands of times. Occasionally the bullet will miss him but fly so close he will hear the *crack* of the round as it breaks the sound barrier. He knows I will not miss again. He's coming for me, his legs are coiled, his black eyes are piercing, mouth menacingly opening to unleash his war cry. His bayonet is fixed to his rifle. He is coming for me; he is coming for my brothers and sisters in arms. If I do not kill him, he will kill me, and he won't stop.

Crack, crack, crack, hundreds of rounds I put through him, my movements becoming instinctive. I am calculating, I am cold. *Crack, crack, crack*, a hundred more. The distance increases, the winds blow harder. *Crack, crack, crack*, a hundred more. He never stops and neither will I.

The targets get smaller; this enemy is far more cunning, stealthy, never exposing more than his head. The outline of his face is dark, he is battle hardened, he is looking for me with his black featureless eyes and expressionless face. *Crack, crack, crack*. Head shots, aim small miss small. When I miss, he turns sideways to let me know but abruptly turns back to face me again. *Crack, crack, crack*, a hundred more.

Every round I fire I learn. Every hit, every miss. I record the wind, mirage, the light, the temperature. I crack on. Every hit reinforces my training. I am educated. I'm not after a diploma. I'm after a small badge with a rifle on it. This is my master's degree. With every miss there is a why, a how. I need to understand so I can get better, without warning, without remorse.

I can feel the change in me over time, autonomy when I get behind the rifle cloaked in my ghillie suit. I shoot in all conditions, snow, rain, dark, standing, kneeling, prone, sitting, in cars, buildings, towers. It is for the kill; it has always been for the kill. Now I know it, now I feel it. I am the killer of paper tigers, of paper men, *crack, crack, crack*. No one shoots back, no one bleeds, no one cries. But right now, I don't care ... all I can hear is the *crack, crack, crack* from my rifle. I am the killer.

*

Master Corporal Barry Nisbet, Sniper
Detachment 63C, Task Force 3-06
Panjwai District, Kandahar Province, Afghanistan
2006

I watch the news before my 2006 tour to Afghanistan. I see the flag-draped coffins being loaded into the CC-130 Hercules at Kandahar airfield as our dead are repatriated. The closer my deployment date gets, the more real the news feels. I have already completed a tour to Kabul in 2005, but Kandahar is different. It is combat. I am a sniper now.

My best friend Jamie Murphy was killed by a suicide bomber on January 27, 2004 in Kabul, Afghanistan. I was not there. When he arrived home in one of those flagged-draped coffins, I met him on the tarmac of (CFB) Trenton. Death and loss were new to my generation of soldiers; sadly, Afghanistan normalized all that. I followed Murph to Newfoundland and laid him to rest. There is not a day that passes when I do not think of him. I met his mom Alice for the first time in a funeral home in Conception Harbour; her voice I recognized immediately. Back in Petawawa hanging out with Murph at his place, he would toss me the phone from time to time when he was speaking with his mom and say, "Talk to Barry" and we would make small talk back and forth. When we finally met, she looked straight into my eyes and said, "Oh Barry." Her voice brought tears to my eyes; her embrace made them roll down my faces uncontrollably. It saddened me like nothing I had ever felt before. War brings loss and loss brings grief. There is no peace without war and there is no war without grief.

A couple years after Jamie's death, our sniper team is in an observation post hidden amongst the jagged fangs of Masum Ghar in the Panjwai District, the mountain's teeth piercing into every unprotected part of my body that touches it, blood sucking. My eyes and gun point northward, watching and waiting. Sweat is amassing in every nook and cranny of my body even though I do not move. My uniform absorbs it only to be blown dry by the sand-filled wind. It is cyclic: sweat, wind, sweat, wind. At each iteration my uniform absorbs what my body expels as the September sun blasts down. I am a combination of digital desert pattern and white salt stains, covered by a thin film of dust that sticks to everything. You breathe it in: every grain that doesn't cling to the inside of your nose turning your mucus black, travels down into you. Afghanistan is at your very core—like it or not it is in you. It has a taste, a smell. All you need to do is breathe. The only way to stop it is when you stop breathing and that sometimes happens without you knowing it.

From our perch I stare across the Arghandab River. At first glance it looks flat and desolate. I have studied this terrain for over a week; it is my new home for now. I have seen its crests and folds appear and vanish with the rising and setting sun. The river is barely a river at all, a little wider than a tank or two, its cool, ankle-deep water running to the evil west. Days before we drove confidently across in LAVs, following a pounding by air and artillery to assault Taliban positions. A frantic hour after our green machines crossed, my right boot, followed in quick succession by my left, plunged into the water as we withdrew across it, following a costly and bloody day for our battle group. Time passes by. My boots dried; the dead replaced by the living.

Sleeping on the ground for days, exposed to the harsh sun, sleep can be elusive even though my mind is so tired. Explosions in the distance jar you awake, and my eyes open. *Where am I?* The C8 resting on my chest reminds me. Falling back asleep to the distant sound of fighter jets high above the star-filled Afghanistan sky is oddly soothing. These wartime sounds replace the peaceful sounds of home. An Apache helicopter firing its 30mm chain gun replaces a woodpecker drilling into a tree. A low fly-by of a British Harrier replaces the drone of vehicle traffic. This is normal—it is best to immerse yourself in it and accept it. These are the sounds and sights; this is the norm. It is a beautiful country wrapped in a shroud of death, destruction and oppression. The sand soaks up the blood of the infidels, the Taliban, and those caught in between, and the winds scatter it indiscriminately throughout the country and beyond.

Nestled up in our perch overlooking the Arghandab River, our satellite phone battery is exhausted like many of us baking in the midday sun. I need to call home to my family to let them know I was not amongst the wounded from our assault during Operation *Medusa*. I begrudgingly go to make my phone call: an 800-metre walk down to the few remaining LAVs in the battle position following our disastrous attempt to cross the Arghandab River into Panjwai. I have my C8 slung across my back; I am wearing a T-shirt, my Tilley hat, boots and pants. My body armour stays behind. Most of the walk I am protected from enemy view by the peaks of the ghar. The last 200 metres or so is wide open. Dust kicks up with every step and the rocks grind under my sweat-stained boots as I step out of the protection of the ghar. To my left across the Arghandab are Taliban fighters hidden amongst the bombed-out ruins of Panjwai. As I near the

LAV I can see the ramp is down with a few guys hanging out at the back, the turret gently traversing left and right as the gunner scans out across the void.

The sound registers in my left ear from far across the river: distant machine gun fire. I don't give it a second thought. My eyes see it, to my right and up about ten feet the rocks mysteriously start to explode and tumble all around. The sound comes next. *Fuck me*, my brain says, *they are shooting at me*. I am angry ... I look to the LAV, and the guys are jumping around, putting on helmets and waving their arms at me to run. So, I fucking run and swing my C8 around, grasping it instinctively. There is no shooting back. Just run. I curse myself for not wearing any of my protective gear. So many ways to die out here—IED, RPG, casual stroll. The rocks continue their sick symphony of destruction above me as I run in a sort of hunched-over position. As I near the safety of the LAV I extend my head forward as if I was trying to win a race. I exhale, my short sprint leaving my lungs in desperate need of more oxygen. Now safely behind the thick green sand-coated armour of the LAV, I take stock of what just happened.

"Those fuckers were shooting me," I say to the guys.

"Yup" someone blurts out, "they sure were."

Laughter erupts as they make fun of the look on my face as I ran towards the LAV, and rightfully so. I'm sure the look of shock and fear painted on my face was quite amusing.

I think that was my first real exposure to direct enemy fire, fire that was just for me, stupid me. Almost shot coming to make a call home to say I was okay. Laughter is a good defence in combat. I made my call home a few minutes later, calmly and coolly as if nothing had happened, because nothing did happen. Both sides have guns, some of us are better at using them than others.

The more time I spent in Afghanistan the more my auditory combat library expanded. The *crack crack crack* was the base. It was always heard in training; when downrange in the butts pulling targets up and down and the rounds would *crack* overhead while I was safely tucked away in the concrete barriers. In Afghanistan that concrete barrier disappeared, sometimes replaced with the canvas of a modular tent, the armour of a LAV, a G Wagon, sandbag walls, mud walls, and a lot of time nothing but the air around you. Space, poor enemy marksmanship and luck were sometimes the only protection. The most wide-open space could shrink into nothingness when bullets were flying all around. The *crack* would at times be a *whizzzz* as a round ricocheted and tumbled around you.

I remember sitting up on Masum Ghar in the later part of Operation *Medusa* when something was fired up at us from across the Arghandab River. It appeared to skip off the dry riverbed and almost as quickly, I heard a *whizzz* to my left and snapped my head in that direction. Three feet to my left was Jody who had snapped his head to his right, having heard the same thing. There was a short "holy fuck" moment that was quickly dispelled by laughter and a casual posture change. Then there is that *crack ptang whizz* sound when the bullet whips just past you, smashes into the armoured vehicle beside you and *whizzes* off in multiple directions. That was an early Afghanistan sound for me.

Our assault across the Arghandab in September 2006 did not go as planned. I quickly found myself in the back of a LAV with our sniper team cruising across the dry riverbed. No plan survives first contact; this we were all about to learn. We had planned to dismount and peel off to a flank. I stared up through the open air sentry hatch at my rucksack strapped down to the turret. Hanging from it was my helmet and flak jacket … great place for them. I had a bush cap and combat shirt on, and *You are a fucking idiot* rang out in my head. All hell began to break loose, vehicle kills, soldiers killed, chaos. After what seemed like an eternity our LAV stopped. We had no idea where we were or what we were going to do. The ramp lowered and I instinctively swung to my left to face the open ground. I was looking back to where we had come from and noticed the Bison ambulance about 300 metres away, just sitting there. Unexpectedly, a wounded soldier, a medic, was thrown onto the floor of our LAV, his shoulder expediently bandaged. I don't think I've ever felt as useless as a soldier as I did at that moment.

Wahhbump. A mortar landed just to my right, the next casualty into our LAV was MWO Barnes. We had nowhere to go and nothing to do, so Jody and I decided to take the wounded medic to waiting Bison. So off we went, walking with our wounded comrade as the LAV's 25mm cannons pounded away, coax machine guns belting out and coloured smoke billowing up from the dead ground well ahead of our position. We walked with our backs to the enemy, the ambulance growing larger with each step. The nose of the vehicle was facing backwards. I pounded on the back of the door, and it swung open. The injured medic crawled in, and the door slammed shut. So now what? We looked back to where we had been and could see vehicles jockeying around, coloured and black smoke billowing about. Our vehicle was gone. So, we took up a knee beside the Bison looking out at the undulating riverbed speckled with green vehicles and tan specks hurrying about.

About a minute after taking a knee came that unsoothing *crack ptang whizz*, bullets hitting the Bison and ricocheting in all directions. There was nowhere to go, nowhere to hide, just listen and hope. *Crack ptang whizzz*, like a record skipping every few moments.

I called out to Jody who was near the front of the Bison and said, "We are going to die here."

"Yeah, probably," he responded casually.

So, we waited. *Crack ptang whizz.*

A few long minutes later a LAV came speeding towards us, dust spewing from the back. It slowed and pulled alongside us. I looked up to see a friendly face in the crew commander cupola and we exchanged *nice to see you're not dead* looks. Then the ramp lowered, and more familiar faces exited, but these faces were sullen, some in disbelief, emotion hanging on them, but I couldn't place exactly what the emotion was.

"Come give us a hand," someone said.

At the rear opening of the LAV, I could see him laying there, lifeless. Loss was what hung on their faces, loss and pain. We carefully picked up Warrant Officer Rick Nolan and carried him to the back of the waiting Bison. The ramp lowered and we carefully guided him in. I remember how heavy he was with all his gear on, not daring to lose my grip. Loss and pain without a sound. We would lay three more to rest that day, loss, pain, grief … *crack ptang whizz.*

Afghanistan created sounds I had never heard before. Sounds of near misses, sounds of injury, sounds of death. I have to think that these rang true for both sides. Our job was to kill the enemy, to inflict loss and pain on them. It was not payback: it was what we were paid to do, it was why we were there. There were teams of people to liaise with the locals, to bring food, to rebuild roads and schools but everything I had been trained to do as a sniper was done with the intention to kill. We did not practise shooting people in the arm or leg: we shot a kill zone, an area comprised of the upper chest and head, a kill shot. We learned how to adjust artillery fire if the enemy was out of rifle range. We learned how to call in fire from aircraft. We gathered intelligence. In my eyes it was all to kill. However long the tour lasted—six or eight months—the focus was on killing and not being killed but you couldn't do one without the other and I know there were times when I focused on killing and other times I focused on just not being killed.

It was always the sounds. Afghanistan outside of the cities was quiet sometimes. The silence was broken daily by the sounds of gunfire or an explosion and the radio would chirp, "TIC." These were the regular sounds. No cars honking, no music, no phones ringing, no traffic, no western normalcy. It was gunfire, explosions, attack helicopters, fast air, outgoing artillery, and the call to prayer echoing across the landscape. It wasn't always us getting shot at, but we could hear it all around us, other Canadians, Americans, Brits, all the others. The TICs would bring air support of some sort, fighters or helicopters whizzing and streaking through the skies. Then the 9 liners and medevac calls … who's hurt, who's dead, do I know them, is it a friend, a close friend, another sniper team, who's out, where are they? … it all just became normal. Like compiling a shopping list.

The worst was the *boom flash*, the detonated IED howling into the darkness and the moan of injuries that left untreated would lead to death. Nights in Afghanistan were virtually silent, no nightlife, very few lights, as if everything was locked down. If you were a local and out at night you were Taliban because you had no other reason to be out. At night I felt safer, hyper-alert, sense of hearing heightened like never before, the green glow of our night vision escaping from around our eyes, eclipse like. The sounds at night carried and echoed, but I always felt safer. I remember the first few steps out of a FOB (forward operating base) on night patrols or insertions; it was as if you were walking out into a landscape devoid of sound and light, lunar-like. I walked point every time and would pick the routes, but we all had a say. The ground would often change your route: walls, ditches, wadis, buildings, animals, they all shaped our movements. The route was fluid.

The Big Bang

We did the majority of our insertions at night, the blackness masking us, the night vision making us superhuman. In 2006 the Taliban were starting to use more IEDs and to great effect, both physically and mentally. The sitreps were constant: watch out for a white Toyota Corolla … VBIED (vehicle-borne IED). We knew the IEDs were out there and although we had put a lot of kilometres on our feet, we had stayed out of their path, mostly because we were operating in an area that did not get a lot of foot traffic. There were times when we would walk two or three kilometres from the outpost and not see another soul: everywhere seemed abandoned, the houses, the fields, it was desolate. We knew there were eyes on us whether we saw them or not. We stayed on the roads and trails mostly; it was as hard packed as it got around there, easy to see if it had been dug up or not. We had a sense for the area day and night. War changes everything, the landscape, the children, me, you.

We left out of Strong Point Centre. It was a dark, cool, star-filled January night. Gord tagged onto our usual three-man team making us four. He recalled:

> *The mission was to get eyes on and report on a possible IED manufacturing site, west of Strong Point West. This would see Recce and Snipers depart approximately 24 ours prior to the clearing force and get eyes on the objective, ensuring that the larger clearing force would have a foot on the ground prior to moving, allowing them more security in movement. It would also provide them with a hostile force laydown and intentions. By this time Snipers and Recce were practised in making deductions based on movement and bad guy numbers in an area. We could identify probable fighting locations, lines of support and egress. Ultimately, we wanted to set up so that we could support the approach and assault and cover any lines of reinforcement.*

It was a battle group operation with a lot of moving parts. A couple of soldiers from the strong point guided us out to get around the trip flares. Through no fault of theirs, they took us further west than our intended route. Once they dropped us, we did a quick nav check.

"Jody," I said, "we need to head south ... we are way too far north."

"Okay."

I signalled to the guys to get up. I always felt a bit of added pressure walking point, but it was reassuring to know my team had my back. Gord Cullen expands:

We all had 100 percent confidence in Barry's ability to NAV. He was meticulous in his route planning, ensuring there were control measures along the way to guide and confirm our movement. A control measure west of strong point west usually took the form of intersecting routes or wadis; for the most part these are the things that our artillery and close air support hadn't changed over the course of the war. Buildings would come and go but generally the intersections or linear routes were unchanged. I often thought of Barry's route selection like an expression of his desire to close with and kill the enemy. Nothing was ever missed; we were always on target.

It was so quiet at night, I could hear my heartbeat, my breath, I could feel the cold metal of my C8 on my right index finger as it rested above the trigger, thumb on the safety. Anytime I stopped, everyone stopped; if I took a knee, they took a knee; we scanned, walked, we listened. As we pushed further south through a grape field, I could see a large wall running east–west. Beyond that wall was a road and more grape fields. I was happy Gord was with us, always calm—a more reliable soldier I have never known. Gord again:

This calm comes from confidence in the soldiers around you. Barry was on point, fearless. I was second, one ear to the evolving situation on the radio and my focus ensuring my sector was covered. K was third, constantly scanning, constantly updating his own situational awareness. Jody pulled up the rear, keeping track of the six and ensuring our discipline was maintained. When everyone is pulling on the rope, there is literally no weight to hold. The machine moves forward, each cog taking its timing and movement from the one in front of them.

The wall loomed larger in our NVGs. The problem with the monocular was that you did not get a lot, if any, depth of field—you would short step and stumble and trip a bit, but the advantages far outweighed this. We could use the IR lasers on our C8s to point out any and all manner of things to each other.

We came to the wall, and I halted us about five metres from it. There was a large break in it with the road on the other side. We closed up into a tight 360, looking out, listening for about a minute. I took a few steps closer to the break and looked at it with NVGs, hard pack before and after it. To the left the wall sort of jutted out and then turned east; to the west it continued to run with more fields to the south. We all had a look at it, then collapsed back into our 360. Jody tried to establish comms but to no avail; not a big deal—we still had about two kilometres to our ORV (objective RV). Recce Platoon was also moving further to our south.

After another quick nav check we moved out—we had all agreed to go through the break in the wall. Gord recalled:

As much as possible these obstacles were avoided until they couldn't be. The walls sometimes soared to eight feet on one side and dropped off to 12 on the other. We all understood that we would step through the wall, not placing any pressure on the soft ground that stood where the wall once was but take an exaggerated step from one side to the other. We were all heavy—we had packed enough batteries, ammo and water to last a while. K was carrying the only sniper rifle and both Jody and I had radios. Double-banked comms on an outing like this was a must.

I stood up first and walked to the wall, gun up, right index finger on the cool metal, thumb on the safety switch. My eyes and head scanning, I took a larger-than-normal step over the threshold, looking left then right and left again as I walked through. Gord was quickly behind me, "bumping me" as I continued west down the hard-packed road. It was clear night, the sky ahead full of stars, my boots barely making a sound—my breathing was the loudest thing. K would come through next and bump Gord. I saw Gord moving with me as K covered to the east. I turned and surveyed the ground ahead.

BOOM! The sound was deafening, a millisecond of confusion as my brain computed what was happening. Then I felt the concussion of the blast. I dropped to a knee, thumbing the safety off. I raised my C8, the butt stock in my right shoulder. I scanned over the sight. I waited to see the muzzle flash from Taliban AK-47s and RPKs, I waited to hear that *crack crack crack*. In that moment, in those few seconds that felt like minutes, my adrenaline spiked, my body was getting ready for what I thought was to come. I heard what sounded like a piece of metal hitting the trees forward and to my left. *Fuck, a grenade*, I thought. I looked for cover. I leapt up but forgot to tell my legs and skidded into the ditch alongside the road … no *boom*, no *bang*, no *crack*. My heart was racing. I could feel the sweat beading on my brow. It was quiet, no flash, no bullets, no grenades. The smell of explosive lingered in the air as the dust settled. About two to three seconds had elapsed since the blast.

Then I heard the low moan. I knew it wasn't Gord, pretty sure it wasn't K. *Fuck, it's Jody.* I called back to Gord, "Do you need me?"

"Yes," he replied, calm, no excitement.

I had been the furthest from the blast. Gord was much closer:

The blast had taken me down to my knees, the rush of dust, dirt and shrapnel blowing past me. Searching for air in the vacuum of the explosion, I looked back to see K on the ground: he was good to go, already scanning his arcs. I moved past him to find Jody on his back. He was screaming that we were not safe here. His composure was mind blowing. The norm during this time of the war was for the bad guys to come out and see what they had caught in their trap. They knew where all their emplacements were and could zero in quickly. The other more disturbing norm was to place a secondary device that would inflict even greater pain on a group coming to recover the prey, a secondary.

I turned and moved. I could see Gord was kneeling, I could see K standing, and as I neared Gord, I could see Jody. He was down, laying on his back.

"I need to call in a 9 liner," Gord said calmly. "Look after Jody". Gord again:

Due to all the moving parts involved in the operation, the radio net was constant. I gave a "Break, break, break, this is 63. Contact IED" over the net. Initially it went silent; unfortunately, not everyone had their ear glued to the headset or handsets waiting for us to talk and call signs reporting on their movement or sending fucking sitreps started consuming the bandwidth. I tried a couple times getting through to Zero with no joy: the stronger signals from vehicle comms or CPs and TIs [tactical infrastructure] were crushing my signal. Now for those who remember, Lieutenant-Colonel Lavoie at 9'er doesn't let call signs stepping on each other eat up the net when a 9 liner is being called in. There is one priority, and you had best minimize or find another fucking frequency to put your adrep in on. With as much brevity as possible I sent my 9 liner and MIST [report] to 9'er who had now taken control of the net. If there was one piece of certainty that the next 90 minutes would provide, it's that the CO is stick-handling the casualty evacuation, and nothing was getting in the way.

I went to Jody and knelt at his right side. He was breathing, moaning in pain, taking short but strong breaths. It was his legs, his feet. His left foot was gone—it was just white bone, flesh, blood. There was still smoke coming up from the hole that used to be the threshold we had all just walked through. His right foot was blown 180 degrees around, hanging on by some skin. He had a compound fracture of his tibia sticking out just below the knee. He moaned in pain, and said to make sure I got a tourniquet on that. He just got blown the fuck up and had the wherewithal to know what needed to be done. Really, that was all that could be done, as we carried minimal medical supplies. So, I applied tourniquets to both legs and cranked them down as tightly as I could. I noted the time, I took his pulse, I held his hand, I checked the rest of him, grabbing his balls and telling him they were okay. At one point I was squeezing his hand too hard, and he told me to stop because it hurt. We waited, the radio buzzed, we waited, his pulse grew weaker, we waited.

Jody kept trying to sit up to look at his legs and feet. I just kept trying to reassure him and to keep him flat on his back, telling him to take deep breaths to slow his breathing and his heart rate. He was losing blood but not a lot that I could see externally. I patched up what I could, but he needed more help than we could give as he laid on the cold, smoldering, blood-soaked earth. Gord kept his eyes up scanning into the darkness and his ear on the radio:

> *Listening to the situation reports on my radio, I could hear the coordination of efforts being relayed on the net. On this roto the casualty evacuation helicopters were reluctant to land outside of TI or not on a hard pack, and especially not on a dirt road in complete darkness. The plan was that the Badger, a Leopard tank minus the turret but with a plow, would push a route to us that an armoured ambulance could move down and extract Jody. This ambulance would move him from our location to Masum Ghar where a Black Hawk helicopter would evac him to Kandahar Airfield [KAF]. I could also hear Captain Macbeth, Recce Platoon commander, convincing 9'er that the patient could move back to our location [our base] as he had a medic and supplies to better treat the amputations. I personally think he had already started his move to us before contacting the boss. The most concerning element was from a Canadian UAV that was reporting on bad guy movement to our north. This, in my mind, was the bad guys coming to check their trap. Normally, we like to have a bit of an advantage in firepower/people over the bad*

guys but in this case, with just K really watching anything, we would be consumed. I kid you not when I say the pucker factor was tight. Would Recce Platoon get to us before the bad guys, would Jody still be gtg [good to go], would they hit a secondary on the way in and be decimated trying to save our four souls? Luckily, elements of A Company had picked up on the bad guy movement and cut off their approach.

I applied a field dressing to his left leg, covering up the stump of where his foot would have joined at his ankle. I had to switch to white light for a few moments and the severity of it all was displayed in vivid colour. No more the subdued green hues of the NVG or the flat tone of our regular red light. The vibrancy of white bone, bloody flesh, charred skin and clothing revealed themselves in an instant. I bandaged the wounds as best I could, trying to keep a calm exterior but inside I knew my friend was dying. The right leg, I can still picture it, that shoe twisted 180 degrees barely attached by a piece of skin. I didn't know what to do, how to treat it. I didn't want to move it and risk further damage or pain. He wasn't losing a lot of blood that I could see and who knows what was pressing together or holding what in place. I wanted to keep it that way so I just laid bandages under and over to keep it as clean as I could, hoping it could be saved but knowing the ferocity of the blast had claimed the leg instantly. Limbs and lives, Afghanistan collected them from combatants and civilians alike.

I knelt and waited, checked vitals, Gord on the radio, K our only security. We had done all we could for Jody. I knelt beside him that cool January night and an uneasiness swept over me. We were in Afghanistan, we had just tripped an IED, our four-man team was down to three and there was no moving Jody. I felt vulnerable: we had made noise, used white light and had remained stationary for over 30 minutes now. I knew help was on the way but who or what else might be coming, I knew not.

We had concerns of secondary IEDs. Recce Platoon was pushing to us as with a medic attached. There was not much more they would be able to do. Jody needed to get the fuck out of here … he was fading but never passed out. He was coherent, talking, basically self-assessing as we waited. Medics were coming from Strong Point Centre as well, plowing a road to us through the fields. All we could do was wait and hope. A UAV buzzed overhead providing information of who and what was around. I think it was a Canadian UAV and probably carried no weapons. We kept waiting, time slows when you feel your friend's pulse weaken, minutes tick by. We needed help.

Recce Platoon showed, having sprinted their way through the fields in the dark to come to our aid. Their medic took over immediately and did what he could. As I relinquished care of Jody, I again became aware of the dozens of more boots stomping all around us, the commotion, the light. I could see Gord didn't like it either: my thoughts were again of a secondary IED and more possible casualties. It was amazing only Jody had been hurt. K had been a few feet from him and other than some ringing ears was unscathed.

In the distance the roar of the big diesel engine tore through the cool night air. The Badger ARRV (armoured repair and recovery vehicle) could be heard plowing through the grape fields to get to us. I still don't know why medivac choppers didn't winch Jody out. The big metal beast eventually bulldozed to the break in the wall and the area was cleared quickly by engineers.

The medics rushed forward. I stayed with Jody leaning over him, thinking I was comforting him but was probably just annoying.

We positioned a stretcher beside him, rolled him up and tried to gingerly get him onto the stretcher. I remember seeing what was left of his right foot hanging precariously off of the stretcher. I could only imagine the pain he was in. We readjusted him and he called out in pain. I've heard grown men complain more about a sprained ankle than Jody did of his multiple blast injuries and broken, splintered bones … his feet were gone. I don't know to what extent he knew what had happened. We loaded him into the Bison ambulance, a dull glow illuminating out the back. The ramp was raised, and they drove off, to Masum Ghar to our south where he would be airlifted out to KAF. We had done all we could out there, each of the roles we filled that night no more important than the other. Our thoughts were with Jody.

Dawn started to break. The mission was scrubbed. So, the now three-man team walked back to the strong point via the newly scraped road. Every step I took I expected to blow up. Every step I felt guilt pressing down on my shoulders, heavier and heavier, as I walked back to the false security of the strong point. Heavier with every step on the dusty road that they had plowed for Jody. That weight on my shoulders shifted to my head. My mind twisted like a bullet down the barrel … *I was first, I walked first, it was my job to get us there safely, I walked over it, it should have been me.* Over and over, it fucked with my head, not because it should have been me, but because in the dark corner of my mind I was glad it wasn't. My selfish thoughts drove my feeling of guilt deeper and deeper into my head to the point that I wanted to hit an IED. I wanted to take the pain away from Jody. But there was no escape from it. I walked on my own feet, knowing Jody never again would.

I felt numb. There was nothing to say. Everyone knew what had happened. We packed up some of the gear we'd left behind and grabbed a ride back to Patrol Base Wilson. After a few hours there we flew back to KAF to be with Jody and see what the prognosis was.

Once in the relative safety of KAF, I could take stock of what had happened in the last ten hours or so, how a life had been irreversibly changed in a flash. We all went over to the hospital. I could feel the apprehension building, the guilt: it had been my job to get us safely to where we needed to go, and I hadn't done that. *It should be me in the hospital bed, it should be me.*

We all went in and saw him. He was drugged up and we could see the bandages where his feet used to be. He had bandages on his hands. I asked him what happened to them.

"Remember when I told you to stop squeezing my hand so tight?"

"Yes," I replied,

"Well, I guess gravel blasted up and tore into my hands."

We both sort of laughed. I guess the squeezing was for me.

The next day I popped over to the hospital to see him. I had gathered up some things for him from his room—we shared a room in KAF that we never really saw: it was more of a storage locker. His bed was raised and he was sitting, just looking at his bandages.

"They cut my fucking feet off," he said.

I don't know exactly when he was told that, or when it actually sank in, or when the meds allowed him to look, to see, to realize. I stood beside him holding his hand. Our eyes filled with tears; I could feel one roll down my cheek. We both just stared at his legs. I never saw Jody get emotional before that and never did again after that. The guilt pushed down on me, but it paled to what Jody would go through in the weeks, months and years to come. He was alive and he was going home.

He flew out to Germany the next day and it would be months until I saw him again. But the war went on and I had to figure out how to get my head back in it. I didn't know how; I didn't want to. I was scared, scared of that happening to me, and I didn't know how to deal with that, the guilt, the fear, the loss.

We had a few days in KAF to sort out our shit and the resupply for the six weeks or so left in the tour. The day before we were due to fly out, I was sitting in our stores/office with Gord.

I turned to him. "I don't want to go back out there," not knowing what he was going to say in return.

He looked to the front: "I know, neither do I."

Maybe he said that to appease me, but it was what I needed to hear, to know I wasn't alone in how I felt. The next day we flew out refocused, resupplied.

Let's just get through these last few weeks, I thought.

Gord recalled:

How do you motivate a small group of professionals to get back on the horse and move forward with what was expected of us? Up to this point we'd had some close calls, been shot at, blown up, way too close to incoming friendly artillery and perhaps a little lackadaisical in leaving footprints on the ground for the bad guys to home in on. But up to this point we had been successful, we had triumphed, killed the bad guys, reported on locations that would later be exploited, gone farther into the darkness and come back unscathed. Now we had seen loss, Jody was still alive, but we were all in shock. In my gut I knew the answer was get back out there and keep the feet moving, but I also knew that in some respect we were all looking for something within each other to grab a hold of to rally behind. In this case it was honesty. If I was to say, Fuck that shit, let's get back out there and give it right back to them, that would be a cop-out. It would have been easy to hide under a cloak of machoism. It would only have dirtied the waters between us. Honesty. We have been close before, but this one was bad. Do I want to get back out there and stomp around the unforgiving landscape of Afghanistan? Fuck no. That shit scared me and made me think that we needed to be more careful, be more restrictive in our support to operations. So, I voiced this, and we talked through it and came to the realization that we made decisions based on the tactical situation at the time, we used proven tactics that we had developed over the length of the tour. We would be okay, we would get back on the horse and complete a number of patrols and missions because we knew where everyone was coming from. I had the confidence that each member of the Sniper Group was able to do his assigned task to the best of his ability and wasn't hiding a fear or would hesitate. We treated each other like human beings, were honest with our feelings and got back in the fight.

This tour, like others, ended, and it seemed no matter the mission, soldiers died, be it from combat, misadventure or accidental. I always went home with a heavy heart.

We had re-integration training in Cyprus. All I will say is what happened in Cyprus stayed in Cyprus. I really just wanted to get home. I wanted to see Jody.

Being back in Canada was odd. I had no gun, no radio, no air support. Sleep was inconsistent: I would wake up in the middle of the night and reach for my C8 that was always on my chest or beside me. Not feeling it caused some minor panic until I realized where I was. That subsided with time. I hated being in crowds, going to the grocery store was stressful, all those people and me without a gun. I had spent over six months thinking that everyone and everything could kill me, and I could not just stop thinking that overnight. If I was driving and saw garbage or a cardboard box on the side of the road, I would drive as far from it as I could. I knew it wasn't an IED, but those thoughts couldn't just be switched off. A car backfired one day when I was walking across a parking lot. I reached for things that were not there. My head was still in Afghanistan but my body in Canada. These feelings and thoughts would dissipate with time, but they would never truly disappear. I would return to Afghanistan in 2010 to do it all over again.

6

The Gorgon's Cauldron, 2006

Sergeant Gordon Cullen, Unit Master Sniper
Detachment 63, Task Force 3-06, Patrol Base Wilson
Panjwai District, Kandahar Province, Afghanistan
September 2006
As told by Mir Bahmanyar

Gordon Cullen, 36, would look perfectly at home in any Norman Rockwell painting of Boy Scouts. One comrade, in 2020, wrote that Gord:

> *is a wild card, not in the unpredictable or uncertain sense, he is wild card in that he makes everything better just by his presence. He brought calm to the chaos of combat, he made your rucksack lighter merely by walking beside you, and made the heat feel almost bearable with his unflappable poise. He exudes professionalism from the soles of his boots to his perfectly coiffed hair that covers his supercomputer-like brain, that is capable of making range estimations, wind calls, and target speeds before most snipers could even see*

the enemy. Watching him set up and manipulate a sniper rifle would be akin to watching Michelangelo paint ... superlative.

As a Unit Master Sniper (UMS), he has also been described as a "stone-cold killer", shooting as many, if not more, enemy combatants with a .50-calibre sniper rifle than his Sniper Group did during one deployment in Afghanistan. But what sets Gord apart from others is his professionalism to the highest order, a non-commissioned officer, cool, calm, composed, meticulous, demanding the best of his men and himself. He also happens to be a great guy. His standards in soldiering and sniping are impeccable. In his career he deployed seven times, four as a sniper including twice as Unit Master Sniper. His deployments to Bosnia in 1995/6 and 1997/8, and to Kosovo in 1999/2000, built the foundation; his three tours to Afghanistan in 2003, 2006, and in 2010—the last two in Afghanistan as UMS of an eight-man sniping group—and one final deployment to Poland in 2013, completed the creation of a sniper leader of excellence bar none. It comes as no surprise to see Gord today serve as the Sniper Program Manager for the Canadian Special Operations Regiment (CSOR), part of Canadian Special Operations Forces Command (CANSOFCOM). Arguably one of the finest elite units in the world, the current record holder in the longest kill shot ever recorded, in 2017 comes from CANSOFCOM.

But it would be in the cauldron of trenchlike warfare of Canada's largest operation since the Korean War that would see his leadership tested and his teams pushed to their extremes. The impending operation was dubbed *Medusa*, like the Greek mythical creature with a head full of snakes who turned mortals into stone when they beheld her vision. And Medusa nearly turned the operation into stone.

The 1st Battalion the Royal Canadian Regiment's Sniper Group 63 took over the area of operations from the departing Princess Patricia's Canadian Light Infantry. Just prior to the RCR's arrival, the PPCLI Task Force had gone hard into the Panjwai District and ultimately set the conditions for the need to launch Operation *Medusa*. They had pushed the Taliban right at the end of their tour and set the RCR up for a really hard start to their own first warfighting tour. At whirlwind speed, and with much contradicting information on enemy strengths, a handover was conducted. The Patricias had stirred up a hornets' nest in the Panjwai District and had suffered several wounded and killed. It became the RCR's job to eliminate the nest.

Back during Gord's first deployment as a sniper to Kosovo in 1999, the sniper dets operated in two-man teams. The threat and semi-permissive environment in Kosovo allowed the det to infiltrate and operate for days without concern of discovery or contact. The current threat in 2006 was greater with the widespread use of IEDs and suicide bombers which presented greater challenges than being directly engaged by enemy forces. Peacekeeping for the Canadians had evolved into peacemaking and the protection of the friendly forces was paramount. It was the snipers who represented the protective sheepdogs and like those dogs, snipers would dispatch any threat to their flock they were tasked to support and protect. With the increased threat and requirement for internal force protection in Afghanistan, the dets now operated in four-man detachments.

The handover was comprised of a Black Hawk flyover of the AO and a tour of the outlying Tactical Infrastructure (the various bases, outposts, OPs etc.). Furthest west from Kandahar was Patrol Base Wilson, just north of Highway 1. This was the closest to the bad guys who were further west. The mountain ranges to the south, Masum Ghar and Sperwan Ghar, were enemy held.

During the first couple of weeks no significant events occurred except of course that everything Gord had been told by PB Wilson's Sergeant-Major was wrong: "I think they are out of mortars. Normally they only mortar during the day but not every day." That night they were mortared, and the following day and night. They had bracketed the patrol base, landing at least two to three mortars in the compound each time. Sixty-three's only protection was a canvas tent, and the sleeping gear was set as close to the ground as possible. If the snipers could have dug into the hard pack they built the camp on, they would have. Instead, the snipers rushed to the only protection they had—the protective skins of the G Wagon until the all-clear signal was given. Nothing was worse than sitting in a G Wagon listening to the *pop* of the mortar launch, counting to ten and waiting for the *whoomp* of the impact. Soldiers being soldiers, it didn't take long for the camp to be gridded into a checkerboard and a lottery began—would anyone get hit? After a couple days of this, the dets began occupying the high features of the camp to identify the spotters. Unfortunately, much of that time was spent listening to the Camp Sergeant-Major bark about the lack of helmets and exposure to enemy observation. This time out, on observation, did afford the dets some inoculation from the nonsense and acclimatization to the weather and area. More importantly it allowed the snipers time to develop the skills that would be required to establish the observed pattern of life in other areas and ultimately become experts on the habits of locals and what their reactions were when the Taliban were present.

At the two-week mark Gord was called back to Kandahar headquarters for a briefing. He left his detachment at PB Wilson. The Canadian compound in Kandahar had essentially two wings to its tactical operations centre. The TOC was filled with radios and monitors and more tech and was where the commander and others received their briefings, updates and intel. It also housed the staff shop. There were probably at any given time 25 to 30 personnel present across the spectrum, from military police, to judge advocates, engineers and a stream of worker bees.

In the TOC the operations officer gave Gord a rough brief about an impending operation and a request for the sniper contribution of the effort. Gord had no idea that this was to be the biggest operation since Korea—operational security was running high. The Americans were stuck in Iraq and the burden of Afghanistan's operations fell on the Canadians and other allied forces. The brief revealed little, but Gord understood it involved the entire battle group—it was infantry-centric—of less than a fully manned brigade but more than a battalion. The breakdown of the brigade was roughly three rifle companies, combat support, artillery, armour support and UAVs plus other enablers. And his small detachment was tasked with providing sniper support for the entire battle group. The operations officer needed to know what assistance the snipers could provide as this was the first time snipers would be called upon to provide direct fire and supporting fire to a large-scale operation. Prior to this, snipers had supported company- and platoon-deliberate operations but had not reached the scale of a battle group offensive. The realization that his detachment was too small dawned on him immediately:

The scale of support was daunting, I found myself going down way too many rabbit holes trying to ensure the snipers supported all phases of the operation. It took a good deal of pacing and white board erasing to finally come to the realization of what we could actually effect and support. We needed to fulfil our role as a force multiplier through long-range observation and interdiction. The gunfight on the ground was not going to be directly in our wheelhouse. It was hard to shake as I knew all the guys wanted to get tested in combat, but this would not be the reality this time. Objective Rugby and its surrounding terrain was dense and interwoven, our optics and observation capability would be significant in providing real-time intelligence, interdicting reinforcing personnel and cutting off squirters.

Gord would have to split his two teams into three to be able to provide proper, effective support for the operation. He thought about the men in his command—their personalities, their abilities and how he should and could create a third detachment without weakening any of the sniper dets. Jim, Jody, Barry, K, Senan, Dave, B and S—all individuals with their own strengths and weaknesses, and all unique personalities. At this time, Jody and Jim were the two det commanders … pulling one member could impact the strength of a four-man team. Who would make up Gord's new detachment so that across the board all three detachments of three men would be equally strong? It was going to be a long night of reflection and decision-making for tomorrow's briefing with the CO. It was time to get out of the office where he was working, a sea can, or shipping container, like a rail steel car. He had enough notes and needed some time to reflect. He believed in a bottom-up planning process. But with his dets still holding in PBW, he would have to make the initial force laydown on his own. And then there was tomorrow's briefing of the CO—the last time it didn't go too well for Gord: his briefing was too long and detailed, rocky might have been the better word. Gord laid down on a bunk bed for the night and finally fell asleep.

By 1030 of the next morning Gord and others received a full briefing on the impending offensive. It included intel on the enemy, location and that, in fact, people were dying the area—the enemy needed to be squished. A complete intel briefing was given on the red force. Present in the commander's briefing room were about 15 members around an oval table with the Lieutenant-Colonel being the highest rank in the room. The operation was to be a slow-burn offensive and was doctrinal in nature. It included pamphlet drops to urge civilians to leave, thereby announcing the impending Coalition attack. A series of pre-attack bombing runs were included. The briefing did miss a few things in planning, crucially the preparatory bombing of the area which was south of PB Wilson and just north of Masum Ghar and Sperwan Ghar, north of the River Arghandab and its floodplain. Gord felt that the prep-bombing and movement to the area were rushed.

Gord proposed three dets of three-man teams to support the effort and felt that that was sustainable for a short period time. His teams would live in a symbiotic relationship with the companies they were attached to. The snipers would provide intel and cover, while the companies would provide muscle and logistical support when needed. For Operation *Medusa* each rifle company was to receive one sniper det. The basic force package meant that Gord's newly created det was with A Company, while Jim was attached to B Company, with Jody supporting C Company. He also was in command and control of all three detachments while leading his own. Gord's det 63A was directly behind C Company on Masum Ghar. Jody's det was on the western edge of Masum Ghar with a U.S. Army Special Forces ODA looking west not north. The main effort was to support the effort against Sperwan Ghar. The third and final det was led by Jim V and was the least experienced team of them all and as such placing it with the B Company blocking force made sense.

For the snipers their mission was straightforward. The idea was that during the initial stages of Operation *Medusa*, Sniper Group 63 was to be detached from its usual attachment to the ISTAR (intelligence surveillance target acquisition and reconnaissance) Company to the rifle companies instead to provide early warning, target interdiction, situational awareness, and be an additional resource to call in fast air and indirect fire support missions. It was not ideal to have created three three-man teams for the operation because of the anticipated prolonged deployment and harsh environment, but it provided the companies with an asset that was capable of projecting either forward or to the flanks of their lines. At least this was the idea. Gord knew all the officers commanding the respective companies and although most officers knew little about proper sniper deployment, a lot of time was spent detailing sniper capabilities and contributions with those officers.

Warning orders were sent out to prepare for the mission at hand. After the briefing Gord ordered his detachment to return to Kandahar. This took a couple of days as a minimum size of convoy was required to travel through the hostile AO. He felt good about his men. He had a high degree of confidence in them but knew sustainability would be difficult because once the detachments separated from their respective companies, to support their efforts each det was more or less on its own. B Company was the intended blocking force and being the only company which would stay static, was the unit the snipers could possibly use for logistical and operational needs. The dets had multiband radios, manifest items and other logistics packed into the trailers behind their G Wagons vital for their mission prep.

Operation *Medusa* was still several weeks away from launch which gave the snipers time to organize and prep. It also gave Gord time to reflect on his teams. Gord had picked S and Senan to form the third detachment. Both were skilled snipers and could pick up the slack if Gord needed to devote brainpower to the manoeuvring and logistics of his other dets. All their training had been conducted through their own dets and no doubt they were concerned how Gord would lead the new team and how he would operate on the operation. Gord knew that the dets themselves were not impacted by the creation of a third one. But he had to not only lead his det as a commander but also oversee all planning and operational aspects as a UMS—he could not afford to lose focus on the overall deployment and conduct of the entire group. But operational and tactical control remained with the dets while attached to their respective companies. The det commanders were responsible to each of their OCs for briefing on their capabilities and constraints. This would be the first time that Jody and Jim would brief an OC outside of a training mission. Although Gord was confident in them, he did review their first back brief prior to delivery. They were both on point for capabilities, sustainment and coordination. This dry run would set the framework for multiple briefs to be delivered in the months to come.

Gord spent a lot of time with his dets, particularly on the roles and tasks of the second-in-command, the 2IC. A 2IC will make or break a team, a difficult but pivotal position. He did consider that his guys might not be able to do the job; after all K was the primary shooter for Jody's det and neither had shot at human beings before. In fact, due to manning issues prior to the tour, Gord had decided to bring in K as a non-qualified sniper. Unfortunately, K had failed off the course for stalking but had shown good potential as a shooter. Another concern was Jim's det as Jim's son in the Recce Platoon was deploying right in front and below his detachment. Gord reminded him not to worry, if possible, about his son going into action:

No plan survives first contact; during my mission planning I wrote this at the top of my white board in the sea can. There were so many factors that could derail the sniper support operation that I was trying to refine. Everything was questioned: what if Jim hears on the radio that his son's det gets into a TIC [troops in contact] with the bad guys during a critical point in B Company's block operation? What if Jody's bravado overtakes the mission that he was given and strays from a sniper task to clear operations? Will they be able to stand their ground when dealing with the OCs or will they look to endear themselves by doing what they think the OCs want? How will they deal with the targeting of real human beings? Trust and confidence go a long way. I had confidence in both det commanders and the det members, I trusted them all to make the right decisions. The OCs being supported were both strong leaders and would take the recommendations of the Det Commanders no matter their experience. It was their game now and my biggest hurdle would be how to ensure that resupply would be achieved. Rations and water would be provided by the supported Company, but our ammunition and batteries where not common amongst the BG [battle group]. I had to ensure three separate bundles where prepared and positioned so that when called for by us they would reach their intended mark. It was my understanding that the initial clearance would take only a few days. Damn you, Sun Tzu.

Egos had to be kept in check as well as his dets' requested items that Gord thought were more appropriate for SOF operators and not snipers. "Why do you need that?" was a common refrain. A lot of the requested items were not to be had in any event. He reminded them that they were there to support the main effort: it was not Sniper *Medusa* but Operation *Medusa*. Their job was to make sure the pointy ends of the spears were able to go where they were supposed to go.

But waiting at Kandahar was the worst. There was too much time on hand despite the rehearsals and kit inspections. The waiting was the absolute worst:

Meeting at the sea cans every morning to update the guys and go over any new details was difficult. We had prepared ourselves mentally and wanted to get on with it. At times the "what if" demon came out to play and had to be put down as fast as he came out. Everyone had their shit wired tight and the longer the wait, the more chance of everything coming unravelled became.

At long last movement to the AO began with a sequenced departure from Kandahar: C Company first, then A Company, while B Company was already in place north of the objective. It was an easy day for B Company. The other companies transitioned through the same areas during their deployments.

The official *Military Chronology of Canada in Afghanistan from 2001–10* reads that Operation *Medusa* began on September 2, 2006 with 800 Coalition troops involved. The PPCLI C Company was situated in the south, coming through the Bazaar-e-Panjwai area, with Bravo Company to the north fighting southward. On one flank, the eastern one, was Task Force 31, composed of U.S. Army Special Forces and Task Force Grizzly, a regular American force. Danish support came with a squad on the opposing flank, while a Dutch company patrolled the northern perimeter. Charles Company's objective was to seize the high features around Panjwai—Masum Ghar and Mar Ghar—and to isolate the town of Panjwai itself, advancing up to the south bank of the Arghandab River which ran northeast–southwest. NATO allies provided air support of fighters, bombers, attack helicopters, unmanned drones and spy planes around the Panjwai area. Objective Rugby, commonly known as the white schoolhouse, in Pashmul was across from the Arghandab River. In charge of the entire operation was the Canadian NATO commander in southern Afghanistan, General David Fraser.

But the veteran NCO Gordon Cullen knew there was nothing stopping the Taliban to squirt to Helmand District once the fighting began.

Charlie Company took the lead in the sequenced departure. Jody's det travelled with them. C Company was to spearhead at Masum Ghar, with its own firebase, and then were to move across the river in its LAVs (light armoured vehicles), covered not only by preparatory fire, but also by support fire from their own firebase. But not everything went smoothly. En route to Masum Ghar at about five kilometres south of the mountain, C Company took small-arms fire from a small group of enemy fighters. When an LAV column of vehicles came under small-arms contact/ambush, they maintained momentum and brought all guns to bear on the initiating area. With little concern of collateral damage to local property or infrastructure, the returning fire resembled a wall of lead. This particular ambush was probably some local fighters looking to get their gun on and were met with everything from 5.56 to 25mm. It was concerning that they had the balls to engage such a combat-heavy force from a fairly open area: not the actions of an enemy supposedly on its heels. Intel briefings had claimed that only a small group of fighters was in the area, wanting to avoid a fight. The consensus was that the movement to their staging area would be administrative but the ambush southside of the river indicated otherwise. Clearly the intelligence was flawed. On the other hand, because of the earlier pamphlet drops, the area featured fewer locals. Since there were lot of LAVs in C Company's packet, they were able to take their time to cut through the ambush steadily. The LAVs engaged everything and broke through the ambush.

Alpha Company followed suit to the same waiting areas where Charlie Company had deployed earlier. But to Gord things did not feel right because of the earlier ambush. So, the messaging was not good. At the waiting area, which had been recced by engineers, Gord went off to see about the final movement orders while the LAVs provided security. One LAV ramp-dropped right onto an old Soviet landmine and blew its tire. Fortunately, there were no casualties, but more clearing was required and the company spent the night in place. But confidence was diminishing. An ambush and now a minefield seemed to bode ill.

The same night A Company's OC received orders to bump up their departure. But nobody notified the sniper det. Alpha Company headed out, leaving in their wake the security element of the waiting area and Gord's sniper detachment. The company had moved 50 metres by the time Gord woke up and immediately got on the radio to ask if plans had somehow changed. The receiver seemed embarrassed or annoyed that nobody from his company had alerted the snipers. This was the final indicator to Gord that this op was a shit show. A Company moved to the side to allow the snipers in their G Wagon to pass on the left and reinsert themselves into the order of movement. The OC gave him a "sorry, man" look as the det moved into line. The OC, Major Wright, was an excellent leader in Gord's estimation but everyone's emotions where heightened and it was affecting the group.

By the time A Company arrived, Charles was already emplaced on the northern side of Masum Ghar overlooking Objective Rugby. A Company had made a left turn behind Masum Ghar and laagered up there with C Company on line to their right. Gord had briefed the OC of A Company that his sniper det was going to overlook the river to provide support for the offensive while also providing overwatch to the south for A Company. As a secondary task Jody's det was also able to provide support to A Company who were the security and reserve force if needed. But the focus of the two dets was north across the river.

On the southern side of Masum Ghar, the snipers' G Wagons were now with A Company's packet while Gord and his det humped up on foot to Masum Ghar. On the ghar, they found nothing but rocks. There was neither foliage nor embankments. Gord's det was still shielded to the north but exposed to the south. He knew that once the sun arrived the men would be punished by it just as likely as they would freeze after sundown. The OP did provide good arcs of fire and ranges into Objective Rugby at about 1,200 metres distance which was the maximum effective range of a .338 sniper rifle. Observation to Objective Rugby and into deeper areas was excellent. Gord's det could see infil and egress routes that Jody's det couldn't and vice versa. The two dets could hand off intel and targets seamlessly. The elements, however, were going to make Gord's detachment suffer. The fact that the det had multiband radios meant the snipers had their own frequency for internal communications. Gord was able to receive updates from the other two dets which also included logistical needs. The bane of a sniper det commander was to have the freedom to make operational decisions but still have to run it all by the Unit Master Sniper. This did not constitute micromanagement but was an issue of quality control.

As part of the force laydown for Op *Medusa*, a JTF 2 detachment and their JTAC along with an ODA team were co-located with Jody. Their focus was west to Sperwan Ghar and north in support of the other SOF units operating in the mission.

Operation *Medusa* began with some precision bombing but not to the level expected. The plan had called for a one-week bombardment before the rifle companies' assault. The preparatory bombing lasted about three days and included aircraft, arty, fast movers and naval gunfire support. But the ground offensive was launched early, supposedly because of a lack of enemy activity—the sniper dets too did not see much activity in front of them. Someone decided the threat across the river was minimal and after one day, when a fast mover hit a few key targets, C Company advanced without any real idea of the enemy forces they would face across the river.

Gord was in his OP as Jody decided to abandon the sniper position and take his team in C Company's LAVs into the assault. Jody knew that Gord would never have approved of this because the sniper det should have provided overwatch and supported the attack with direct fire and movement to lead the attacking elements. But being in the Sergeant-Major's LAV 30 metres away from an enemy meant that they no longer operated as snipers but as regular infantry. It was the wrong decision. Gordon had not been contacted and had no idea of Jody's movement off the ridge. The snipers' contribution was nullified. They had become regular infantry with limited ability to influence the fight if at all.

"I always supported the guys in making decisions, good, bad and ugly. This one was horrific. 63C after initial contact and subsequent manoeuvring became part of the casualty collection team, running casualties to the CSM's LAV and dodging fire."

But Gord's det was in awe as they saw a G Wagon with Frank Mellish in it lead the charge, followed by a front-end loader, then C Company's LAVs. He was listening in to the C Company reports to Zero, the battle group. What happened next was a catastrophe. A well-laid and patient ambush was executed by the enemy who had waited for the G Wagon to enter a tall brush area where it literally got hammered by RPGs as the whole frontage lit up with barrel flashes and smoke. Ferocious fire was incoming from the northern side of the river. Jody's det scrambled and managed to help wounded soldiers into vehicles. Gord's det saw the depth of the Taliban defences: low brush and tree lines were littered with outgoing enemy fire. The LAVs returned fire but were so close that the vehicles could not depress their barrels enough to be effective. There was a lot of confusion about where the front line was as fast movers roared in for supporting fire.

This disaster occurred directly at the 12 o'clock, Objective Rugby, of Gord's position. As the firefight unfolded, his detachment could not open fire because any round that fell short could have injured the struggling Canadians below. The ferocity of the ambush caught Gord off guard. As it stood, he could only advise on movement and provide target grids for artillery or air. S was the shooter while Gord served as spotter with Senan on the radio. A Company was still providing security to the south. But it was a mess to the det's front.

As the SOF's main effort was to the west, Jody's desire to be imbedded with the assaulting force had left the west side wide open when previously he could have shot squirters trying to escape the battlefield and had a genuine impact on the battle space. Instead, as events developed along with Jody's realization that he had become decisively engaged in a battle that he was not equipped for, his det became a casualty evacuation detail. Since Gord had been left completely out of the loop, all he could do was relay the movement his det saw in depth and communicate it to higher for them to better understand the developing battle space.

As soon as a TIC was called, air support had come on station, loitering in the skies and dropping bombs in depth. Gord's det tried to ID the enemy trench line but C Company was too close at that time for them to call in fast air. One American jet flying west to east parallel with the trench line did drop a 500lb bomb that landed behind a wall where the Canadians were taking cover. Gord saw a big puff of dust but no explosion. By a miracle the bomb didn't go off, luckily for the dismounted soldiers. There was a great deal of confusion.

Gord relayed to higher the enemy status: how much depth and movement, the lines of egress or resupply and heavy weapons such as recoilless rifles. His det was using the .338 and so he preferred to be at least 1,200 metres distant in any engagement so as not throw rounds at nearby friendlies. Being too close, he instead delivered as much real-time intel to C Company. He also relayed to Command that Masum Ghar was a hornets' nest and that whoever had provided intel was wrong: "It was very frustrating to not be able to contribute more to the actions at Objective Rugby. The enemy trench line was approximately 1,000 metres from our position; the proximity of the fighters we could see to the friendly forces was too close to confidently engage. Focusing on the depth positions and flanks was all we could do to reduce the enemy."

The madness ended quickly as C Company withdrew within 90 minutes. By September 3 Charles Company had suffered four casualties at Objective Rugby, the white schoolhouse: Sergeant Shane Stachnik, 2nd Combat Engineer Regiment, W/O Richard Nolan, 1RCR, W/O Frank Mellish, 1RCR, in the lead G Wagon, and Private William Cushley, 1RCR.

To be fair, had Jody been in place, he would not have made that much impact on the actual operation but the det could have contributed to the overall suppression and interdiction of the enemy. Gord saw geographically where the enemy was but could not locate any bodies even though he witnessed all the C Company actions. Whenever Gord saw an RPG being launched, the snipers could not get on target in time. In any event, the retreating Canadians were still too close to the enemy.

Jody's det got back to their OP and then finally became effective via air and arty support. Now Gord's and Jody's dets regained the ability to shoot across the river. The rules of engagement were simple: everyone across the river between them and B Company out of PBW was a bad guy and could be shot at. Gord felt better now, considering they were back to their original mission and capable of contributing to the battle at hand even though it had resulted in a withdrawal. But he was angry too. It took a few days to see Jody in person. In the meanwhile, on the radio to Jody, Gord said they'd talk about Jody's decision to abandon his OP to join C Company's assault across the river, but right now Gord didn't want to do this on radio.

There was a lot of Taliban movement in Panjwai but out of sniping range at about 2,000 metres so Gord employed the vector binoculars that were married up to a GPS, which allowed the det to call in devastatingly accurate fire missions to the guns and pinpoint grids to fast air and rotary wing assets. People moved around or into compounds. A group of 15 enemy fighters tried to move west, all dressed in black, with proper distancing and in military fashion. They took a halt, formed up in the shape of an exploding cigar, as Gord called in triple 7s (M777 howitzers) on a fire mission. They hit accurately: the first round was spot on as four guns fired three rounds of 155s each. Their formation was maybe 75 metres in length. Twelve rounds obliterated the area.

Jody also conducted similar fire missions with the ODA JTAC on location. Because of the SF JTAC, the firing solutions and missions came in quicker, as that was one of the primary functions of a JTAC.

The next day played out just like the previous. Jody spotted enemy fighters on the west that Gord couldn't engage because of a terrain feature and Jody's det called for air and arty fire missions. Any heat signature now was hit. The gloves were off.

C Company in the meanwhile reconsolidated to the southern side of Masum Ghar right below Gord's det. Once back in place, C Company then formed a firebase made up of LAVs that eventually would support the push from the north—but that was still to come.

The target area was finally softened up and this is when the original operation should have been launched. Airpower was really in now, however—it dominated— with jets and bombers coming in from Iraq to drop loads along with strafing runs by A-10s and Apache helicopters. The snipers called in several Apache strikes with the pilots confirming the targets and attacking without hesitation. Someone from each det was always watching for enemy activity or was on the radio calling out targets. During these two weeks the snipers got to sleep every two to three hours for a short while, which was a challenge to sustain.

Operation *Medusa* was big and long and all the dets proved exceptionally useful. The planning phase had sited them well: they saw almost all the way to PBW. But friendly fire rendered C Company combat ineffective. Emotions ran high when C Company got strafed by an A-10 "Warthog". Senan was on optics looking across the river, while S and Gord were on their backs watching the strafing run.

"We had been watching the A-10s circle overtop. They would pop chaff on the south side and strafe on the north side, over and over again. Then we saw one not pop chaff. We saw smoke come out of its nose and felt the ground below erupt. Normally you would hear the burp of the gun after the seeing the rounds impact. Not this time."

They felt the impact of the rounds and saw soldiers running, crawling and screaming. Gord did not permit his det to go down to help with the wounded: "The terrain was too steep and completely exposed to the enemy. We had to keep looking out while the focus turned in on the company position. Soon the skies would be littered with medevac helicopters and our main effort was still the protection of the area." He thought that the enemy would use this as an opportunity to launch additional attacks. And he felt enough people were helping below that it was best for the det to keep eyes on target.

It happened on September 4. C Company RCR BG was hit by A-10 fire, killing Private Mark Graham and wounding 30 others, making the company combat ineffective. The casualties had piled on for the RCR in two days. It was an ongoing brawl. The Canadians had been repulsed in the early stages of Operation *Medusa*.

The plan now called for a push from PBW with B Company and Recce, and an American task force to push south to Objective Rugby. A Company left on a mission, with C Company as a blocking force. This meant that A Company took Gord's G Wagon the det's only way for resupply. C Company on the other hand resupplied Jody and the attached JTF guys helped them as well. Gord's det, however, became dependent on ANA (Afghan National Army) SOF guys on the east who had to go to the local bazaar for supplies. Gord handed them cash to get bread and pop for a couple of days before resupply finally arrived from C Company. During all this they still called in strikes while trying to stay undercover, not only from the enemy but the elements beating mercilessly down on them. The detachment was burnt red from the sun.

The sniper dets were still able to do their job and provided coverage. In fact, they became expert at calling in fire missions in under one minute. On occasion, the Taliban tried to cross the river at night; other times they would take potshots from farming areas where water had receded and they could cross. But three .383 rounds put them in their place. The sniper det may have killed some Taliban but could not be confirmed.

Another time, one Taliban in a doorway came out and loosed a burst at the Canadians. He got into a rhythm of shooting. S and Gordon worked out the shooter's timing and each time he came out they said a *bang*. On the third time they took the shot, and he never came out again. Again, they could not confirm the potential kill. There were a couple more times like this, deterring or killing the Taliban who tried to cross the river.

This period saw the dets working with helicopters—right out of the training manual. A compound in a grassy area was proving aggravating but just like in training, Gord called in the helo call sign—the call sign was underneath the helicopters, visible when it hovered above—and talked the Apaches onto the target to take out two or three bad guys in one location. The helo moved south to north across the det to about 600 metres out when the enemy fired on him. The helo backed out and confirmed three solid signatures and engaged them, while another pilot came in too and engaged the Taliban fighters with the full complement of weapons. The entire grassy area and mud hut was obliterated. There were several similar occasions over the two-week period.

After a ten-day period, perhaps complacency or thinking they had superior combat power kicked in on Gord. His det was on the side of the mountain and Gord got a little too relaxed. One day all was quiet to their front, with nothing happening. Gord got tired of lying on his stomach. He sat up and gazed out at the scene of destruction below. As he was looking back to Senan and S who were on optics, he suddenly saw a puff of smoke and felt his head on fire. Something very hot had just blown past his head. Senan mouthed "WTF!" as S screamed for Gord to get down. An 82mm recoilless had fired and impacted just south in an adjacent farmer's field. Instantly, they tried to get the recoilless rifle targeted but Gord was unsure they hit it. Arty support was called in, but the enemy was fast: they had fired the one round and were gone. That was a big complacency check.

"Just because they aren't shooting doesn't mean they aren't watching."

Jody and Barry called in on radio to see if all was okay. The recoilless rifle was in the back of cart being towed by a horse. When the det saw the *poof*, they called in air, but they didn't want to light up the cart because it was on the move. The idea was to see where it went—back to the compounds and Sperwan Ghar. It parked at a compound. The initial call to not call in an air strike was made higher up in the hope of discovering a C2 node (command and control). It was then destroyed by fast air assets.

The most memorable event was a white phosphorus night. Normally Canadians were not allowed to use this deadly weapon on humans, but it was all-out war and everything across the line ahead of them was the enemy. A-10s and arty fired American white phosphorus rounds into the area including the white schoolhouse and other compounds. One old guy stood in the door as his roof and trees were on fire while an A-10 cruised like a shark around the northern side of the river, strafing everything. The old man had to decide to either make a run through the strafing runs or stay inside the burning house: he never came out. Gord wished the old man had been in range so he could have made the decision for him and sent the old man on his way. This was the only time Gord felt bad: "You looked at him and could see from his body language that he was in a complex situation—he wants to leave but doesn't want to die but knows he will either way." In the end it was a miserable death.

From Gord's perspective the overall plan for *Medusa* was decent, with an assault force, a blocking force, and depth with A Company, not just rear security but ready to support. Everything was in place for a successful mission but sending C Company into the assault at least two days early was a horrible mistake that led to more horribleness. The PBW unit moving south took three days to clear the area because the operation was a wake-up call to the Taliban. The Brits in the west saw an influx of movement from the east. The north–south clearance fell just short of Objective Rugby. Call sign Saxon (the current defence minister, then a major) was briefed by Gord on the back of a Hummer to clean up south to north with Saxon's ANA forces which were about company sized. They walked across the river and north, and seemed pretty gung ho. The op crawled to the finish line.

The disabled G Wagon and LAV were still on the northern side of the river, and the attempted recovery with a Zettlemeyer was abandoned. The det could see blue flashes of enemy welders at night as they cut into the LAV. Instead, the det lazed (laser range finder) the blue welding sparks and called in a fire mission.

The official entry for September 17, 2006 saw Lieutenant-General David Richards announce the successful completion of Operation *Medusa* against the Taliban in the Panjwai District near Kandahar. An estimated 500 Taliban had been wounded (and some killed). A local farmer reported that "The bombing and the fighting destroyed our mosque, our homes and our vineyards ... the Taliban are gone, but so is most everything else."

Canadian NATO commander in southern Afghanistan, General David Fraser, explained that "There has been battlefield damage largely because of where the Taliban went. We will go back out there, and we will help rebuild that."

Medusa was pretty amazing given the zero experience they all had. Gord reflected that not a lot of Canadian soldiers get to actually execute their jobs. A modern sniper might not get any opportunity to practise it. There was a great deal of satisfaction for Gord, and he would always go back to that situation throughout his career. He had cut his teeth during the op with many lessons learnt that would prove vital in his 2010 deployment. Gord's after-action report described the two weeks of his detachments during *Medusa*:

TF 3-06 ISTAR COY SNIPERS:

The first two weeks of OP Medusa saw the sniper detachments assisting their respective companies with shaping and information gathering ops. Once the initial push was made to the North side of the river the sniper detachments assisted with target interdiction through fast air, all arms calls for fire and direct engagements.

Due to the Taliban's strong foothold along the River and a series of unfortunate Incidents rendering C Company battle ineffective the Battle Group re-focused its efforts in the North. The Sniper detachments remained in their locations along the south side of the river assisting with long-range situational awareness and providing cut-off for the Battle Group to the West of Panjwai/Pashmul.

Upon the success of the Battle Group push from the North and the effective link up of the ISTAR group and the U.S./Afghan forces in Pashmul the Sniper Detachments re-organized under ISTAR and returned to KAF [Kandahar Airfield] for rest and refit.

Now, with a strong foothold in the south of Pashmul, ISTAR Coy tasked the sniper section along with Recce Pl. to conduct dismounted patrols along the newly ploughed route running north to south across the Taliban peninsula. This would complement the screen being emplaced by the Recce Sqn and support the Commander's main effort.

The tasks, implied and stated, for the Sniper Group were to provide a covert presence in order to gain info on movement, deter insurgents and eliminate any Taliban threat observed in the area of the ploughed route.

The Sniper Group took two very classic approaches to the situation. First and foremost was to maintain a foot on the ground through active patrolling and hasty ambushes.

The second was to establish OPs along the ploughed route and in the vicinity of the route.

These operations were conducted until the groups move with ISTAR Company to Sperwan Ghar.

Op Medusa provided the Sniper Group with a quick introduction to war fighting vise peace keeping. It also provided the group with an insight into the need for a dedicated supply line and clear avenues of communication when detached.

Ultimately, in such a diverse group as ISTAR Company it is the personalities and their ability to bend and reform to meet the needs of higher that enabled the Company to be so successful.

7

Other People's Guns

Sergeant Gordon Cullen, Unit Master Sniper
Detachment 63, Task Force 3-06
Panjwai District, Kandahar Province, Afghanistan
October 2006

Post-*Medusa*, the force laydown had changed significantly. Charles Company and elements of ISTAR Company had taken over Sperwan Ghar from the ODA. A Company was centered on Masum Ghar with CSS (combat service support) elements and the forward TOC (tactical operations centre), while Bravo Company had placed its HQ at Patrol Base Wilson (PBW) with its platoons spread along the newly plowed Route Summit. Although there was still a persistent IED and Taliban threat throughout the AO, much of it was now focused east of Sper and Route Summit. Strong points had been established along Route Summit, conveniently named Strong Point North, Centre and West, which provided coverage for the construction of the route and tied the battle group's forward line of troops from Highway 1 to Sperwan Ghar. Still reeling from their dislodgement from

Panjwai, the Taliban had been trying to focus its efforts on disruption operations, their focus to slow the construction of Route Summit through IED emplacements and harassing the strong points using hit and run tactics. These shoot-and-scoot hits were initially insignificant in size and effect, but perceived successes had rallied the bad guys in the area, so much so that "reliable reporting" indicated that additional fighters were starting to filter back into the area from the west.

At this time, we were located at Sperwan Ghar. We had been providing support to the ODA and their operations west to Zangabad and were again now grouped with ISTAR Company to assist with the definition of the enemy westwards and support battle group operations. I had been getting the intelligence updates through daily orders groups (O groups) with Charles Company.

One night, from the top of Sper where we had established ourselves, we could see an area north of us erupt in heavy fire. This was far more significant than anything we had seen in the previous weeks. The next morning, we found out that Strong Point West had come under intense and sustained fire from west of their position. This wasn't the two to three fighting-age males (FAMs) spraying down the position and then disappearing into the maze of walls and buildings, but coordinated engagements by trained fighters, incorporating fire and movement as well as the use of RPGs on armoured targets. As the UMS, I saw this as a warning order. I returned to the top of the hill and disseminated the information to the guys.

Sper had been active in the past but having the entire Sniper Group there was not required. We came up with a couple COAs (courses of action) that would support Sper and see a three-man det move to Strong Point West to enable the platoon of infantry there. As we were mid-tour at this point, I was undermanned due to the guys rotating home for HLTA (Home Leave Travel Assistance). Although the leave was only about 20 days at home, the travel back to KAF, doing admin in KAF, travel to our support base in a second location and reverse at the other end, meant at least two snipers were gone for 30 days at a time.

With this in mind, I kept Detachment 66C intact and planned to take the two remaining members from 66B with me to support B Company. I guess I expected this to happen within a day or two of the attack on West. I was sadly proven wrong. Normal SOP for us in the Sper OP was to have one radio on the company net and one on the BG's (battle group's) or Zero's net. This normally gave us situational awareness (SA) on the immediate AO and the BG's AO. After about four days of anticipation, we started to hear traffic on getting snipers to PBW to support B Company. Our bags were already packed with the appropriate gear to sustain ourselves at someone else's tactical infrastructure (TI) for a couple weeks. To take a step back, after disseminating the info on the attack and coming up with a couple COAs, I had briefed OC ISTAR on my desire to send snipers to support B Company. As we were under the hat of ISTAR, I still needed to ensure I passed all my plans through him for furtherance to the CO and Zero. From what I could gather from his debrief, he supported the plan that saw me and two other members deploying to enable B Company. Now back on the radio we heard him telling Zero that the loss of three snipers would degrade the capability of ISTAR Company in Sper. I was completely taken back by this revelation, to the point of getting my gear on to go down the hill and confront the OC. I was quickly stopped in my steps when I heard 9'er, the battle group commander, break the air, acknowledging the OC's concerns but restating that a sniper det would be moving to PBW to link up with OC Bravo and project into his AOR (area of responsibility).

This was shortly followed by a message that two Black Hawk helicopters transporting a dog handler would touch down in ten minutes to pick up the snipers. Quick time estimate meant that we had three minutes to get down to the LZ with all our gear. Fail to plan, plan to fail. We grabbed our prepped equip and met the helicopter as it touched down. A quick five-minute hop northeast to PBW and we were in orders with OC Bravo. He had arranged transport to take us south down Summit through Strong Point North and Centre and then on to West. The Platoon WO gave us a quick lay of the land and asked me where I wanted to bed down. The southernmost position of the platoon's defensive position provided good observation of the area from where they had come under attack and also had suitable infil routes to get into the area west.

The strong point was a series of interlocking compounds that had been heavily damaged in the prosecution of Operation *Medusa*. The troops had been fortifying their positions with sandbags. Fortunately, the construction of the mud huts and grape huts was sufficient to stop most small arms and RPGs. I talked to several of the section commanders about what had happened and where they thought the centre of the attack had come from. I was also curious where they thought the enemy's infil routes were. They were a wealth of knowledge, providing numbers, weapon types and avenues of approach. We also visited all their OPs to ascertain what each of them could see and affect with guns and observation. For the most part the position was well laid out with interlocking arcs of fire and observation. There were a couple trouble areas which the guys knew were out there but without UAV or air could not see into. Knowing the enemy fairly well by this point, I was aware they had an outstanding knowledge of their terrain and how to use it. If there were dead areas that the platoon couldn't see, the enemy would exploit them. In many respects they were the masters of their craft and could get in close, wreak a little havoc and disappear without a trace. Strong Point West was part of a former village that sprawled along the corridor where Summit was being built to the east, with a large graveyard to the west. The graveyard would later prove to be a larger kill zone than it already was.

We remained static for a couple days, getting the lay of the land to the west, examining maps and photos to develop a plan to infiltrate west and prosecute the enemy who had launched a wall of lead at the platoon.

On the evening of the second night the position came under attack from across the graveyard. It started with sporadic small-arms fire that I perceived to be exploratory. The bad guys had no night vision so to define one of our positions they would let some rounds rip and see what happened. The platoon at Strong Point West was used to this tactic and held their fire until the entire platoon could coordinate return fire. They used the optics in their LAVs to scan the area with thermal, determined a grid of the enemy, and unleashed a mad minute of heavily concentrated fire. From 25mm down to 5.56mm they tore the surface away from the earth and reduced the walls by a couple of feet. Surprisingly, the enemy countered from another concealed fire position with a smaller, concentrated attack on the centre of the position. This was super ballsy as West was a fortified position with LAVs and a full suite of platoon weapons that could be called upon to annihilate an area. They demonstrated a determination that we hadn't seen since *Medusa*. The second attack ceased suddenly, and the night fell quiet again.

The next morning, we presented our intentions to deploy that night to try and identify the enemy infil routes and tentative OP locations from where we could interdict them. The plan gained acceptance from the OC back at PBW and was supported by the section we were bunking with. The plan in general (big hand) terms would see the three of us push out from our current position, move south to the base of the graveyard, before swinging west and then north to the opposite side of the graveyard. This is where the initial attack had come from and seemed like a solid start state for hunting the enemy. Most of our movement could be covered by the machine gun and OP in the southern corner of the compound and a small QRF would be on call to provide support should we need to be extracted. At this point only foot patrols had pushed west of the strong point, no roads had been cleared or plowed, and the intersecting wadis made it impossible to move our LAVs across. For this reason, we limited our exploitation into enemy territory to no more than two kilometres. Depending on our success we had planned subsequent exploratory patrols using different routes into additional sectors until we had defined the entire frontage of the platoon.

Prior to departing we had some concern about the supporting OP's IFF (identification friend or foe) recognition. Normally we would only turn on our strobes or crack an IR glow stick if we felt we might be targeted by friendlies or were in contact ourselves. For this quick jaunt we decided to crack an IR glow stick and put it in our right leg pocket. The material in our pants would dim the signature of the glow stick under night vision enough that it wouldn't wash out our NVGs and would still be visible to the OP—the right-hand leg pocket also because we would be doing a right hook in front of the OP and would not need to move it during the more dangerous part of the patrol: more often than not, if we came under contact, it was on the infil.

At 0200 Senan, I and B departed south out of the compound in that order. By this point we had all worked together and were somewhat familiar with each other's nuances outside of what we had covered in rehearsals. Initially confident in our stealth and ability to move effortlessly through the night, we were startled to see that the claymore used to cover dead ground below the OP had been turned inwards facing back at the compound. No more than 20 feet from the OP and compound, a stealthy individual or individuals had reoriented the claymore. Fuck, that's a bit of a game changer. Senses became heightened, movement a little more deliberate, as we radioed in to advise on the claymore which would be re-sited the next day. After a quick listening halt, we became very aware of the raw iron taste that sat in the back of our throats in the presence of freshly buried bodies. We knew this was one of the graveyards where fighters had been buried post-*Medusa* and could ascertain from the flags that some had been distinguished people but the numbers of freshly dead under the stones was surprising. This compounded our level of awareness and imposed a certain level of doom … walking amongst the dead.

We moved south to a predetermined point, conducted a quick map recce and started west. We could see a few fires still burning in the fields and in a couple compounds. Many of the roofs of the buildings and huts were made from thatch and the petrified hardwood found in the area. They would most likely smolder for a day or so. Moving slowly between a wall and a wadi, careful to examine the ground for fresh footprints, signs of IEDs and ensure we left as little sign of travel as we could, I heard B come across our internal comms.

"Stop, I got something."

He had picked up a couple shadows against a wall in one of the compounds. Given the factors to this point, we decided this needed further definition. We gathered in behind cover and B disseminated what he saw: looked like a couple dudes sitting around a fire, but he could only see the shadows on the wall. Why would you decide to camp out in a kill zone, the night after an attack? Afghan locals may be simple in their lives, but they have been around long enough to know that this is not a good idea. We sent in a quick sitrep to B Company with our intention to manoeuvre around the compound to further define what we had out here. The compound, about 50 metres from our position, had several external doors and was enclosed by broken walls. We could see a fire burning inside, where most likely the roof had caved in. However, we could not see into the open area so we decided to move around to the south where there was a large gap in the wall that should afford us a good line of sight. We moved off, keeping our profiles low, not sky-lighting ourselves against the moonlit background. We made good speed and found a depression in the ground from which to observe. Confirmed, there were at least two FAMs inside the compound with positive ID on an AK-47 leaning against the wall. Do farmers carry AKs? Sure they do. Do they carry them within a kilometre of a Canadian position that came under attack the previous night in an area that has been contentious and ground zero to heavy fire?

Nope.

I updated our position and began looking for a way to get eyes into the compound without getting into a gunfight. To stay light and retain our capability, only two of us had carbines while the third man had a long gun. If there were more than two in there, we could find ourselves in a position we didn't want to be in. Further, given the tenacity of the enemy in previous encounters, there was good chance that other fighters could be in proximity and able to provide support to their brothers. After a good look at the compound and surroundings, it was apparent that we could not get eyes into the compound without entering. I called back to B Company to see if there was air on station in the vicinity. Luckily there was an A-10 who was coming over to get a look into the compound. Perfect, he could confirm the target and then take care of it. We could peel back, watch from a distance and deal with anyone who came to help the targets. The A-10 confirmed the target but was getting low on fuel: he would need to go off station and refuel. We didn't want to sit on these guys all night. They could be waiting for reinforcements or were part of a larger attack which we could get caught up in. Neither was desirable.

So, clearly the airspace was free as no other air support was available. At this point in the tour there were four M777s at Sper. We had a lot of experience employing them and I felt super-confident in their ability to bring fire to bear on the target. We backed off about 100 metres east into a built-up area that provided us with positive line of sight onto the compound and sufficient cover to protect us from any shrapnel. I called in the grid, direction and target description of the compound, a point target for their purposes. The gun line was quick to reply. They were uncomfortable with dropping bombs so close to our position.

"Danger close."

Understandably they could not see the cover we had and did not want to get into a blue-on-blue situation. They requested ground commander's authorization to drop and pushed the initial target grid by 100 metres west. From our perspective west was an add, east a drop and north and south were right and lefts. I gave my name and permission. We could hear the report of the gun at Sper. No one in the compound moved. The round impacted 100 metres west of the compound

"Drop one hundred." Back to the original grid.

Again, the report of the gun and four seconds later the impact just right of the compound. This was one gun firing one round. The compound was well within the lethal radius of that round and an additional three guns would make sure of that. Still no movement ... perfect.

"G11 [artillery call sign] target round, fire for effect."

Now deep in my mind I know they make the call on how many guns and how many rounds. I can give them a repeat, but the initial volley was on them.

"63 [Gord] ... G11. Four guns ... four rounds fire for effect, shot over."

I think my voice shook a little when I gave the "Shot out" in return. I also know from past experiences that they are super-accurate, but this was the first time I was downrange of the enemy when the rounds were inbound. I maintained visual of the compound, forcing my eyes to stay open. I could hear the air breaking from the inbound volley, the ground literally shaking the instance before the first four rounds impacted and then exploded with a violence that I have never witnessed. Shrapnel the size of dinner plates flew through the air, sounding like Harleys passing our position. The ground was enveloped, turning the compound inside out in a ball of flame. It didn't matter that I screamed "Fuck!" at the top of my lungs because the next three volleys of four rounds were right behind the first. We pressed deeper into the earth, hoping it was bombproof, giving each other uncomfortable glances. The guns were devastating; my head was swimming in overpressure and noise as I waited for the dust and smoke to move off of the compound so I could assess the damage. Annihilation, nothing better describes it. It was like looking across an open area that had been bulldozed, difficult to really say where the centre of the compound was anymore. I called in the BDA, battle damage assessment, describing the target effect with the obligatory "Good shoot".

As we were moving back towards the compound, the A-10 that had gone off station to refuel was back. He caught the last piece of our BDA and confirmed that there was a crater two feet from the target position that he had confirmed earlier, and added, "Ya, I would say that was a successful engagement." We laid up short of the to see if any bad guys would come and investigate. After an hour or so no one had appeared, and I really didn't blame them. I wouldn't go anywhere near the place if I had heard the wrath that had just delivered the "fuck you".

We decided to take advantage of the stillness and carried on with our original task. We pushed back on our original route west to the southwest corner of the graveyard and turned north. Here we found several fresh—within a day or so—flip flop and boot prints running both north and south along the moondust path where the sand was so fine that it was like walking on the moon, or at least what we perceived of it from the pictures: when you placed your foot down, dust would puff up all around your boot.

Doing a quick assessment, we ascertained there were around ten sets of prints that had traversed the path. It was too hard at night to figure if they were all in one group but suffice to say this was the infil route we were looking to exploit. Approximately one kilometre north on the trail we held up to identify an area we could occupy the next night to ambush the bad guys using the path. Again, given the threat and skill of the enemy, we didn't want to walk into and clear the OP tonight. We wanted to ID an area that would provide cover and concealment, had line of sight to most of the target area and afforded good infil end exfil routes. Just north of the field that bordered the northern side of the graveyard was a small compound on the edge of a group of compounds that could have all the essential elements. Again, going in and confirming these things that night would leave footprints or signs that the enemy could pick up on and emplace a shitload of IEDs or lay in ambush in proximity. Better to just leave it until we needed to occupy. We had a quick chat about the tentative OP, routes in and out and a rehash of the fire mission. I believe the consensus was that we had a new appreciation for what "danger close" should mean.

We called into B Company and let them know we were on the way back. The sky would start getting lighter soon, so we moved with a bit more haste. The return route would take us west to east across the graveyard with a large mound of earth known as the Ant Hill as a reference point. The early morning stillness of Afghanistan is like nothing else I have experienced—

no chirping birds or insects and no mechanical noises in the background. As we started into the graveyard, I heard the sharp cycling of the action on the machine gun in the OP.

What the fuck is going on now?

We put ourselves behind the Ant Hill, which we knew was blocked from view. I gave the boys the signal to put our strobes on. Clearly, with all the things that had happened that evening, the OP was a little on edge and we later learned the position had been put on alert. I should have expected it. I was about to come on the radio to let the OP know we were coming across the graveyard with strobes on when the OP broke air calling in a contact: four FAMs with weapons moving from behind a wall west of the graveyard. Given this description, that was right behind us. We scoured the area but couldn't see or hear anything. I called the OP to confirm the contact. I could hear him talking to his buddy Randy in the OP. Randy has a distinct voice and at this point it was very loud. He was describing our movement behind the Ant Hill and was sure there were four of us. Fuck, fuck, fuck … Randy was on the gun and targeting us! *Motherfucker, no more tonight.* I unclipped my strobe from my harness and held it in my hand.

I came on the radio: "Randy, this is Gord … I am behind the Ant Hill. I am going to step out with my strobe. Don't fucking shoot me."

"Roger," replied Randy.

Stepping out, beads of sweat were running down my back. Randy is a really good shot. I could hear him say "Got him" and then the radio confirmation. We regrouped and made our way across the graveyard to the compound. Randy was having a good laugh when we got in, so I told him to go fix his fucking claymore.

We decided to rolex, to push, our next patrol in 24 hours. Let the area settle a little, confirm all the supporting plans with B Company and prepare—no point rushing to failure. Given the enemy we had encountered the night before last, we had requested UAV support to cover our infil into the proposed OP location. UAVs were invaluable when properly employed. They could loiter overhead and feed us real-time intelligence on what was happening around us. For example, I could lay up on the corner of the building and get the UAV to tell me what was around the corner and further down our route. It could also monitor our peripherals, acting as early warning on movement.

Departing the compound at 1230 hours, our initial route would take us east across the graveyard, basically parallel to the route we had taken on the last patrol. We confirmed communications with the UAV, working through the JTAC attached to B Company. Everything sounded in order, there wasn't any movement west of us and our infil route appeared to be clear. Our objective was north of our position, but we wanted to take a long dogleg into the area for security reasons. We would be occupying the OP for 24 hours, so we wanted to make sure we took our time getting in.

Just short of the tentative OP, we held up in behind a mosque to conduct a listening halt and confirm what we wanted to do upon entry. We held here for a good 20 minutes. All appeared to be good, so we hopped over a low wall and into a compound with three attached buildings, all oriented south to north with their windows and doors only facing south. We cleared all three, taking note of which one would afford us the best observation onto the north–south route. The center building had an oversized entry that would allow us to view most of the route from 400 metres out. As it was the middle building, it didn't have any windows on the east or west side, which provided deep shadows in the back of the room. Senan and B set up and I called in the OP report, and once set, we started into OP routine. At this time our UAV had come off station and was RTB, returning to base. Throughout that night and the next day, we observed no movement along the route. We were scheduled to collapse the OP that evening and move back into the compound. As we were collapsing the OP, we received a call on the radio. A Predator drone which had been loitering in the area had observed a lone fighting age-male with an AK-47 slung across his back 60 metres west of our position.

Concerning, but not devastating, we quickly finished our preps to depart. The intent was to cache our gear in place, move out, dispatch the bad guy, wait for a bit to see who else was around and then call in the QRF to exploit the scene. Not so lucky—as we were preparing to move out to take out the bad guy, we received an update that the one FAM had moved west to a compound about 150 metres from ours where he had met up with four more FAMs with weapons who were now moving on our position. Change of plan. The B Company JTAC let us know that the Pred was going to strike the group of five FAMs and we needed to hunker down. No problem … the Hellfire missile impacted in the centre of the group dispatching them all and giving the walls of our building a good shake.

Another update came across the radio. More bad news. Another eight FAMs were moving down the same trail, all armed.

The Pred was looking to engage them too but was concerned he would have less success as they were better spaced. This left us trapped in our OP with eight agitated FAMs inbound. The JTAC was giving us a live talk-on of what was happening. The group was 50 metres from our position, beginning to recover the bodies from the first strike. It would appear they were unaware of us. They were moving the dead back to a casualty collection point approximately 500 metres west at the corner of a grape hut. The Pred waited until all the bodies and the group of eight were gathered at the grape hut and launched his second Hellfire. The strike was unsuccessful, and the group dispersed. We were told an A-10 was coming on station to assist. At this point no further updates on the enemy location were being given. Where did they all go? IOT (in order to) ensure the A-10 knew our position. I was told I needed to go outside of my building, take a knee and hold my rifle over my head with a strobe on.

Are you seriously kidding me right now? You want me to go outside when you don't know where eight really pissed-off bad guys are and take a knee in the open?

So, I went outside, took a knee and got sparkled by the A-10. A couple minutes later the A-10 picked up the group moving south from the grape hut which the Pred had struck. This was our cue to move back to the B Company compound. A bit of a risk, but essentially our best opportunity as we knew the enemy was moving south and there was air cover should any more show up. Our route back would parallel theirs, separated by a few compounds. Then we would turn east back to friendly lines. The A-10 made a number of gun-runs on the group, approaching from our 6 (north) and strafing the group. We were confident the guy driving the plane was good to go but we all had the blue-on-blue at Masum Ghar on our minds. We moved with best speed back to the graveyard, ensuring we still examined areas for IEDs. The enemy group must have changed direction west. We were just about to turn into the trail that would take us into the safety of the compound when we saw the A-10 bearing down on us from the east. It was directly in line with us, and we could see the smoke coming out of his nose. Senan jumped off the trail, landing in the fetal position as we heard the report of the 30mm cannon unload overhead. Although B and I had a good laugh at Senan's expense, we were all a bit unnerved.

I later had the opportunity to view the Predator feed from this event. It was a frightening realization. We never understood how the initial bad guy ended up in our vicinity. Turns out he was making his way to the compound where the group of eight came from when he saw our footprints in the sand on the verge of the path. We had made every effort to rock hop and conceal our movement, but we had made a mistake. The video had him bent over at the waist investigating our prints. He then moved back and grabbed the other four guys, showed them our trail, pointed at our group of buildings and would have rolled us up had the Pred not been around. I expect the whole group was gathered to launch another attack on Strong Point West. The Pred had stayed on station as an observation platform throughout the engagement. I was able to see the second strike and the subsequent gun-runs from the A-10. All the bad guys perished in their move west. No further attacks on Strong Point West occurred for at least a month.

Although we weren't able to dispatch any enemy with our own systems during our initial time at the strong point, we were able to disrupt their activities by putting ourselves out there. No other dismounted patrols had pushed that far out. We would return to Sper in a week to support another push west to Zangabad but our time at Strong Point West was not over; we would return in January to conduct additional missions and push even further into the heartland of the enemy.

8

U.S.Eh

Corporal Barry Nisbet
1st Battalion, Royal Canadian Regiment
U.S Army Ranger School, Ft Benning, Georgia
2003

I can feel the rungs of the ladder in my hands; they are cool, not cold. It is just a ladder; climb it and shut up; it's only 35 feet high, climb it and shut up. The murky water gets further and further away with each rung I ascend. On top of the ladder, I am welcomed by a six-inch-wide balance beam. It's just a fucking beam. Midway on the beam is an obstacle, you could say: two steps up and two steps down—they're just fucking steps. So, walk down the beam, take a couple steps up and down, and walk some more. Basic skills. Three and a half storeys up, that murky water looks flat and concrete-like. So just walk, I tell myself, and I walk. Don't look down, just walk. You can walk, right? I walk, I get to the steps, take a step. You know how to do that, right? I do, up and over I go. Now walk to the end. Fuck, I got this. I get to the end of the beam and look at the long rope extending to a pole in the water with a large wooden "Ranger" tab hanging in the middle. Although the rope sags slightly, the height difference is minimal compared to the beam. I am not afraid of heights, or water. I am young and believe I am indestructible. So, I just need to commando crawl to the tab. I opt for the under approach and wrap my legs around the rope, my body hanging below. I put my left arm over the rope so that it falls into my elbow joint: I'm locked in. With my right I start pulling, pull, pull, I'm eating this thing up, I'm smashing this, and the tab is looming larger with each pull. I reach it in an instant. This is where I stop, hang down and request permission to drop—it's all going to plan, I'm strong, I feel good. I unhook my legs and as they pendulum down, I make the mistake of transitioning my left arm from its locked position on the rope and try grasping the with my hand to hang freely. *Fuck, I did this too fast.* My head knows what's about to happen and it's telling me something bad is coming. My body tries to disagree with my brain but it's all in vain. I feel my right hand pull off the rope as my legs continue their swing, my left-hand straining to hold my 197lbs. I see my fingers extending and there is nothing I can do about it. I'm falling, I'm fucking falling.

I try to sound off on my way down: "Ranger 156, request permission to …"

I'm an out of control flailing mess of woodland camo. I plunge into the murky water, it hurts, my head slaps hard as I impact the water on my left side. I pop out of the water and take a laboured breath. I make the short swim to the ladder to exit Victory Pond. I have done the name no justice. There is commotion near the ladder, the instructors clamouring around. I think to put out a helping hand that never comes. Drenched,

I put both feet on to dry land. Calmly one of them asks me if I'm alright. I take the bait, thinking there is some sincerity in his voice. My head is ringing, my left side feels as if it was slapped by a 2x4, pride hurt the most.

"Yes, I'm okay," I say.

Then the real head-ringing starts. Out of nowhere I'm surrounded by instructors, inches away from my face. They are ravenous, like a pack of wolves, they all want their piece of me, and so it starts.

"Who the fuck told you that you could fall off my obstacle?"

"What the fuck is your roster number?"

It is 360 degrees of welcome to U.S. Army Ranger School … with a splash.

That was day two or three, I think: Victory Pond Water Confidence Course Class 5-03. Sleep was a luxury, yelling commonplace, walking a speed rarely used, hunger lurking, which would take hold like I'd never known. My weight was diminishing. Sixty-odd days to go.

There were six Canadians blended into this sea of this woodland-cam-wearing, "hoooah"-shouting, god-loving, testosterone-filled group, the six of us only discernible by our CANADA name tape in place of the U.S. ARMY above our left breast pocket and our use of "eh" in most sentences. Our name tape was usually covered by the strap of some heavy ruck or piece of gear, so we assimilated for the most part.

At this stage some hopefuls had already been beaten by the PT test, or just the general tempo of it all. Out of us Canadians I was the lowest rank. As a corporal, my unit had put faith in me to get this done, to come back with that black and gold Ranger tab, with some experience to pass on. They told me I was the first corporal from Canada to ever be sent on the course—whether that was true or not, I did not know or care. I had been joined by two captains, two lieutenant and a master corporal from other units. Rank was non-existent on the course that chewed up souls and skin, exploited weakness, blistered your feet and your mind with self-doubt and worst of all, self-pity. Self-pity sent you home. I just kept telling myself, *You fought to be here so just don't quit.* Inside my cap I wrote my roster number 156 and drew a small maple leaf in case I forgot where I came from. There were times on the course I forgot where I was, times I didn't know up from down, left from right, if I was sleeping or awake, times I just wanted lighting to strike me to end it all. But just don't quit.

My class consisted of various ranks and experiences. We had Air Force PJs, Ranger Battalion "Bat boys", some SF, Marines and other foreign students. Every time before chow we would form up in front of the chin-up bars and one person was selected.

"Repeat after me" and we would recite the Ranger Creed, hopefully mistake free. Mistakes = push-ups and we didn't pass a chin-up bar without ripping off seven. My first meal in chow hall was epic: there was no menu, you lined up and grabbed a tray with food on it. As I did this I turned casually and took a step to grab a seat.

"EAT!" an RI (Ranger Instructor) screamed at me.

I stared blankly.

"EAT!" he repeated.

With a petrified look on my face, I grabbed my fork and started shovelling. By the time I sat down I was almost done. The only time we didn't have to double-time was walking back to our barracks after chow. I suppose they didn't want piles of puke strewn about.

You figured things out fast at Ranger School. I listened, I watched, you quickly see who's strong and who's weak. You see the spotlight Rangers who burn bright when being assessed or when an RI was around. They would quickly extinguish when not in an "assessed role". Then you see the ones who just go, always on, always trying, helping, pushing, doing more, fully knowing the hazards of their chosen profession. I pushed, I tried, I did more, and although I didn't always burn the brightest, I always burned, or so I thought anyways.

Friendships usually start with some commonality. In Ranger School this was no different. As the RIs assessed me, I assessed the other students. They threw so much at us in the first week that it was pretty easy to see who had some experience and who did not. I could see the students who were physically strong and, more important, mentally. I knew this was going to be an extremely physical course and had been warned by others who had gone before that this paled in comparison to the mental aspects. The mind is weak: it takes everything in, the cold, the hunger, the yelling, the physical exertion, sleeplessness, and it tells you to stop, it tells you that you have had enough, it gives you a reason to quit. This will happen well before your body gives up; you just have to convince yourself of that. We will all be tired, hungry, angry, stumble and fall. But you need to get back up and carry on. So, I looked around, I watched the other students, I saw them fall; some sprang back up repressing what their mind was telling them. Others fell with a look of discomfort and pain, slow to get up, allowing their minds to convince them how hard it all was, wallowing in pity and self-doubt. You need to shut out the doubt.

I don't remember the exact moment I met Green Beret Sergeant Joe Healey. He was tall with a thick "American accent".

He had just finished Q Course (SF qualification) a few months prior. It only took a short time for me to see his head was in the game. No doubt. He was confident but not cocky and exuded kindness and compassion. He knew this game that we had embarked on, how to play it, and he played it no matter who was watching, always on. Although my memories of Ranger School have faded, the ones most embedded had him in them. Years later those memories would embrace me in a far-off land.

As the first phase of Ranger School wound down, our bruised and battered bodies welcomed the eight hours we had away from the screams and glares of the RIs. We Canadians banded together and headed back to Fort Benning. Sleep was all we wanted, but we needed to get our kit squared away for the next phase and that ate up precious hours. We hit an all-you-can-eat buffet, but I could barely get down a chicken breast and some salad. I was 17lb down after the first phase and all the hunger I had felt over the last three weeks or so failed to materialize given my opportunity for gluttony: fuck you hunger. I watched the other guys wolf down plate after plate after plate, jealous of their filling stomachs. Those hours sped by and my hunger remained.

The next thing I knew we were back under the gaze of the RIs, on a bus heading to the mental and meteorological fog of the mountain phase up in Dahlonega, Georgia. We ascended and descended mountains and rock faces in various ways. We learned basic mountain skills, and with our knot and belay tests behind us, Class 5-03 shrunk in size a little bit more. The pounds continued to fade and what little fat reserves I had left were being devoured by my body in a desperate fight for calories. Tired and hungry, we moved on to some platoon-level operations.

One generally sunny day our platoon had just finished hitting an objective and fell back into the ORP (objective rally point) to take up our firing positions on our rucks. That signalled the actions on the objective "assessment phase" were over and the leadership roles would change for the next phase of the mission. Roster numbers were called out with your position, and you had a few minutes to debrief with the outgoing, gather kit and unfuck yourself. Part of the unfucking was untying para cord. Everything was tied off. It was a nightmare, bowlines tied off to every single piece of kit that could possibly be lost.: M4 tied to web gear, helmet tied to web gear, NOD (night optical device) tied to helmet. You name it, it was somehow tied off to some other piece of kit that was tied to another piece of kit. If it wasn't tied off to your body then it was tied off to your rucksack; there was para cord everywhere knotting and tangling—more lessons in rope management, I suppose. This was all made more difficult by our painfully cracked fingertips, which we sealed with drops of crazy glue: it does the body good.

The next assessment phase was patrol base occupation, set-up and routine, or try to stay the fuck awake through the night phase.

"Ranger 156, platoon leader," an RI yelled out.

It did not sink in immediately, probably because I wasn't expecting to hear my number and platoon leader in one sentence.

"Ranger 156, platoon leader," they called out again.

Fuck me, I didn't need to check the inside of my cap. I leapt up and doubled over to the RI who had called out my number. I felt the eyes of the other students fall on me; in my head they were all saying, *That's that Canadian corporal.* I felt a tinge of pressure push into one ear and a bit of trepidation seep into the other but all along I could hear that voice in my head repeating over and over: *Just don't quit, shut out the doubt.*

We had gone over patrol base operations in classroom sessions and on other missions. The basics were like those in Canada, but as a corporal I had never been in charge of the whole show before, and never assessed at it. I needed to think, to remember what I knew and what I'd been taught. There were steps and checklists to follow, leader's recce, in route, out route, dogleg, OP, clearance patrols, claymores, M240B machine gun at the apexes, firing positions, interlocking arcs of fire … a lot to do but I didn't have to do it alone. We had our *Ranger Handbook* to guide us. I had scribbled notes on every piece of blank paper in it. More important, we had each other to rely on: we all had tasks to do—the platoon leader, platoon sergeant, squad leaders, team leaders—with pressure on us all.

I would be lying if I said I remembered how it all went. I know I was hungry and tired just like everybody else. The sleep deprivation and lack of calories messed with my memory but there are always things, good and bad, that stand out. It wasn't raining or overly cold when the main body of troops occupied the PB (patrol base). We did our listening halt as everyone settled into position. After a few minutes the squad leaders, platoon sergeant and I collapsed into the middle and met the RIs who had been assessing our actions so far. Their faces were expressionless as if they were sitting at a poker table—no tell, no hint of how they thought things were going, just blank and emotionless.

"So how long you need to set this thing up?" an RI asked.

Joe Healey was my platoon sergeant, my right-hand man, in the mix beside me. We all knew that faster set-up equals earlier chow and maybe, just maybe, an extra precious few minutes of sleep. But it needed to be done right. I don't remember exactly how long we decided we'd need, but when I told the RI, his blank stare turned into a smile, followed by laughter.

"Okay, we'll see," he said. The RIs got up and walked into the fading Georgia sun. They would return with the darkness, our other habitual nemesis.

The RIs never really left—they lurked, they watched, they evaluated. We couldn't always see them, but they were always nearby. So, we just got at it, squad leaders, team leaders—we all just did what needed to be done, or so I hoped. The squad leaders were on the team leaders and team leaders on their teams. The sun was down as I did a final walk around the patrol base. I checked with each squad leader and did a walk-through of their positions. We were on time and, so far, looked to be on target. I reminded the boys the RIs were about to come through and to please, please try to stay awake for a little bit longer, the same pleas that had been verbalized to me countless times before. I was so tired that I was awake and felt as if my military career was hanging on this moment. Head up, gun up, NODs down. We were all shattered, zombie-like, by this point, the darkness luring you to sleep. Okay, things looked good. I remember Joe being around, double- and triple-checking; good was not good enough for him. He was a star. We needed to keep the beasts at bay and those which lurked, waiting for us to falter.

The RIs reappeared out of nowhere in an instant. "Alright, let see what you got," one said casually, as if he held a royal flush to my pair of deuces.

We started our clockwise tour of the patrol base. I tried to make as much noise as possible to let the guys know we were coming. *Stay awake boys*, I screamed in my head, hoping they would hear. We walked the first squad, looking good, 240B at the apex, staked in, range card tied off, tabless wannabes diligently manning the gun. Onto the next squad: firing positions are good.

"Dig those shell scrapes deeper," the RI grunted. As we neared the next apex, the 240B position, I heard it, soft at first and as we got closer the three separate sounds merged into one. I was behind the RI, so I know for sure he heard. Three people snoring blending into one. *Fuck me, my 240B team is out cold.* I leapt in front of the RI and delivered gentle kicks to the helmets of my 240 team and loudly asked if they were good to go.

Startled, they all responded, "Yes, sergeant."

The RI laughed and said, "That's one way to take care of it".

It happened to us all at some point—the rack monster would just come out of nowhere and carry you off to sleep town. In Florida phase I drifted off, my pillow the butt of the 240B. The alarm clock was the RI ripping off a burst as my head jerked back and forth. I barely woke.

My heart sunk. I couldn't shut out the doubt. It leaked into my head, slowly at first, then faster and faster as if a tap had been turned on. I thought for sure I had just failed. I returned to the centre of the patrol base, dejected. Joe met me in the darkness, and I told him about the dream team on the 240B and how I'd persuaded them to wake up. He laughed and told me you can't control what others do and the RIs know that. In my head we are a team, we live and die as a team and I felt like I had died, I was the platoon leader, I was in charge.

I settled in for a long and sleepless night. The "enemy" would probe us, blanks ripping off all around us. We would return fire as best we could. Para flares would shoot up into the sky then float earthward, casting mischievous shadows all around us. The real enemy was sleep and it was relentless, night and day. The RIs would walk around the patrol base taking NODs off sleeping Rangers' helmets and pulling magazines out of their rifles resting in their hands. This continued all night—blanks, flares, another set of NODs down. I tried my hardest to summon the sun, for light, for this iteration to end and as the sun finally came up, my platoon leader time came to an end. I did not get a wink of sleep that night and I don't think anyone who was being assessed did either.

The sun warmed our bodies. Who knows where exactly we were up in those mountains. The platoon began to take stock of our missing equipment and as we did the RIs appeared with a bag of items they had collected throughout the night, which were usually returned with a "minor minus". Collect too many of those and like a piece of plastic, you were recycled back to day one of mountains. New roster numbers were called out, followed by the untying and tying of kit, crazy glue tube passed around, and so the cycle was repeated, day in and day out.

I remember lining up that morning for the water check, the RIs making sure we had drunk the six litres of water that we carried with us … 12lb of water. We got it from whatever source we could find, purified with iodine and sometimes a few drops of bleach. As I waited for my canteens to be checked, I stood and wondered if I had done enough. They didn't tell you if you had passed or failed. You just waited to see if your number got called out again. Time rolled on so slowly in Ranger School.

As the ascents and descents of the mountain phase came to an end, we all gathered back together, the final mission completed. The RIs called out six roster numbers, mine and Joe's were two of them.

"Get your gear and get on the truck."

We did as we were told. *Fuck, am I getting recycled?* In the back of the truck the six of us shared blank stares as we drove back to Camp Merrill. When we arrived, the instructors' mood changed—they weren't nice but weren't yelling. They directed us to a small building with our gear and we all shuffled over as fast as our blistered feet and battered bodies would take us, "

"Just walk," an RI blurted out. "Fucking relax."

It's gotta be a trick, we thought, and *Fuck it if it is*, so we relaxed, we walked. We got to the building and waited. A few minutes later a couple RIs came over and gave us all a can of Coke and a Hooah energy bar. Then it started to sink in: *We did good, I did good, real good.* No one said it but we all knew it. We had been rewarded for it in the best possible way, calorically. I knew it would be short-lived bliss. I remember drinking that sweet can of Coke. Joe and I looked across at each other and just smiled, drank it down and chewed up the Hooah. We had survived mountains and would soon be parachuting into Florida, the swamps, snakes and gators all waiting to make our acquaintance. I was down a few more pounds, my uniform sort of just hanging off me; my body was not all that happy with me. *Just hold together, don't quit, we got this. You can get by with a little help from your friends.*

Florida was wet, cold, it hailed all the time. We killed and ate a chicken during survival skills training, and I got cellulitis for the second or third time. We paddled, humped and jumped. Hunger plagued all who had not recycled a phase, real sleep eluded us, the swamps kept us habitually damp, and the rains soaked and chilled us to our protruding bones. But the end was in sight.

At the end of Florida things relaxed a bit. We got our care packages and were actually allowed to keep them. On the other phases they would hand them out and you'd have 30 minutes to devour whatever your body would take. I remember guys getting jugs of milk in the mail and chugging it down. All sorts of baked goods—favourites from moms, wives and girlfriends—flowed freely. It was morale, the food was warm, and the opening of a care package closed another phase. At Florida, as we cleaned and turned in kit and weapons, we had our super-supper. For five bucks got you two hot dogs, chips, a chocolate bar and a soda. I spent ten bucks. No one yelled. I sat at a picnic table with Joe and others, and we ate and laughed because it was over—we had endured it all. We had about a 150-metre walk back to our barracks after our feast and as I stood up and took my first stride, my stomach twisted and knotted in extreme pain. I doubled over in agony, both hands clutching my stomach. It took me about 30 minutes to get to the barracks, but no one yelled. I could only muster a few steps before having to stop and bend over as my stomach crippled me. We got to sleep, just two of us up on fire watch. We had beds and a pile of junk food at the door free for the taking.

The next day we loaded into a C-130. My web gear was loaded down, not with ammo but with junk. Pop Tarts fit into my mag pouches and a jumbo bag of Skittles in my utility pouch. Life was good and only diabetes could kill me now.

I was proud and in the worst physical shape of my life. There are tougher military schools and training courses out there, but just let me have this moment. Let me bask in the black and golden embroidered glory as my father pins my Ranger tab on my shoulder beside those murky waters of Victory Pond that I had plummeted into two months before. Let me remember the hunger, the pain, let me remember how I pushed, ran, humped, pulled, carried, lifted, paddled, climbed, slept, walked, crawled and defeated doubt. Ranger School to me was about not letting my mind convince my body to stop. If you've been there and done that, Hooah to you. If you haven't and think it's easy, then go and try: don't recycle, don't buy MREs for $100 in the field for an extra meal, don't be a spotlight Ranger. Shine when the RIs aren't watching. Just go and be a Joe, a GI Joe Healey.

In those short 63 days friendships would begin and end before they really got started, emails exchanged and eventually lost. Afghanistan and Iraq continue to rage, friends die, tears fall, try to forget and hope to remember. Rangers of a feather ...

*

Master Corporal Barry Nisbet, Sniper
Detachment 63C, Task Force 3-06
Panjwai District, Kandahar Province, Afghanistan
September 2006

I think the U.S. has about 50,000 or so SF members across the military, which is about the total size of the Canadian Armed Forces—Army, Navy and Air Force. So given we were on a U.S.-led mission in Afghanistan, we were going to cross paths with some of them.

As Operation *Medusa* lingered on, our little OP high up on the ghar was home, rocky, dusty, home. A JTF 2 sniper det and JTAC were located beside us, watching another objective. Their time came to an end, and they disappeared into the distance.

Thankfully they had shared their "body bag" resupplies with us: thanks boys. We missed their companionship and knowing they had been nearby made us sleep better at night. It was again just the three of us. We were informed an American ODA team, Green Berets, was coming up to run an operation. They arrived around midday when I was in our OP, scanning across the Arghandab River into Panjwai. I could hear them in behind our position but didn't pay much attention. They were establishing a position higher up the ghar. They dropped their rucksacks at our position to go and recce an OP of their own.

My two hours were up, and I went down behind our position to get a little shade and something to eat. We had been there almost two weeks now. We stunk, salt from our sweat stained our uniforms. I sat and sipped on a bottle of warm water and surveyed all the U.S. rucks laying on the ground, their name tapes sewn on at the top. As I scanned, one jumped out at me: HEALEY.

I turned to K and said, "Ha, that was the last name of my good friend at Ranger School." I didn't really think much else of it.

A while later I curiously looked west up the ghar at the small dots coming back down the mountain. They were featureless and faceless, just grey specks. As they descended, I could eventually make out arms and legs and M4s. As the distance closed, I could make out heads and unshaven faces. One in particular stood out: he was tall, wearing a Red Sox ball cap. He got closer and closer. I was fixated, I did a double-take.

"No fucking way," I said to myself, "NO fucking way."

As the ODA team settled back around their kit, I looked at the figure hovering over the HEALEY.

"Hey hoser," I said casually.

The battle-hardened Green Berets all just sort of stopped and looked at me, probably thinking, *Who is this asshole Canadian?* Joe looked over at me, a bit perplexed, then a smile spread across his face. You just can't make this shit up. I stood up, we reached out our hands to shake, then laughing pulled in for quick soldierly hug. You just never know. For me it was momentous in the mountains of Afghanistan.

Joe explained to his team where we'd met: Class 5-03, U.S. Army Ranger School. What were the chances? This reunion seemed to meld our two teams. Many of the other Green Berets had also been through Ranger School. Joe shared a few of our Ranger School stories and in a roundabout way, he vouched for me with the rest of his team. We ended up sharing space and shifts on the OP. This worked out great for us as it bolstered our three-man team up to nine or ten as they used our lower position as a comms/resupply point for their OP further up the mountain. We spent about a week together up there. Joe and I spent some time in the OP on shift. We had trained together and now we were ready to fight together. Ranger School was not the be all end all, and I'm sure it meant different things to anyone who completed it. But everyone felt the hunger and sleeplessness. Completing it was a gut check, and the ODA guys knew that. Joe and I reminisced as best we could, but that was training, this was war. So, we made new memories up on that ghar: some joint ODA/Canadian sniper kills. We could see and spot, they could call and drop, almost like it was meant to be. Taliban be damned—you shall feel the wrath of our Ranger School reunion.

Eventually all good things come to an end. Then there was three—three Canadian snipers sitting up on the ghar. We had hosted and been hosted by two Special Forces teams over our three weeks, had been dead centre in the failed crossing of Arghandab during Operation *Medusa*, and had been woken by an A-10 Warthog mistakenly strafing the Canadian lines below us. Almost got shot to make a call home to say I was alright. I can't imagine how badly I smelled. I wanted a shower, a bed, a hot meal and some cold water. I would cross paths with Joe again in FOB Sperwan Ghar. And as the tour wore on, just as our Ranger School friendship had ended so would our combat friendship. Joe, I hope you made it out safely, back to whoever was waiting for you. I know, like me, that not all your brothers did. *Pro Patria, De Oppresso Liber.*

*

Sperwan Ghar

After 23 days or so, and an exploding battery fire, we left Operation *Medusa*. Pack for three days we were told for that one. We flew back into KAF for a well-deserved shower and some much-needed laundry. I threw away most of the socks; they had been worn, sun dried, worn inside out, and they stunk, perhaps caused by some fungus that was growing on my feet. After stinking out the medical facility, I was given some cream and told by a kindly medic to try to keep my feet dry for the next week and to not wear boots. The next day we were loaded up into G Wagons and driving through Kandahar City out to our new FOB, Sperwan Ghar. I stood in the turret of the G Wagon manning the C6, boots tied tightly.

Sperwan Ghar dominated the area; it gave us 360-degree views of the ground around us. To the northeast was Masum

Ghar and north of that the mostly dried-out Arghandab River and Panjwai. We lived at the top of the hill, in what we thought was some sort of water cistern, a concrete bowl about a 30-metre diameter with three-metre-high walls. This would be home, and it was pretty luxurious considering. We conducted a lot of overwatch and over time developed our bowl into a pretty comfortable oasis, by war-torn Afghan standards that is. We were lucky to be situated in a U.S. area of operations; there was at least one and sometimes two ODA teams operating out of the FOB. We had our own M777 155mm howitzers and our reconnaissance and armoured recce elements all deployed here. ISTAR is what our company was designated, intelligence surveillance target acquisition and reconnaissance, but I won't get into the politics of having an armoured CO. From time to time the ODA boys would venture up the hill to have a look and a chat. Ryan, a U.S. Air Force Special Operations JTAC, took a particular shine to our position and to all of us polite Canadian snipers. As he got to know us, he realized our capabilities went well beyond that of pulling a trigger. We lived on glass; we watched the area day and night. We knew the areas the enemy used and the areas they avoided. We watched and learned their pattern of life, their POL. We conducted a few joint patrols with the ODA teams as they probed and felt out the local Taliban fighters. There was a particular feature a few kilometres to the west, Zangabad Ghar. A mission was spun up to push west and take the ghar and then push further west; it was ODA led, and they requested a sniper detachment to support. We were only too glad to assist.

One evening, we marked and recorded the ghar with artillery, the M777, the shots came from directly behind and below us. We could lean back and watch the rounds fly overhead and follow them to target with the binos—a mixture of delay, impact and smoke was used to record the target. I have to give the artillery props: you guys and girls delivered.

We attended orders with the ODA, packed, prepped and repacked. Our role was to move with the main body, deploy to provide overwatch if the ground dictated and call and adjust artillery fire. There were a few elements involved: a mechanized group would push north and then west down to the north of the ghar; our dismounted element would push on foot through the fields and villages to the base of the ghar. I have nothing but respect for our American brothers and sisters in arms, but they can sometimes march to the beat of their own drummer, or in this case to *Ride of the Valkyries* blaring out of their Psyops Humvee as the operation kicked off. Throw in a couple Huey's and surfboards and well you get the picture … Taliban don't surf. There was no doubt to everyone outside the wire that something was coming.

Walking outside the wire was an awakening of sorts. There is danger in the camps but being inside always gave me a sense of security: I was with my sniper family. As I crossed through the line of wire to the outside, everything just changed. Hypersensitive is the best way to describe it: I could hear more, smell more, see more, feel more. Outside the wire everything was danger—the air, the ground, the women, the children, the garbage piles, the overturned earth, the cars, the dogs—and everything had potential to kill you. For once we were not the first in the order of march: we were midway, near the command elements. As we snaked our way westward, I knew we had our guardian angels high above on Sper, watching, guns and glass trained on the ground we covered and the ground we had yet to traverse. Knowing Gord and B were watching our six was comforting. Maybe not eyes in the back of our head but the next best thing.

We continued our slow walk westward up and over walls, through deep centuries-old grape fields, where a few onlookers would steal a glance before scurrying away, undoubtedly to update the Taliban on our direction of travel and size of our group. It was slow going. They knew where we were going. it was no secret. As we drew closer to Zangabad, ICOM radio chatter increased, and the ODA interpreter translated what he wanted us or thought we needed to know. There was chatter about ambushing the infidels, but this was nothing new. We neared the edge of a large open area about 500 metres west of the base of the ghar. We knew the Taliban were out there, watching us, waiting for an opportunity to IED our route. After a quick chat with the ODA captain, our sniper det pushed a little south and hastily occupied a compound. We cleared it quickly and got up on the roof. Eyes and glass scanned the ground around us. ICOM chatter increased. We decided to shoot first and the decision was made to call a quick-fire mission onto Zangabad … stir the pot a little. Jody called in the pre-registered target from the previous day. *Whump, whump, whump*, the triple 7s spewed out their cargo, 155mm shells hurtling down on the ghar—*whump, whump, whump*, the sound was rhythmic, it was a short flight time, *whump, whump, whump*, rounds on target, rock and dust filling the air on the top of the ghar. The fourth or fifth volley went screaming northwest just over the tip of the ghar and exploded out of view; we could see the dust clouds fill the sky from behind the ghar. The ICOM spewed panic, chaos screaming out in Pashtun from the little black hand-held, as the interpreter tried to keep up with the cries and explain to the ODA captain what he was hearing. Apparently the "long" rounds had crashed into the main body of the Taliban fighters laying in ambush as we made our way up the ghar, the mixture of airburst and impacted 155mm shells shredding them. I had no remorse for the Taliban cries on the radio: it is Afghanistan, it is just war, you kill us we kill you; it is history, it repeats. We unleashed another "long" salvo for good measure.

We scurried off the roof and fell back into our OOM (order of movement) and continued to push westward for the base of the ghar. Maybe we had just picked a fight or maybe we had just ended one, but they now knew exactly where we were going. They would regroup; they were a tenacious and cunning adversary.

As we neared the ghar the smell of high explosives hung in the air as the dust from our barrage slowly began to settle to earth. The ICOM grew quiet, the eyes on the back of our heads, so we marched on, waiting for the inevitable *crack, crack, crack* of AK-47, RPK and RPG. We walked and waited, anticipated, and we pressed on.

We reached the base of the ghar in late afternoon, the sun still prominent in the sky. We hadn't really walked all that far, but it had been a slow and methodical walk. The ground guided you, could trap you and then explode and kill you. It was nice to see the solid rock of the ghar, better to feel it under your feet, one less thing to kill you … you hoped.

We began our walk up. The rock had looked smoother from a distance. The topography changed from smooth and wind-worn to jagged and gravelly along the ridges and folds. We walked as best we could, staying in cover because of the failed ambush to the north. Eventually we had to crest and clear the ghar: no surprises, no boobytraps, no gunfire. The ghar was a chunk of ancient stone that looked like it had been accidentally dropped from the heavens; it didn't fit with the landscape, but it was here, and it was ours. We owned this piece of real estate with just a few words spoken over the radio and some accurate and a few lucky 155mm rounds.

As we continued to push west, we observed two FAMs (fighting aged males) to our north. They were behind a low wall, tactically moving eastward, with heads popping up here and there. K found a decent-enough spot to set up, extending the legs of the bipod on the 338, while I grabbed the Leupold spotting scope and set up to his right and slightly behind him as best I could. We started to gather a bit of an audience as the ODA guys saw what was unfolding. I grabbed the vectors and lazed the wall: 980 metres, light wind, mirage right to left, I glanced at my wind and spin drift chart. K and I agreed on 1,000 metres DOPE. They were definitely behind the wall, just not sure how far. Jody and I agreed on a wind call and K dialled it in, never taking his eyes off the target. Only one brave soul remained, a kilometre away from us. I could make out his light blue shalwar and dark brown scarf around his neck. He was watching us, then his head would bob down behind the wall, then he would pop up again a short distance to the left or right. He came up again, a little further behind the wall. K was instantly on him again.

"You got him?" I asked.

"Yep," K replied. His breathing was slow and methodical, timed; inhale, exhale, his words came out just as he exhaled. He did not move from the rifle, and the rifle did not move …

"Blue man jammies, brown scarf."

Inhale … exhale … "Yep"

I saw him bring a radio up to his mouth, an ICOM, "Radio left hand."

Inhale … exhale … "Yep."

"Winds are good," I said. We had done this hundreds of times together, paper or people, it didn't change. I knew what was coming next.

K exhaled, "Stand by."

"Send it," casually departed my lips.

Trigger squeeze, squeeze … *Pheew*, the 250 grain round spins down the barrel out of the suppressor at over 3,000 feet per second, just over a second and a half to the target. The spinning stabilizes it as it speeds downrange. I pick up the swirl of the round in my spotting scope, the shockwave visible as the round is supersonic. I watch is as it reaches the culminating point of its trajectory, right of target and slowly coming left and in line with our friend. The round dips below the culminating point and I lose the swirl, my eyes locked on him, his head tantalizingly up above the wall. Suddenly dust kicks up from the top of the wall directly in front of our friend. He drops. We do not see him again. The round has hit the top of the wall; another inch or so up and it would have plunged into the bone and flesh of our Taliban voyeur. Inches from a one-kilometre head shot.

"Hold point two up if we see him again."

K had already cycled another round into the chamber. "Already doing it," he said.

I could hear the disappointment in his voice. He had seen the puff of dust on the top of the wall as his scope settled back on target after he had fired. We stayed on the gun for about another ten minutes, watching, hoping for one more shot. Sometimes miss by a country mile, sometimes by an inch, but a miss, nonetheless. Not K's, not mine, ours.

Day was slowly turning to evening. This was our home for the night. The ODA started to establish a perimeter and a quasi-patrol base along the spine of the ghar. We had Afghan army and police with us: the army was generally okay, but fuck the police—pretty sure they were 50/50 Taliban. Jody, K and I found a nice little depression towards the west end of the spine, which would be home for the three of us and possibly JTAC Ryan if he so chose. We settled in. K pulled the 338 out and we immediately started to range and break down the ground we could affect with rifle fire, noting some potential infil and exfil routes. We had about 180 degrees to cover with most of the ODA and Afghan forces in behind us, making a ring with 360-degree coverage. We ranged and named some prominent features so we could use them as a reference if needed. They would come in handy.

The sun was just starting to kiss the horizon. K was standing just a few feet in front of me, surveying to the west, the sun harsh and bright. The Taliban timing could not have been better: *swoosh* from the left, *swoosh* from the right as two RPGs ripped across the sun-smeared sky in front of K, who swore, upset that his picturesque moment had been interrupted by war. Then the small-arms, AK-47 and PKM, fire started; you couldn't see anything to the northeast as the bright setting sun burned your eyes. Bullets skipped and ricocheted all around. K jumped on the gun, and I took my place to the right with my spotting scope and began to scan for targets, muzzle flash, smoke, movement, as the RPGs continued to streak across the sky and small arms cut through the air.

Moments later JTAC Ryan rolled into our hacienda, radio in tow. "I've got air stacked up all around us. I need some targets." He sat back and started to scan.

I picked up the vector laser binos attached to our DAGR (Defense Advanced GPS receivers), which would allow me to laze a location and get a ten-figure grid reference. I think we all saw the first POO (point of origin). White smoke billowed out from the vegetation to our southwest; a quick map check confirmed a narrow wadi running east–west. I centred the vector bino reticle on the POO and pressed the buttons beneath both my index fingers, and instantly the DAGR displayed a ten-figure grid. Quick confirm on the map and I held it up to Ryan. It was as if he was on the phone with his mother as he just calmly and coolly provided the grid to the pilots, confirming the target,

"Tally target," chirped out of the radio … "cleared hot."

We had built up trust with Ryan and it was reciprocal. We had adopted him into the team when he was out with us—he loved to watch, to look, and most importantly to drop bombs and he was really, really good at it.

You didn't hear it at first, you saw it, grey, dust, debris, destruction, and the sound following as a 500 pound bomb impacted the earth.

"Good hit, good hit," Ryan called out to the pilots.

Pooff, another launch further east down the wadi, reticle on target, laze, grid to Ryan … grey, dust, debris, destruction, sound. What I could never forget was just how effortless Ryan made it all seem: he was controlling multiple aircraft, multiple targets, and it's as if he was sipping a beer in his backyard. In American terms he was a stud. The more bombs Ryan dropped the less intense the small-arms fire became until eventually all you heard was attack aircraft circling above us—it was a comforting sound. Then all the sound just gave way to silence, the planes left, the shooting stopped and the darkness grew. Now the Taliban knew where we were, which was more than we could say about them. The ODA set up a perimeter of claymores and ran two to our hole, and told us roughly where they were pointing. Ryan decided to spend the night with us ... he had a surprise when it got dark.

"Hey, you ever rope in a Spectre gunship?" Ryan asked me.

"Uh, nope" I said laughingly.

"Well, tonight you can."

The heavily armed AC-130 Hercules only came out at night. Spooky was its nickname. It was slow, but it was a flying armoury with its 105mm howitzer and 40mm Bofors cannon mounted on its left side. The radio crackled. They were inbound. You could hear the drone of the turboprop engines in the quiet night sky. Ryan gave me his "rope", an IR (infrared) laser the pilots would pick up with their night vision.

"Okay, so make big slow circles in the sky and when I tell you tighten them up ..."

I did as he said. Spooky ID'd our positions and scanned the areas all around us. We had him for a few hours and I prayed the Taliban would come and try to fuck with us in that time. We had our thermal binos out, humming as we scanned for targets but to no avail.

You hear the fighters, the choppers, but the sound of the Spectre is unmistakable, the low rumble of the four turboprop engines; it does not tear across the sky, it's like it bulldozes a path through the stars. It only flew at night, blacked out. It was not a guardian angel, the four engines more akin to the Four Horsemen of the Apocalypse. Ryan chatted with Spooky and advised of a few hot spots nearby, one being an old, abandoned building about 700 metres from the base of the ghar to the south. We had received small-arms fire from it during the ambush. Ryan called the Spectre onto target, and they lit it up with a massive IR light to confirm the target. It's an odd sound hearing a 105mm howitzer getting fired from thousands of feet above you, in the dark. The round growled as it chewed through the air, the growl getting louder and louder and then *boom...* impact. Sparks flew as the round crashed through the thin metal roof of the abandoned building.

"Good hit," Ryan said into the handset. Can we get some 40 mike mike (Bofors 40mm cannon) into same target?"

Three rapid pops echoed out of the dark sky above ... *bang, bang, bang*, the rounds impacted the roof sending debris and sparks into the air.

War can emit many emotions. Tonight was happy. I stretched out on my therm-a-rest, feeling the rocks digging into me. The only thing I took off was my helmet, the C8 laying across my chest, vectors and DAGR laying beside the .338 that rested beside K. In my head I went through a quick WTF do I do if we get hit, visualizing where things were and what I needed to do. Satisfied with my mental response, I closed my eyes. The low rumble circling high above filled my ears with peace, as soothing a sound I have ever fallen asleep to, given the circumstances of course. I didn't count sheep. I counted the bombs we dropped that day and drifted off to a well-deserved few hours of sleep as that spectre of death watched over me from above, warning the

Taliban to take the night off. I don't think the Taliban slept quite as well as we did.

The night passed without incident. I would sleep, wake up and take my turn on shift, scanning the area around with thermal and night vision, looking for heat and light sources, worrying more about the Afghan police inside our patrol base than the Taliban outside.

Darkness began to release its hold on the sky, a sky that held more stars than I had ever seen before. No light pollution. There's that perfect time in the morning, just as one end of the sky begins to lighten and the other end is still blanketed in darkness and stars; it was calming, a fleeting few seconds that showed the perfection of that part of the world, that part of the world we would soon reshape with some pinpoint 2,000lb JDAM (Joint Direct Attack Munition) bombs. The earth keeps on turning. The bombs keep falling. And we all hope our hearts will keep beating.

That morning the mechanized group pushed up to us. They had struck an IED the day before, but no one had been hurt. One of our other sniper teams had deployed on ATVs (all-terrain vehicles) with them and had come up the ghar. Our team had been prepping to push towards the west end of the ghar to cover the ODA's further advance westward.

The three of us stepped off. I was comfortably back on point. We replaced our helmets with ball caps—looking back, not the safest choice. It was full sun now, and there was no hiding as we walked down the southern slope of the ghar and onto the road. Gravity pulled us down the ghar with ease. That hyper-sensitivity took back over; we had plenty of eyes watching our backs. My eyes were watching the front, the left, the right. It was constant, continuous, you got no break, your eyes saw, your brain computed, your feet moved, each step taking us a little further away from the safety of our group. After a few hundred metres we headed back up the ghar; it was lower here as the feature bled off to the west. As we got closer to the western end of the ghar, we found a piece of ground on the top that was basically a slit in the rock, giving us decent cover from the north and south. There was no hiding our presence—we had to hide in plain sight. As we settled in amongst the rocks our radio crackled and chirped. Just to our north Taliban were observed up in a 30–40-foot mud tower: they had binos and were observing back to the main body up on the ghar. The main group called out the contact, we followed along on the radio and identified the structure. I quickly zapped it with the vectors and plotted it on the map. It was 741 metres from our current position. I knew Ryan was on his JTAC net getting a hold of whatever air assets we had nearby. K had the 338 out and I was off to his right on the spotting scope. Jody was keeping an ear on the comms and relaying info to us as it came in. A Rockwell B-1 Lancer was circling high above. It was armed with a few 2,000lb JDAMs and wanted to lighten its load (a 2006 Honda Civic weighs about 2,700lb just to give some context).

We were over 700 metres away, give or take, and I think the danger radius was somewhere around 340–360 metres of a 2,000lb JDAM, so we really had nothing to worry about, as long as the bombs were on target …

"Thirty seconds," blurts out over our radio.

I start to count down in my head. We were all peeking over the jagged rocks, eyes on the target. At about ten seconds we decided to get down … nine, eight, seven, six, five, four, three, two ... you could hear the sound of the bombs whistling to earth ... one ... the two Honda Civic-sized munitions exploded within a second of each other, as the earth shook, revolting in pain. We popped our heads back up. The plume of smoke and dust rose hundreds of feet into the air, debris raining down all around the tower. But it stood, the stone and mud tower built by hand stood. Much like the Taliban, it was defiant to our technology, to our will, to our way. I could not imagine being on the end of that, the concussion reaching us nearly a kilometre away. This was Afghanistan: shoot us with a gun and we will drop a fucking bomb on you. No fight is fair, the Taliban did not fight fair. They wore no uniforms. One day they carried a shovel and smiled at you and the next an AK as they closed an eye to get a sight picture on you. They could not go toe to toe with us and when they did, we decimated them. We hunted them from the air and from the ground, with thermal and night vision, with precision-guided GPS bombs, Special Forces, drones, Royal Marines, mortars, howitzers, helicopters ... the list goes on and on. They fought us with small-arms fire, RPGs, recoilless rifles, and of course IEDs. Ingenious, low tech, lethal, they fought for their country and lives. I fought for my life, my fellow soldiers and their country as well.

PART THREE

Afghanistan 2010
Task Force 1-10

9

Textbook, 2010

Sergeant Yves Bedard, Sniper Detachment Commander
Detachment 66B, Task Force 1-10
COP Shakare, Nakhonay District, Kandahar Province,
Afghanistan
August 18, 2010, 1000 hours.

Our team was currently working Bravo Company's area of operation. Bravo was responsible for the northeast portion of the Canadian battle group's area of responsibility (AOR) which was southwest of Kandahar city. It was the gateway for all troop supplies, coming through on the main supply route (MSR) that ran on the northern part of the AO. Unlike their sister company who had one large central FOB, Bravo had four outposts (TI) to man to the southwest. The main one was COP (combat outpost) Sohja, situated along the MSR called Lake Effect; COP Shakare a few kilometres west, also on the MSR; COP Patricia located at the northern edge of Nakhonay; and the unfortunate and isolated COP Ballpeen that was located on the southwestern side of a village. As far as I recall, Bravo was tasked to disrupt INS (insurgent) activity coming up from the Adamzai chain to the southwest, as well as protect the MSR, vital for resupply runs. At this time, it was mid-point in the tour and I was way over being there. To be honest, I hated the country and everything it stood for or, should I say, didn't stand for. Due to the revolving door of tours, our soldiers were burning out.

I had to sign a waiver to volunteer as this was my fourth tour in a fairly short period of time. I was pencilled in as detachment commander for 66B; due to personnel rotation, it also meant that I had all the sniper experience for the team. It wasn't even a question to sign the waiver: my brothers were going so was I. I had already seen firsthand what "qualified" snipers they could dig up, people who had somehow managed to pass the course but were never competent enough to actually stay with the sniper cell. There was no way I was letting some forgotten, useless relic take charge of my team. Even now as I fought a headache and cursed the unrelenting sun constantly beating down on us, there was no other place I would want to be.

We had been in this AO for a week or so. I recall at the start of tour we were getting bounced around quite often to help with various ops and just to get the general lay of the land. I had been here with TF 3-06, but everything was changing—the layout was the same, but we had lost ground. The enemy no longer had an identifiable line in the sand. They had given up any thought of conventional warfare and were now bleeding us with IEDs and shoot-and-scoot ambushes. Even if we were eager to jump into the fray, the start of our tour was relatively slow.

Earlier on we had been sent to COP Ballpeen as they were getting hit almost daily to the point of getting overrun.

Unfortunately, the snap decision to get us there ASAP meant walking in through the village at daylight with a patrol. Word must have spread about the soldiers carrying long guns because we spent five relatively quiet days at Ballpeen. It wasn't until we were pulled away for another task that they got lit up again. This constant movement made it difficult to really get a sense for an area as every AO was different but since spending more time in one area, business had now started to pick up.

I had just woken up and was standing outside our shelter, stretching. We had been out for the past few days and had come back prior to first light. Dehydration was always a challenge in a wasteland like Afghanistan, so I decided to head over to the common area where they kept all the water and IMPs (individual meal packs). Mess tents and showers were a luxury. I was happy to find an unopened box of pop-tarts instead of yet another IMP. I was about to crush my second bottle of piss-warm water when one a section commander poked his head round the corner.

"Hey, you guys busy?"

We had a standing task at that point, that when not involved with ops we were to assist keeping the MSR safe by disrupting INS activity along it whenever possible.

"Not really, what's up?"

Watching the MSR wasn't very exciting, so I was looking for any opportunity to pitch in.

"We have a patrol going to go to Fathollah tomorrow and could use a hand if you're available. The last couple times we tried to go in we got ambushed and we're expecting a fight."

Funny thing about information, unless it's shared, it's fucking useless. I had been studying maps dotted with INS activity trying to figure out how dated the info was (to best deploy a det to disrupt the insurgents) and here he was a giving me first-hand information that we could act on.

"Yeah. Let me just check the latest op orders but it shouldn't be a problem." I couldn't make it appear we were desperate.

"We're planning in ten minutes if you want to join us."

"Sounds good."

No question we were going out on this one. As a sniper team attached to a company, we were there to support them where we could; unfortunately, it was rare if they ever came over to see what we were up to, so I was glad he did.

I went back to the shelter where the guys were lounging—it wouldn't be much longer before the place was a sauna and they'd be forced out. I grabbed a map and orders book and then gave Pete a quick nudge.

"Pete," I whispered.

Pete was the point man on our four-man team. He walked point on every mission without ever complaining or hesitating. He was an excellent soldier, always positive and motivated and knew his job well.

"I fucking hate you," I told him.

"C'mon man, why?"

This is typically how I woke him most mornings: as much as I respected him someone had to keep his ego in check. After all, it was his first tour in snipers.

"Get up. We may have a gig. Get some food into you. I'm off to the orders tent."

I heard Colin sit up. "What's going on?"

Colin was the primary shooter. He carried the .338. Another new member to snipers, Colin was a fit and motivated soldier.

He was quiet and reserved most times, but you knew he was just a wild card waiting to drop.

"I didn't think you cared, you soulless bastard."

Colin responded, "I don't if it means I can go back to sleep."

"I'm going to do some mission planning. We might be going out so get some food and for fucks sakes, clean those pants when you get a chance."

I walked over to my 2IC Justin and gave him a nudge. He was usually in a coma-like state, so I gave him another kick.

"This better be good! I was having the best sleep in days."

I was fortunate to have Justin. As the 2IC he was also detachment commander-qualified which meant he knew exactly what needed to be done. Although this was his first tour as a sniper, it wasn't his first trip to the suck.

"Fuck your junk, get up sleepy bear," I said.

We had come though battle school together, so I had known him a long time which made it easy to work with.

"I heard ya. Five more minutes, mom."

And with that I left to go plan a mission, I had no doubt that they would be squared away by the time I got back. We were always ready to go at a moment's notice.

I met up with the 22A section commander who started laying out a tentative plan. He had been tasked to go to Fathollah to link up with local elders and clear some grape rows suspected of having IEDs in them; however, he was fully expecting a fight and wanted input on how we could fit in. Since we hadn't worked much with the sections directly, the best plan would be a simple one. They had planned to walk in to Fathollah from the east in the open, essentially inviting the INS to come out and play. After slightly adjusting their proposed route in, we had a tentative plan. I got timings for final orders and made my way back to the tent to brief my team. I could hear the usual banter, two of them ganging up on the other as always. As I entered, they went quiet.

Justin spoke first. "So how soon do we leave, B?"

The kit was ready with a map laid out, but it seemed every time I came back from some type of orders, we were already late. Not this time.

"You're going to love this."

"Let me guess. We go in and clear out an entire village and give them the nod when it's safe," Pete said.

Funny guy.

"Wrong AO, Pete. This will be either very good or very boring."

I laid the plan out for them: "Two Two Alpha is tasked to conduct patrol IVO [in vicinity of] Fathollah. They have been hit multiple times and are expecting a fight which is why we have been asked to tag along. The section will leave at first light, and we will tag along, which enables them to rest the QRF and not have them on standby all night."

I could see Justin's wheels spinning. "Yeah Justin, means you can get some more sleep."

"Fuck you, I was thinking of the poker tables later."

Often, I thought us moving around the AO so often was a good thing. It prevented us being lynched by our own guys as these three degenerates played some of the dirtiest poker I'd ever seen and between them probably accounted for one soldier's combined tour pay.

"Nice try. I want everyone rested and sharp." I continued to lay the plan. "Six Six Bravo will fall in at the rear. At a designated point we will break off from the patrol and head directly north to our ORV. Two Two Alpha will continue east toward Sohja and buttonhook back west towards the objective which should give the INS time to react."

No point in sneaking in if you were looking for a fight; they won't come out if they don't think they have the advantage. This should give us plenty of time to set a final firing position. We had experience in that rough area, and I had already pointed out a tentative location for us to set up. Fathollah was at the northern end of B Company's AO; it had three roads meeting up plus two wadi systems as well as a third wadi system to the south, which we could exploit to cover ground unseen and develop a position. The way Fathollah was laid out, an approach by 22A from the east would force anyone wanting to get eyes on, or ambush, the patrol to be position in the southern part of the village, which hopefully would put us directly on their flank.

Justin looked up at me. "So, where's the part that we get fucked over and left for dead?"

We were used to not having close support. At that time artillery was a last resort and you'd better be getting overrun before calling for it. A QRF was on five minutes' notice but usually took them longer to get going and they were never guaranteed to get there due to IED threats. And the only air assets I can remember were American. I'm pretty sure our Griffins only had enough lift to take fuel or ammo but not both so unless you were lucky enough to have a Predator on standby, you were on your own.

After going over the plan in detail, I left it open for input. In a small group like that, as team leader I had final say but if no one was comfortable with a plan, it was probably because it was a shit plan. Listening to your team was vital. This, however, was a walk in the park compared to most other missions so with a promise of action, everyone was in good spirits.

"The section is giving order at 1900 hours. We are all sitting in, so we know what to expect from them."

Sitting in on section orders wasn't exactly standard, but I felt it was more important that we all knew what their actions on would be for us to best support them as our piece was simple. After weapons maintenance and rechecking kit for a third time we bedded down for the night as morning would come quick.

*

August 19, 2010, approximately 0600 hours

We were all standing just inside the COP gates, ready to step off. The section had beefed up with engineer assets and a medic and looked like they were carrying as much ammo as they could. They were eager for some payback. I checked in with the patrol commander. He was busy briefing the interpreter and some of the ANA troops who would tag along. They had not been invited to orders as none of them could be trusted. It was obvious some of them had allegiance to the INS and would tip them off as it was not uncommon to have locals at the gate inquiring about the patrol/mission that had yet to deploy. I took the time to go through final rehearsals and get everyone dialled in.

After some delays due to comms, we didn't step off until 0700 and of course the sun was beating down on us. I couldn't remember the last time I went out this light for a patrol. Usually, we had three days of food, water and ammo, and all our observation kit stuffed in our rucks, but this was a rare in and out. We still had enough equipment should this drag out overnight, but we had thinned out significantly for this one.

It took around 45 minutes for the patrol to shake out and complete the first leg, moving carefully as the IED threat was always high. In all my time in the suck I don't even want to imagine the number of IEDs I've walked past unawares. The second leg saw us turn northeast and start back toward Sohja. The objective at this time was approximately two and a half kilometres to our north and could be seen intermittently through the wadi system. The locals would have finished any morning prayers and just started the day's work by now; it wouldn't be long before everyone knew there was a Canadian patrol out and about.

At about 0815 we reached the point where we would detach from 22A and head north. The break-off leg hadn't been picked arbitrarily on the map: it was a point along the patrol route that put the most vegetation and rubble between us and the objective, hopefully allowing us to get into position unseen. That was always the goal but in a country like Afghanistan they didn't sit around indoors watching TV. The landscape was their TV and their ability to pick out small changes in that landscape was unnerving. Usually by this time, the locals would be walking around or sitting on walls starring at anything that caught their eye but today, with the patrol having no doubt been noticed walking south of them, they were slower than usual in their daily routine. I'm sure the locals were keen on figuring out where the patrol was heading so that they could head the opposite direction: patrols had a knack for attracting bullets and explosions.

Pete was now looking back at me, expectantly. With a quick nod, he turned and tapped the patrol 2IC which meant, "We're off, you got the six". A quick scan to make sure no one was tailing us or observing us, 66B started heading north. We had passed the no-return point anyways—couldn't always be helped but knowing that you have been compromised is better than not knowing. Luckily it seemed everyone was fixed on the patrol lead who were now breaking cover of the wadi and in full view of Fathollah. I was pretty confident that we had made a clean break but was always ready for worst-case scenario.

We made it to our ORV in good time, ahead of the patrol getting to their last leg into the objective. This meant we would have plenty of time to not only set up a good position but to range likely enemy firing positions should the patrol come under contact. While the team was getting the kit ready to move forward, the observation balloon picked up three FAMs on the western side of Fathollah speaking on cell phones. Cell phones weren't uncommon in Afghanistan; they didn't have running water or toilet paper, but you better believe everybody had a cell phone.

Now the balloon was essentially a weather balloon equipped with video gear attached to a cable leading down to a trailer parked inside a FOB with two soldiers posted inside. It was like World War I tactics. Due to the elevation it could achieve, it was effective at scanning the surrounding area. Unfortunately, the equipment was only as good as the soldier operating it. The operators, so far removed from the action, would never have the same motivation as the patrol trying to stay alive. Not to pick on the operators but they were not trained snipers or recce patrolmen and likely never left the wire. At this time, however, I was pleasantly surprised that they made an effort and had called in these males with cell phones. Most times the equipment would be used by a sun-fucked CSM to make sure the guys' pants were bloused or they would be calling in stuff that I considered completely irrelevant and three guys with cell phones wasn't exactly groundbreaking but the fact that they were not gathered with the entire village to the east to observe the patrol and were instead on the far side of the village, was interesting.

A quick tap of my earpiece and Justin gave me the thumbs-up: he had heard the description of the FAMs, and another forward hand motion indicated that he and Colin were ready to get into an FFP. A quick glance over the berm to get my bearings and I had a pretty good idea where they were. There was a gentle rise, likely a long-collapsed wall, that was slightly in shadow. It would afford some concealment and protection from fire from the north as well as hopefully allow the guys to see through the thin line of vegetation to our front. I motioned to Pete's metal detector in case he wanted a sweep done but the location appeared to be completely random and with a shake of his head, Justin confirmed he was good and off they went.

At this time the patrol had reached the RV for the final leg in and had huddled up for quick confirmatory orders in case they got hit coming in. I looked over at Pete; he had the six and was confirming best exit routes should shit hit the fan. There wasn't much to use for cover however but doing anything was always better than doing nothing.

I pulled out my map while listening to the radio traffic. Unlike my counterpart in 66A, I could rely on my 2IC to be competent enough to spot. which left me free to keep track of the battlefield with my own eyes instead of broken radio traffic.

Prior to leaving I had sent artillery coordinates for a linear fire mission on the wadi system to our front. I wanted to confirm our location. I had already been on the wrong end of a short drop and wasn't keen on repeating the experience. Everything looked good, almost too good, then for some reason I pictured an en (enemy) mortar landing in my lap. I'd found that it was usually best not to ignore a gut feeling so I decided to take Pete up and slightly east of our primary team to see what kind of arcs we could get. We found a spot that afforded good observation on the entrance of the village as well as the grape rows that 22A would have to clear. From here Pete and I would be able to keep track of friendly progress as well as employ the AR-10 effectively should they come under contact.

"Pete, what do you think?" I pointed to the entrance.

"Three," he said, the number of meals he was thinking about.

"What?"

"Three IMPs I'm crushing when we get back. I'm starving!"

I knew he was still eyeballing the range.

"650 or so should work and you get salmon meal only."

"Agreed. Not on salmon. That shit is gross."

It was right about this time when we got the first ICOM hit. (ICOM was the means of communications the enemy preferred when they wanted to coordinate an attack or rally more fighters. It was a short-range radio that could be intercepted. Interpreters who went out with patrols often carried one and scanned all channels attempting to gain a heads-up if enemy were in the area. They translated what was being said and relayed info to the section commander.) The interpreter at COP Sohja had also picked up the same communications and Zero (Bravo HQ) was now passing that over the comms just as 22A had just started on their final leg to approach the village. ICOM was indicating that the enemy was going to ambush the patrol from the garden with had two larger-calibre guns.

Now a garden could mean a lot of things in Afghanistan; for example, a courtyard with a blade of grass could be considered a garden. The enemy were concerned about us listening and used coded speech, so I was worried about the weapons mentioned, hoping they meant PKMs and not a recoilless rifle. No mention of explosions so that was good. I could see Justin and Colin in position to my left.

"Pete, I got to go check on Justin. Keep eyes on the entrance and to the south of the village if possible. If it pops, you're clear to engage any threats."

Quick pat on the shoulder and I cautiously doubled over to Justin. Still believing we hadn't been noticed, I tucked in behind Justin who was on the scope relaying ranges to Colin. It was about 500 metres to the southern wall and 680 metres to the entrance of the village.

"Justin, you getting that traffic?"

"Ambush in the garden, so original. I bet you I'm looking at this garden right now. C'mon, take the bet. I could use some poker money."

I was concentrating on listening to what the patrol was planning; they were all over the comms attempting to get guys in the right positions, amped up and expecting an ambush any moment. I scanned our western flank which was open ground for two kilometres. I was always expected company, even though attacking a sniper team over open ground would have been absolutely brilliant.

"I got three guys here in my garden, one in white the other two in dark greens and blues. Looks like they're staying low, hopping walls and carrying something," said Justin.

The description matched the three the balloon had hit on earlier. I knew Justin couldn't give me a better description of what they were carrying because it would be covered in cloth. They knew our ROEs and wouldn't risk carrying a weapon out in the open as it was a good way of attracting a Hellfire. Unfortunately for them, however, we weren't constrained by quite the same ROEs: nobody covers a shovel and uses tactical movements to dig a ditch.

Once Colin was put on the threat, Justin gave me a grid.

"Let me know if you see them again."

I attempted to relay this information to the patrol, but they were still going back and forth on the comms. We were carrying a smaller, less-powerful radio which meant I was getting stepped on while transmitting. I flipped to the alt for Zero and relayed that we had observed three FAMs as described earlier enter a walled section to the south of Fathollah carrying what ATB (appeared to be) a covered weapon while moving tactically toward the patrol. No sooner had I finished my transmission than Justin observed the ICOM.

"White man jammies Colin, ICOM."

That was strike three.

"Seen."

I had the elevation and correction ready in my head, but they knew their job and Colin reached up and dialled in. Zero broke the comms traffic and advised the patrol that ICOM indicated that the enemy was there in the garden and observing the patrol. Zero had barely acknowledged my earlier transmission about what we were tracking, and I still couldn't get through to the patrol. Ideally, when working with other groups, prior to a shot being taken, I like to give them word so they can expect it. I've been in situations where I had to fire overhead at the enemy moving towards a patrol only to have that patrol turn and dump all and any ammo at the nearest unsuspecting grape hut. To me a suppressed .338 sounds like a well-hit golf shot with a titanium driver and it wasn't likely they would hear that at this range, and we weren't firing overhead. Comms was getting to be an issue yet again. I wasn't going to let our lads get shot up because of poor radio discipline.

"Justin, do you still have him?" I asked.

"No, he's down again but still in the same spot. I can't see the other two."

Time to make them rethink their life choices.

"If the ICOM guy gets up again, send him to whatever god he chooses."

I knew that because of the walls, they would only have an upper torso to shoot at but at this range, with no wind, it was quite manageable. I caught Pete's eye and gave him the sign for eyes on enemy so he could also expect the shot. I was pumped: fighting in built-up areas was always a crap shoot finding good positions, but we had selected a good one and the team was dialled in.

The next few moments seem to slow right down. First, I heard Justin say, "He's up", followed by Colin's "Stand by", quickly followed by "Send it". The shot left the barrel before Justin finished the command and I leaned in to hear the result.

"Hit! Uh, at least I think it hit."

"What do you mean, did you hit him or not?" I asked.

At this range it wasn't exactly rocket science to spot.

"Well, I seen the round go right at his head and he dropped but then it looked like it hit the wall behind him and low."

"If you missed at that range then you're both fired!" I laughed. "Remind me to give you a refresher on terminal ballistics. Now was it a hit or not?"

Justin knew what I meant. The round, once passed through a medium, would likely have exited on a separate vector, stripping the jacket on the way. Either one could have caused splash on the wall.

"B, it hit him in the ear, I'm positive."

I had no doubt it had. It happens so quickly you only have a small window to make the call and, unlike Hollywood, the enemy didn't go down flying in a fountain of blood.

"Keep watch and observe for the other two."

I radioed in to Zero to inform them of the shot.

The patrol was still advancing in the open and openly talking back and forth on the comms. All I got from Zero was a quick "Roger out". We weren't the focus right now and it's likely they weren't paying attention to us at this point. I looked over to Pete again and gave him a thumbs-up. He smiled, no doubt thinking about his next meal.

"B, I have two guys near where the ICOM was. They're in shadow but looks like they could be the other two. What's the call?"

As much as I wanted to dust every last one of them, we weren't murderers. I wasn't going to take the chance that they weren't civilians coming over to see the commotion we'd just caused.

"What are they doing?"

"They're just standing there looking around, kind of this way, not carrying anything."

"Keep eyes on and let me know where they go. If you see a weapon, let me know."

I really wanted to have at them, but information could be more important than two low-level thugs. Besides, to demoralize the enemy, someone had to be left to tell the tale.

The ICOM hits went cold. The patrol finally did reach the grape rows unopposed and started their task of clearing it for IEDs. None of the locals ventured out to greet them; they had the ability to disappear at a moment's notice and it was likely that they now knew the patrol wasn't alone.

"B, got 'em again. They're moving west now. Holy fuck, they have a wheelbarrow and it looks like they have our ICOM guy loaded."

I was always impressed on how fast they could move with a wheelbarrow full of shit.

"Track them. Let's try to identify their egress routes."

I pulled out my map and marked it down for future reference. As quickly as it started, it was over.

The patrol finished clearance of the grape rows without incident and started on their return route which came by our position. We continued to observe Fathollah for signs the enemy would come back at us. The locals had gathered in the garden to the south and were sitting on the walls watching us. Had the enemy still been planning an attack, they would have been in hiding so I was confident we were good to go. The rear of the patrol came by; we had packed up by then and were ready to rejoin them. I approached the patrol 2IC but he shrugged with one palm up, which I understood as him telling me he didn't know what had happened with the attack. I smiled at Colin and gave him knuckles and then fell in with the patrol back to COP Shakare.

The walk back was uneventful if not scorching hot, but I wasn't thinking about the sun at that point. We made it back in record time and immediately went to drop our kit.

"Guys, that was absolutely textbook but I'm a little freaked out right now," I said as we dumped everything on the floor.

Pete somehow already had food in hand. "Why's that B?"

I tried to look shocked. "Because everything went exactly as planned!"

We all laughed, mostly because I was right as nothing ever went to plan. As I exited the tent, I called over my shoulder, "Justin, get us sorted and I'll attend the debrief. Good job, guys."

The section had already started their after-action brief as I entered the tent. They were discussing what they had accomplished and how the clearing had gone. The engineers had located a small device that they were able to take care of but there really wasn't much to talk about their end.

The section commander looked over at me. "Thanks for the help, guys. Sorry we didn't get any action—not sure what happened there. I thought for sure they were going to hit us ... then nothing."

I knew my next line would fly right over their heads. "I guess we must have changed their minds." As dry as the red desert.

I got a couple looks as I gave him my issues with the comms and not being able to relay what we were seeing. As I went into how we had observed the ICOM controller, I got a couple more looks. Once I had told them that we had given the INS with ICOM an earful, I got a couple smiles and high fives out of the lads sitting in. Up to that point they had no idea that we had got one and that the mission had been successful. The debrief wrapped up and I was pulled aside by the platoon commander.

Word came down that they were looking for snipers to assist with another op near MSG and an LAV would be waiting to take us to COP Sohja to catch our helo out.

As I returned to the tent to break the news I was thinking, *How many ambushes have we thwarted?* We just went about our business doing what we could to support but what we did largely went unnoticed. I'm not one to tell stories. I don't do this job for the recognition. You'll never hear me claim to have killed two enemy at 800 metres with my C7 and shitty optics IOT get myself a medal of valour. That shit didn't matter; what mattered was getting my team and as many guys as possible home in one piece and eventually leaving this Godforsaken place behind. That would be my greatest accomplishment. I was proud of my team today. We had been on much harder and crazier missions and would undoubtedly face more hardship before our tour ended but they had performed their duty well and professionally. We had likely prevented friendly casualties and the threat of us being around would keep the enemy on the defensive for a little while. It just goes to show what a small group of highly trained snipers could accomplish with a single, precise and decisive round delivered without warning.

10

All Good Things Must Come to an End, 2010-2014

Sergeant Barry Nisbet, Sniper Detachment Commander
Detachment 66A, Task Force 1-10
Patrol Base Shoja,Panjwai District, Kandahar Province,
Afghanistan
October 2010
As told by Mir Bahmanyar

Sergeant Barry Nisbet, fifth-tour combat veteran, lit a cigarette outside of his tent as he watched Taliban mortars target Patrol Base Shoja. Soldiers scrambled for safety. Unperturbed, he kept smoking. Another shell detonated. He estimated this one at 75 metres. Shrapnel sliced wickedly through the air. Another deliberate inhale, another long exhale—defiance in the face of danger. He took in the unfolding drama, the camp, the dirt, the heat, the mortar rounds exploding. Why he didn't run for cover he did not know; he wasn't suicidal. What he did know was that right then, something inside him clicked—a long overdue decision made. In an instant, his military career was over. He would not re-enlist. He knew the war was winding down for the Infantry. Canada was tired of the endless war. A war without progress. Canadians though knew very little about combat operations in Afghanistan. And Nisbet knew that in the bigger picture of the war, he'd had a tiny piece to play, one bullet at time.

The troubling thing now was what he was going to do during peacetime. Train young soldiers who had a different work ethic? Men who were unwilling to suck it up and put up with tough training he had gone through? He loved his job, man did he love it, but the army was changing faster than he was willing to. It was a new generation of soldiers—a new mentality—and it was one he did not like nor was willing to accept. Barry Nisbet was old-school in a new world. He was that tree that could not bend, a tree that would not break in the unforgiving storm of change.

*

Three Months Earlier
Task Force 1-10, Patrol Base Folad
Salawat, Panjwai District, Kandahar Province,
Afghanistan

Patrol Base Folad was enclosed by a series of HESCO containers, large grey squares filled with sand or dirt, piled one or two high. It formed a massive perimeter wall, topped with nasty concertina wire, entrapping the soldiers like animals in a zoo. Animals that nobody came to see, but that a few locals wanted to kill.

The environment was tough, just like the locals. The heat, the dust. Especially the dust. It infiltrated everyone and everything. Every time Nisbet bit down, he felt the grains of dirt shattering between his teeth. He dealt with it because he had to and, more importantly, because he wanted to. He wanted to be there. He wanted to be at war.

Folad was situated just north of Salawat, an ancient village of a few thousand inhabitants in the district of Panjwai of the Kandahar Province. It was one of the deadliest places for Canadian troops and was considered one of the most heavily IED'd areas in Afghanistan, limiting the mobility of the Coalition forces. South of Salawat village rose the dominant mountain, Salawat Ghar, where in the previous year, Private Sébastien Courcy of the 2nd Battalion, Royal 22nd Regiment, the Van Doos, had been blown off the mountainside by an IED, possibly an old mine from a previous conflict. Salawat Ghar was barren and rocky and looked like nothing the soldiers based in Folad had seen before. Sergeant Nisbet, however, had been on similar mountains. He had traversed those beasts on previous tours, remembering how their sharp teeth mercilessly ripped through clothing and skin, how hard they were to climb during the day, let alone at night with limited visibility. People did not appreciate the absolute darkness and stillness that embraced Afghanistan at night.

To the east of the mountain was the village of Karakolay, and to the south was Nakhonay. All villages were considered extremely hostile; the entire province was the birthplace of the Taliban, their stronghold, their centre of gravity, and their centre of opium production and distribution. Good thing Folad had the HESCO walls protecting its animals.

For the most part, in late summer of 2010, Patrol Base Folad was manned by 8 Platoon, Oscar Company, 3rd Battalion, Royal Canadian Regiment (RCR), which was attached to the 1RCR Battle Group. The company commander was Major S. Brown, who was well liked by Nisbet. Brown knew how to command; he recognized that he didn't know everything. For that reason, Nisbet had confidence in him as a commander. Oscar Company had been getting hit almost every time they walked out the wire and Nisbet was happy that his team had been sent by his boss, Unit Master Sniper Warrant Officer Gordon Cullen, to help the beleaguered troops.

WO Cullen commanded two sniper detachments in his unit, 66A and 66B, and was on his third deployment as a sniper in Afghanistan. Snipers were transient, not attached to anyone in particular, homeless but with a home. Most of their gear fit in a shopping cart. They went where they were needed, always on an hour's notice to move. If an area flared up and UMS Cullen felt the teams' skills could be used, he would send them into the hotspot.

Cullen remembered the reasons for having sent in 66A to Patrol Base Folad. Someone had been taking potshots at the base, there was an increase in IEDs, and there were a few shoot-and-scoot scenarios where the shooters outran the Canadian troops before they could react, or they simply disappeared after initiating contact. In Cullen's experience after word got out that snipers were in one of the bases things quieted down, especially when they dropped a fighting-age male in a field at 600 metres. It was a clear sign to the enemy that there were men with eyes and guns on them at a distance beyond their own capabilities to effectively return fire. The bad guys did not like snipers. This was confirmed by intelligence reports of intercepted enemy communications. Patrol Base Folad had two sniper-qualified soldiers that the UMS had issued a .338 sniping rifle and supporting equipment to, but they did not have the experience his sniper detachments had. At a pinch those two shooters provided Oscar Company with a rudimentary level of overwatch. The decision to finally launch one of his detachments came when one of the sniper-qualified soldiers was almost shot in the head. Warrant Officer Cullen sent 66A.

Sergeant Nisbet was the commander of sniper Detachment 66A in charge of three sniper-qualified corporals. His most junior guy was Dee, the other members were Tom and Harry. Dee was the man Nisbet counted on the most—he was the point man. Air was their preferred way of travel. There were less IEDs in the sky, Nisbet joked. The risk in the air was minimal in comparison to travelling mine-infested roads, as the use of IEDs had grown exponentially in recent years. Nisbet loved the Chinooks; nothing compared to seeing them come in, the twin rotors whizzing around, throwing the sand and dust into a frenzy. He always felt safe in them although the thin aluminium skin was designed for weight reduction and therefore afforded no protection from small-arms fire to those sitting inside. But it beat driving. The snipers always sat at the back of the transport helicopter where they boarded through the massive ramp. The air crew's rear machine-gunner was perched on the very edge of it. The ramp always stayed open and looking through the opening was like watching 3D HD TV. It was iconic, a defining image of the war in Afghanistan. The Chinooks seemed effortless in the air, but they looked as though they shouldn't even be able to fly. They were big, ponderous machines, intended as a medium-sized transport helicopter but exceptionally capable, especially given the elevation and weather conditions prevalent in Afghanistan. The Chinooks delivered the snipers to another grey, spiral–encircled zoo—the patrol base.

The team arrived at Folad midway through their deployment and conducted the odd patrol and overwatch out of the tower located in the camp. But it was never good to think of it as halfway home because sometimes the end was just a step away—a mine, a bullet or a grenade. Nisbet always found it easier to accept that death was near, all around, all the time. It put him at ease; it helped him focus on what he was there for, but he did realize that his attitude probably hurt those waiting for him back at home in Ontario.

The snipers' mission was to kill Taliban, plain and simple. Whenever someone asked Nisbet about being a sniper, it was always about killing, about how many he'd killed, about the distance of the kill shot. But to him, sniping was much more than that. It was life itself, part of his inner core, his DNA. Most people can be taught how to shoot. Give them enough rounds and they will eventually hit. It's science, muzzle velocity, bullet mass, internal and external ballistics, temperature, humidity … the list goes on. To be a sniper, a good sniper, according to Nisbet, was about mastering all the skills. It was about fixing problems, knowing how to use all the equipment in the day and in the dark, when one is cold, miserable, hungry and sleep deprived, when the smell is so bad that even the goats get offended. It's about embracing the misery, befriending it and ultimately welcoming it.

Off the eastern tip of Salawat Ghar lay a small village belying its deadliness. It was close to an intersection that was so heavily IED'd the troops did not dare patrol through it. It was also a potential staging point for Taliban operations. The village was about a two-klick (kilometre) walk which provided enough time for the Taliban to prepare and emplace IED ambushes on likely areas of ingress and egress by the RCR soldiers. Something had to be done. The operational plan devised by Major Brown and staff seemed simple enough. The patrol was going to walk into the village and see what would come out to greet them. The sniper detachment was to be tactically positioned to spoil any Taliban ambushes by killing them first. Time had come for the Canadians to assert themselves.

The Plan

It is a common misconception that soldiering is simple. In fact, it is one of the most complex, difficult professions in the world. It also requires a mental and physical toughness not found in the civilian world. A seemingly simple patrol, so often seen badly done in Hollywood movies or TV shows, requires a lot of planning and training, with experts who have spent years learning the craft of combat arms—from ensuring all the gear is serviceable and available to planning contingencies and support from various assets that require experts and manuals setting forth the operational procedures. Additionally, there are radio channels, call signs, codewords, medical evacuation protocols, and much, much more. This simple plan hatched by Major Brown was no different in its complex planning requirements than a larger combat operation. Lives were at stake.

Sniper Detachment 66A was given a few days to plan their part of the mission and to observe Salawat Ghar from an old bunker just to the south of the patrol base. There was a small observation post dug into it. Nothing special, just a hole in the ground with a few sandbags, and although it was outside of the safety of the grey HESCO wall, it was still within the outer perimeter of the patrol base itself. But the only thing separating them from the enemy was a concertina wire fence. From the bunker the team glassed the mountain for days, looking for any movement and possible OP positions for the team to occupy during the impending mission. Nobody should have been up on the mountain; it was just a rock with major elevation. Anyone on it was an enemy.

Nisbet scoured over intel reports to see if the ghar had been used as a position by allied troops on previous tours. Of course, it had been, and not to his surprise, Nisbet read the report of a Coalition soldier, Private Sébastien Courcy, who had struck an IED while climbing it. Since it was the only real high ground in the area, it was bound to be IED'd. Night optics and thermal binoculars revealed no enemy presence.

After a couple of days of patiently observing, 66A went into mission planning: routes in and out, and all of the what ifs, including the what-if-somebody-got-blown-up, as had been the case on Nisbet's 2006 tour when Jody M stepped on a mine even though Nisbet, Cullen and one other member of the det had successfully moved through a gap in a wall leading to a trail. They planned for every contingency, but an old military adage always had to be kept in mind: Murphy's Law—if it can go wrong, it will.

66A took the .338 Timberwolf rifle as their primary sniping platform, along with C8 carbines, 9mm Browning pistols, fragmentation grenades, smoke grenades, first aid gear, radio, back-up comms, batteries, water and food, and more, but they still needed to be as light as possible because speed was their security. No matter how light the snipers were, and they were not, the Taliban would be lighter and faster since they carried far less equipment. They knew how to move, it was their terrain, their backyard. Nisbet always had to keep a potential run-in with the enemy in mind when planning ops. But 66A still carried 80 pounds of gear on the upcoming mission. During the planning phase the team usually developed three COAs that were presented to the ground commander who generally decided on what best suited the overall plan. Nisbet, being a veteran and having the experienced UMS Cullen, always knew which one the ground commander would pick. He and the UMS formulated the plans in such a manner to make sure of it. After all, they were a small, eccentric element within the structure of the army and knew how to best deploy themselves within the overall operational plan.

The infiltration route to be used was not far from the PB, around two kilometres, but 66A gave themselves plenty of time to move in unseen and unheard. The plan called for the sniper detachment to scoot down to OP Khyber which was at the southwestern edge of the mountain in the back of a LAV the day prior to the main patrol heading out from PB Folad. OP Khyber was a small but permanent observation post set up and manned by the Royal Canadian Dragoons (RCD) Armoured Recce. It wasn't much to look at, just some sandbags and wire with a few Coyote Reconnaissance Vehicles on hand. Their task was to maintain observation on the road that ran along the base of the mountain. The OP provided good views onto the southern side of Salawat Ghar.

It was a clear morning at PB Folad. The snipers slept in a section of a modular tent, no AC, no fans, crushed rocks for a floor. Nisbet neither had feelings of impending gloom nor doom, nor any expectations of grandeur. It was just another day, another operation, his det had a mission. He pulled out his can of chewing tobacco and put a pinch of Skoal in his mouth and tossed the can to Dee who did the same. They had gone through the orders the night before. It was routine without being routine; it was exciting without the excitement. It was simply time to go to work.

The team loaded into a LAV III, capable of carrying nine to ten people including crew, for their drive to OP Khyber, and Nisbet hated it. He preferred walking and taking his chances out in the open rather than being confined inside a big steel coffin. But walking wasn't an option. Nisbet took the air sentry hatch in the back of the vehicle, reducing the coffin-like feeling by just a bit. He looked around, taking in the beauty of Afghanistan and its people. It was a beautiful country with some of the kindest people he had ever met. They were an ingenious people. They could make something out of nothing. An old oil can could be crafted into hinges, and two boards, two nails and four tiny pieces of foam could be made into a deadly, almost undetectable pressure plate for an IED. They knew war better than he ever would and that made him respect them. It was a short ride, an uneventful ride, his favorite kind. Nobody liked driving in-country.

OP Khyber

The vehicle pulled into OP Khyber and the snipers unloaded, trying to blend in as best as they could but the long gun they carried always attracted attention. Nisbet linked up with the lieutenant commanding the little outpost to discuss the plan of action. This was followed up by a reconnaissance in a Coyote to survey the area his detachment was going to insert into because things were always bigger and different once seen up close.

The terrain was craggy, rocky, jagged and steep. Knowing that a soldier had hit an IED up there played over and over in the det commander's mind. There was a balance between risk and reward, a balance that was in constant flux. As the sergeant of the team, he had to weigh and make such decisions. Part of mission success was coming back for the next mission.

Nisbet arranged to have a UAV overwatch when they made their insertion that night while the RCDs would provide direct fire support since the Dragoons could maintain observation for most of the team's insertion route. But this came with its own difficulty because the passage of friendly lines was sometimes not so friendly. Blue-on-blue incidents were devastating. Nisbet remembered being wakened by the A-10 'Warthog' attack on Masum Ghar in 2006 which killed Private Graham. Sometimes, sleep-deprived soldiers who did not always get the best handover instructions when they came on shift could accidently engage friendly units passing through their lines. Nisbet wanted them to know there would be good guys out and about that night. He had no problem avoiding Taliban gunfire, but he took issue with having to avoid friendly rounds. Artillery units had also been contacted during the planning phase and would be once again when the operation started. Nisbet was confident calling in fire support because of his experiences in 2006 when calling for fire was a fairly standard practice. By 2010, the rules of engagement had changed from defeating and killing the enemy to winning the hearts and minds of the locals based on the newly espoused counterinsurgency doctrine under American General Stanley McChrystal. Receiving permission to blow up targets and enemy personnel became nearly impossible. Snipers had to be far more reliant on their own means when operating in hostile territory.

It was a good plan, but as always it had risks. They were used to dealing with many of them. Snipers operated in small elements, cut off, away from the larger units, alone. It was what set them apart. It didn't make them any better; it just made them different. They accepted the risks but mitigated them wherever they could.

66A spent the remainder of the day sitting in a small bunker in the OP glassing the ghar and just bullshitting. As it got darker, they tried to find a spot to lay down. They hadn't brought much in terms of sleeping gear as they needed to travel light, just a thin Ranger blanket to fight off the night chill. It never really got cold but the drop in temperature seemed to make it always feel colder than it really was. Nisbet tried to doze off but whenever he was about to fall asleep a Coyote vehicle would start up and the reality of where he was kicked back in. He heard one of the other guys moving around which usually set everyone else in motion. They had about an hour before they stepped off. So much for sleep.

It was a clear night with good ambient light for their night vision. Nisbet got up, boots tied and double knotted. Professionals rarely, if ever, took their boots off outside the wire. He went through his checklist: night vision gear, comms, infrared laser, GPS, the odd feeling in his stomach. Nisbet went over to the command post prior to their departure and had a quick look at the ghar using a thermal camera from inside a nearby Coyote. There was nothing unusual, no hotspots indicating people or animals. Their UAV support was suddenly called off—nothing unusual there—so the snipers would be going it alone for the most part. They were used to it. Priority did not usually go to a few snipers going out for a walk—at least that's how things were in 2010 in Afghanistan. The QRF was on a 15-minute notice to move from PB Folad in case 66A was engaged by Taliban forces. One had to add at least 20 minutes of travel time for the QRF to get to the snipers which would render them fairly useless since a four-man team did not last long against an attack by superior forces, as happened most notably to a Navy SEAL team in 2005 in Afghanistan where only one man, Marcus Luttrell, survived by sheer luck and with the aid of local friendlies. Nisbet and his team had to rely on themselves. Four snipers against the world. This was always the team's default, self-sufficiency. They needed to rely on stealth, they needed to be what they loved being: snipers in hostile territory, experts at silent infiltration.

It was a still, clear night. Salawat Ghar shot up out of the darkness to their north. It separated them from the target village also just to the north. There were a few small outbuildings on the southeastern base of the ghar. They appeared to be abandoned but Nisbet and the team had to assume they were occupied. A series of flat fields, like plots, ran west to east along the base of the mountain. They looked solid and undisturbed, less likely something explosive was lurking beneath. The knowledge that a soldier had hit an IED loomed large. Their route would take them about 500 metres north to the base of the mountain which they would skirt for about a kilometre before starting the slow climb up. They then would set up an ORV and scout out an observation post to hunker down into and wait for morning. If things went as planned Detachment 66A would be perched up above, watching and waiting as the night gave way. Then, at first light, the infantry patrol would leave Patrol Base Folad, walk east and then south into the village. Nisbet went through his checklist again: NVGs, laser, final comms, odd feeling in his stomach ... and into the darkness like ghosts they went.

The Insertion

Nisbet always remembers the sound of the first few steps he took when he walked out of the wire. The silence, the crunch his boots made as they pressed down into the ground, how that odd feeling in his stomach disappeared. The switch went on, his senses heightened, an eerie calmness transcended. He had come to terms with death a long time ago. He had seen it, had lost friends, had seen limbs blown off men. But it was always at the instant, those first steps outside the wire, that he truly came to terms with his mortality. It helped him focus. Nisbet didn't want to die but accepted that it was always one step away—a feeling that he never felt replicated since his military service ended.

As they moved past the wire the darkness embraced them in its protective cloak. Everything glowed green through their night vision, depth perception lost. The ground that looked so flat began to undulate beneath their feet. Salawat Ghar grew higher with every step, each sound amplified in the darkness. Afghanistan was an exceptionally quiet place, even during the day. The hum of the Coyote vehicles dissipated with each step. No one talked, each man immersed in his own silence. They stopped a few hundred metres out and pulled into a tight all-round defence. As the last man moved in, they knew they had a few seconds to get comfortable and then they were like statues, quiet, unmoving, frozen in time and place. Nisbet closed his eyes to heighten his hearing, to adapt to the new surroundings away from the sounds of the vehicles stationed at OP Khyber.

Nothing. It was quiet, a good sign, no enemy alerted by their movement. A minute later Nisbet gently tapped Dee on the shoulder and Dee took the point to navigate the team forward. Dee was not just the point man but also the team's navigator. Nisbet kept a pace count in his head, counting each step, to see how far the team travelled because relying on GPS could be deadly should batteries die or satellites become unavailable. Navigating by terrain and pace count was an art in itself and vital for the survival of the team when technology failed.

The route they had planned the previous day was based on maps and satellite images, but it was nothing more than a guideline, a very general line on the map, essentially marking their movement from point A to point B. How that route was executed on the ground was ever-changing because the ground dictated movement to a certain degree. Some terrain was not navigable by vehicle but on foot the det could pretty much go anywhere even if it was hard going. Each member of the team did his best to watch the point man and to follow him in his steps to avoid potential IEDs. This was more difficult at night; walking head down was not an option. In hostile terrain each sniper needed to be aware of the surroundings to avoid potential ambushes or emplaced mines. The head acted like a swivel, looking left, right, a quick check behind to make sure everyone was following, while watching ahead for any hand signals. If the lead man stopped, everyone stopped. If he motioned for silence, everyone went quiet. If he got down, everyone followed suit silently. Spacing between members was crucial to avoid injury or death by one bullet or one single explosion: if the det was spaced too tightly, a single blast might get them all. Best case was that only one guy got hit and that the rest of the team could deal with it. Worst was everyone got hit and they would bleed out into the night because no one would make it to them in time even if they were able to communicate effectively. The formation had to be just right to maintain distance and visibility. They continued the slow, methodical walk to the base of the mountain.

A few wadis crisscrossed the route as they covered the ground relatively quickly and in absolute silence. The ghar now towered above them as they reached the first flat, hardened field. Nisbet liked the ground: it was even and easy to walk on because it was relatively smooth. Even in the darkness it was easy to see the flat surface. The whole area was a completely different hue in their night vision, a greenish Mars-like environment. It felt comforting to be walking on the hard ground, since it was solid and no enemy would be digging anything without the team seeing it. But these fields didn't last forever. It was just a temporary reprieve from the constant IED threat.

Dee suddenly stopped and the det froze instantly in place. The point man glanced back at his sergeant, indicating he needed to talk with Nisbet. Nisbet signalled to Tom and Harry to hold their positions, and they automatically took a knee and covered their arcs, guns up, scanning. Nisbet pushed up to Dee and both crouched. Just ahead of them Dee had spotted a few small outbuildings.

The team moved slowly, cautiously, toward them, watching for any sign of movement and listening for any noise indicating human presence. They approached the first building up the left side, Dee held just before the threshold of the doorway. Nisbet tapped Dee gently, indicating entry into the building which Dee did effortlessly through the doorway, C8 assault weapon at the ready. Nisbet followed behind him and moved swiftly to the opposite corner as they had trained to do by "pie-ing" off the room with interlocking arcs of fire.

Empty.

It barely took seconds. They had done it countless times. They quickly cleared the remainder of the structures and moved on. The flat fields ended as the rocks grew larger beneath their feet, slowing their progress. But they had time.

As they approached the eastern edge of the ghar, a large re-entrant loomed up at the southern face while just to the east, high up on the ridge, a rocky outcrop glowed ominously in their night vision. *This is going to suck*, they thought. But a moonlit stroll up a mountain at midnight, heavily armed, outnumbered, two kilometres from friendly forces, a minute away from bleeding out, a step away from been blown up—there was no better place to be.

When using night vision, distance seems shortened and so the climb looked relatively easy plus they weren't carrying all that much gear. The plan was to ascend, spend the day supporting the patrol if needed, and come back down under the cover of darkness. As they started to climb, they quickly realized that although the area was not likely IED'd, they had to sacrifice some of their stealth because the rocks they dislodged tumbled down to the bottom. The higher they climbed, the longer the rocks rolled down the re-entrant, crashing and bouncing all the way down.

By now 66A was out of direct fire support from their RCD comrades at OP Khyber. Their only defence was the guns they carried and the artillery on standby. There was no air support, but Nisbet expected aircraft would be deployed to their location if his team got into a firefight with the Taliban. They were exposed but the likelihood of coming under contact was minimal. The real risk was falling: the higher they climbed the more the likelihood of a fall meant a painful death. After about an hour of picking their way across the unstable ground, they made it up and across the re-entrant to the rocky outcrop.

The det again pulled into an all-round defence and listened to their new surroundings. It was silent. After a minute Nisbet got on the radio where he called the Oscar Company command post and, using a codeword, let them know that 66A had reached the ORV. They had achieved the first part of their mission.

The ridgeline carried on higher to the west. It was the highest point around, but it was an obvious position and probably the first place the Taliban would look when the snipers went loud and started shooting. Nisbet decided to push a little to the east where it looked like the terrain levelled out somewhat. There were several places to set up an OP. The satellite imagery they used during the planning phase confirmed Nisbet's thoughts on the location for the OP. He also knew that the company CP was tracking the team's progress so minor adjustments were fine. 66A had picked a tentative ORV from the map during their battle prep, one where they would be less exposed and had defendable high ground should the proverbial "shit hit the fan" and the Taliban attack. Dee and Nisbet prepped to recce the OP position. This was a standard operating procedure (SOP) to go on a leader's reconnaissance before moving the team into its final fire position or OP. Nisbet gave Tom and Harry, who stayed behind to guard the equipment, a contingency plan. It essentially covered what to do if he and Dee did not come back or came under fire. There wasn't much chance of Taliban sitting up on the ghar so Dee and Nisbet only took pistols and ditched their body armour. The risk they were taking was to get blown up and if the blast didn't kill them, the fall would. Nisbet and Dee thought, *Fuck it, mission before self.*

The first 50 metres took them about 30 minutes. They crossed a rock face at about a 70-degree angle. Every step was painfully slow. They made sure their feet were locked into something solid, then grabbed a hold with their hands, and only then moved one foot at a time, inching across. Falling at this point was almost certain death and if by the odd chance they survived the fall, it would be a lonely and painful wait for help, assuming the Taliban didn't arrive first; after all, they were playing in the Taliban's backyard. They dragged themselves across the rock face and finally managed to get into some more navigable terrain. They spotted the village below to the east and north. Further to the northwest they made out the dark void that was Patrol Base Folad. This was an excellent spot to observe the impending operation to be launched out of the patrol base.

They found a good position to set up their OP. It was flat and provided good cover to the north and east. They were slightly exposed to the south, but Nisbet thought the RCDs should be able to warn them of any approaching danger. The two snipers surveyed the flat position as Nisbet got down on his hands and knees and gingerly ran his hands over the semi-sandy patch. He pulled his knife out and tried to prod the ground: it was compacted rock, difficult to dig but this was the spot.

Usually, a sniper team wanted to keep their eyes on the objective from the moment they first observed it. This was done for a few reasons—most important, it was about watching for a pattern of life which allowed them to provide real-time battlefield intelligence. This night though both snipers headed back to the ORV, exhausted, to gather up the rest of the team and equipment. Time was on their side because the bait, the patrol, was not set to step off for a few hours yet. Nisbet and Dee made the trip back to Tom and Harry where Nisbet briefed them on the position and the very daunting move to the OP, a move made more difficult by the added 80lb of gear they had to carry this time round. Nisbet advised Tom and Harry not to look down.

Contact: The Man in the Light-Blue Man Jammies

Grid Coordinates QQ 4152 9001; 0251 hours call for prayers heard, 0625 hours,

one round @ 610 metres, 1 x FAM blue MJ blue scarf with ICOM radio.

It had been slow moving but 66A safely made it to the OP position with about an hour of darkness left. The patrol members back at PB Folad started to wake.

"Gun up and eyes on."

Nisbet and Dee took the first shift, Nisbet scanning the area using thermal binos. He was looking for hotspots and he found them. Dogs meandered around some of the buildings. Nisbet continued into the large grape field to his north, hoping to catch a glimpse of the mysterious Afghan liger, a combination of a lion and tiger that roamed only at night. A mythical beast? Who knew. It was a running legend throughout all his time in Afghanistan. He did not spot a liger that night.

Nisbet and Dee produced a quick range card and scouted the ground around them as night began to give way to day. The radio started to crackle, the patrol back at PB Folad going through their radio checks with the CP. Nisbet had already called in his OP report, comprised of basic info of their position, arcs of fire and visibility. The staff at Folad's CP plotted the information on their operational map. The outgoing patrol would have an idea of where the sniper detachment was and what they were seeing on the ground. The snipers settled in and watched. Cooking fire smoke from the buildings in the target area drifted lazily into the sky. There was no movement yet.

The area directly below to the north was full of grape fields running east to west; further north a long road and walls ran in the same direction. Walls, thick mud walls, were everywhere. Every compound had walls, roads were lined by walls, the grapes grew out of the mud walls in the field. It was a maze down on the ground and the dismounted patrol would have its work cut navigating through it. The snipers' job was to keep watch, to warn the patrol of any danger, and if needed to kill.

Sergeant Nisbet scanned the road to the east. Another road intersected it, running due north into the large open area that separated the village below with another to the north. A main road ran east to west towards PB Folad and it too was under observation. Further east, it ran out of view and into another village where it joined the crossroads littered with IEDs. Nisbet could just make out the edge of it. It was not their concern today, but eventually it would be.

The patrol conducted its final radio check with the command post and prior to stepping off, they made contact with 66A. Nisbet gave them a sitrep on what they had seen so far: a few grid coordinates of the buildings where the smoke was. Nisbet watched the patrol push out of Folad and move east down the road. The soldiers of the RCR knew they were being watched and not only by their own snipers. Nothing moved in Afghanistan without being seen, sometimes not even the snipers, no matter how hard they tried to insert stealthily. Afghans did not have TV, no internet, no video games; instead, they could pick out the smallest change in the scenery that they had spent their entire life watching. Nisbet figured that his team would find out soon enough if they had been discovered—with AK and RPG fire. Nisbet thought the question the locals would be asking now was where the soldiers were going this morning and what would transpire along the way.

It wasn't long before the snipers caught their first glimpse of a fighting age male in the village to the northeast. He was dressed in light-blue man jammies, a long shirt that went down to the knees and wearing pants which made the whole ensemble look like man pajamas. The FAM wore a dark beard. Detachment 66A didn't know it at the time but the FAM would be the first to die that day and not the last. They called out his presence to the patrol. The calm voice of the OC acknowledged over the air. The patrol covered ground quickly and began to push south through the grape fields. Their movement slowed as the terrain forced them northeast of the ghar. They were about 400 metres away from the snipers now as the sun rose.

The smoke from the fires rose straight up, giving snipers an indication of the wind speed and direction. The shimmer coming off the ground eased to the left as Nisbet and Dee checked where they had last seen the FAM in blue. They talked about a wind call, they chirped back and forth about the shimmer and how the spin drift of the round would negate each other at about 600 metres out. They agreed on .1 of a mil right. It was never hard and fast. They would make an initial wind call for the current conditions and monitor, make changes when they needed to or just apply a hold, in fact aim slightly off target to compensate for the wind direction. Sniper stuff. They were tracking their man in blue who, one way or another, had been alerted to the presence of the patrol. However, he had not been alerted to the sniper detachment. Nisbet and Dee lost track of him as he moved west towards the patrol. They feverishly scanned the ground, anticipating where he would come out. His movements indicated he was not just out for a morning stroll.

Snipers are professional voyeurs. They hide and watch, they evaluate and anticipate. They try to think like the enemy who are dedicated and formidable adversaries. The enemy knew the rules of engagement, they knew when the Coalition forces could kill and when they couldn't. There is a difference in how people act when they are being watched; they let you see what they want the observer to see. However, when they don't think they are being watched, they expose themselves: either they are the enemy or they are not. It is easy to tell but impossible to explain; one just knows. That doesn't mean snipers kill on a hunch or a feeling, they have their strict rules of engagement to follow and follow them they do. The man in blue was the enemy—he knew it and so did Dee and Nisbet. He just needed to show it to them.

The lead elements of the patrol were almost directly below Nisbet and his detachment. They knew the det was up on the ghar hidden somewhere amongst the rocks. Dee spotted the enemy first and called it out to Nisbet. It was the man in blue. Nisbet quickly ranged him using a rangefinder.

"606 metres," whispered Nisbet.

He heard the clicks of the elevation turret as Dee rotated it. Dee didn't have to look at it—he just knew how many clicks it took to adjust. They made another quick wind call at .1 right. Nisbet made out the FAM's features through the binoculars. The man was in his late 30s, had a dark beard and was wearing his light-blue man jammies. There was a wall directly behind him running north–south. Nisbet saw blue man jammies take a step back. Nisbet focused on the object in the FAM's right hand. Bingo! The Afghan raised it to his mouth—a small antenna protruded from the top. It was a handheld ICOM radio. Nisbet knew Dee was on him.

"Dee, you see that?" whispered Nisbet.

"Yep." Dee usually didn't say much.

Blue man jammies' movements were deliberate, calculated. He did well hiding from the approaching patrol but was not doing a good job at hiding from the snipers, which made Nisbet confident that his team had moved into their position last night undetected. Dee had the laser-etched crosshairs of the 12-power Schmidt & Bender scope centered on the enemy's chest. Nisbet felt the adrenalin surge through him. Dee felt it too.

Nisbet took a deep breath. He was just behind Dee. He had the binos resting vertically on a small rock. Dee was in a semi-prone position, the .338 Timberwolf resting gently against his shoulder. Too much pressure could cause a slight pulsing in the muscles that would reverberate through the rifle and magnify at the tip of the barrel, throwing the bullet off a hair that would only be magnified with distance and result essentially in a miss. The FAM moved the radio up to his mouth and Nisbet saw his lips move. He was reporting on the patrol—to whom they did not know—maybe to set up an ambush or to detonate a command-wired IED. But Nisbet knew blue man jammies was dead: he just didn't know it yet. There was no time to warn the patrol below of what was about to transpire.

It was now up to Dee. His breathing was slow and deep, waiting to be two-thirds exhaled—then he'd squeeze the trigger. It would be a bit of a surprise when it went off.

"Stand by," Dee whispered as he ex-haled.

Nisbet focused in on the soon-to-be-dead man. "Send it." This was their language. They had uttered it thousands of times during their sniper training. It was instinctual. If there was a better phrase in the English language, Nisbet had yet to hear it.

Three pounds of pressure exerted on the trigger was all it took. The firing pin snapped forward, indenting the primer, igniting the precisely measured powder in the cartridge and starting the 250-grain 338 calibre bullet in motion. The right-hand twist of the lands and grooves of the barrel turning the bullet as it sped its way down the barrel. The spin added to the bullet's stability, accuracy and penetration. The gases from the ignition of the powder were trapped by the baffles within the suppressor as the bullet exited. The bullet was now free of its cage and had only to defeat the grip of gravity as it hurtled towards the man in blue. The right-hand twist of the round produced a slight amount of spin drift to the right at 600 metres. The fall of the round was minimal as it cut through the morning air at over 3,000 feet per second. It was over in less than half a second. The FAM's lips were still moving when Nisbet saw a puff of dust on the wall to the left of the man in blue. Nisbet called a miss, but the bullet had in fact deflected to the left as it went through the man's body. In his haste Nisbet gave Dee a correction to the left instead of the right but Dee corrected him. Nisbet replayed the shot and sequence in his head. He saw the hit as blue man jammies spun to his right and went down. There was no chance they had missed at 606 metres, no chance.

Shoot, communicate, move were the principles of combat. The shooting was done for now. Nisbet grabbed the radio and called out, "Contact, one FAM engaged."

The patrol had jumped as the high-power round cracked through the air, snapping through the sound barrier as it passed overhead. The sound a suppressed .338 round makes is, well, like the sound a suppressed .338 round makes—it just doesn't really sound like anything else. The soldiers of the RCR reacted as they should have and were relieved to know it was the sniper det who had fired the round.

Dee chambered another round. "No way we missed the man," he snapped at Nisbet. Nisbet agreed.

Thirty seconds later they saw movement in the area where the guy in blue man jammies was. Two FAMs came over and picked him up. They each grabbed him by an arm to drag him back to the village proper. Nisbet and Dee saw his toes dragging in the dirt. He did not move, his head slumped forward, his arms flopped around the necks of his comrades. A large dark-red circle stained his back as his friends dragged his lifeless body away, the circle growing in size. And then he was gone.

Nisbet reported the grid of the contact to the patrol as the command post plotted it. They visually followed the Taliban as far as the ground allowed, noting the grid where they lost sight.

Far below the snipers the dismounted patrol dusted themselves off as it was quickly passed down the line what had just happened. A life taken meant a life saved. Nisbet and the detachment heard yelling coming from down in the village. The news of the kill had travelled fast. Nisbet hoped that the story in the village was that Mr. Blue had been shot by the patrol and that no one would be any the wiser of them hiding high up above the village. The last thing the det needed was Taliban forces manoeuvring onto them as the patrol moved further away.

The patrol continued to push south and then swung back east at the outskirts of the village. From there they pushed back north into the village and mostly out of view of the sniper team. The patrol provided sitreps while they made their way through the maze of buildings and fields. The response they received from the locals seemed positive; the locals seemed happy with the patrol and its presence in the village.

The ground has a way of funnelling movement, and the Taliban knew it. They always knew where enemy soldiers came from and where they were going. Therefore, the patrol was telegraphing its movements and there was no way to avoid it. The best practice was to change direction multiple times, and carry sledgehammers to make holes in the walls to avoid the easy route which was always assumed to have been IED'd.

As the morning drew on, the pattern of life picked up. People tended to their animals and worked the fields; just another normal day for them. Nisbet and the det felt pretty secure up in their little nest. They couldn't see the patrol anymore but were tracking their progress with the location updates provided by the patrol to the CP at PB Folad.

The lead elements were nearing the large open area north of the village to hit the road and head west back toward Folad. They were tired and hot and had been humping for hours. The snipers then spotted a couple of heads up on a rooftop east of the patrol's last position. They were about 1,200 metres out and were more than a little curious about the patrol. Due north of 66A's OP, the team noticed a build-up of foot traffic in the nearby grape fields: eight to ten FAMs were moving east with a sense of purpose.

Nisbet had moved the det slightly after the first shot, half anticipating an RPG to be lobbed up in their direction. For the most part they were packed up and ready to move if needed. They had taken up another firing position about seven to ten metres from their first spot where they were slightly more exposed, but they needed to be there to cover the patrol back to the PB.

The patrol had now cleared the confines of the village and was moving west along the road. About 200 metres to their front was a road that ran north–south which they had to cross. Nisbet knew that the patrol would treat it as an obstacle and go through their drills. The road ran for a further 300 metres before intersecting with another road near the grape fields closest to the snipers. It was an absolute maze of walls and walled roads. Things picked up now, as 66A tracked multiple FAMs moving through and around the grape fields. No weapons were visible, but the fighting aged males weren't out to tend to their livestock or their fields. The snipers relayed this information to the patrol who could see none of this unfolding. Nisbet's detachment were their eyes. It was clear the patrol had all the attention from the FAMs. Det 66A switched off on the gun and Nisbet feverishly worked the radio, trying to make sense of what was developing. He radioed the patrol to stop and hold before they crossed the road because none of the snipers liked what they saw. They had lost sight of three or four of the FAMs at this point and those still visible were being more deliberate in their movements as they drew closer to the patrol. It was clear that they were setting up an ambush: the road running north would be their kill zone when the patrol crossed it. But they were unaware that their movements were being tracked and passed down to the patrol. All Nisbet and the snipers could do was wait and watch. They called out potential targets and quickly broke up the ground and ranged a few prominent objects, so they were all on the same page identifying key terrain. Whatever was going to happen next was going to happen fast. The enemy fighters were looking for some payback from earlier this morning—no one liked to lose.

One of the FAMs drew 66A's attention immediately. He was slightly detached from the group and about 400 metres to the det's north, walking west–east on an elevated trail in the grape rows, which paralleled the trail but were lower by about three feet. He carried something in his left hand wrapped in a blue cloth, a common tactic used by the Taliban to hide whatever they were carrying from the UAVs surveilling the area. The snipers watched him intently: he looked hurried, almost panicked, as if he was late for something. Suddenly he stopped and put the long, cloaked item on the ground. He reached down and partially pulled off the blue cloth, exposing the barrel of a PKM machine gun. It was clear he was moving to engage the patrol. He picked up the machine gun and his pace quickened as he moved to his intended firing position. He would not make it. He moved oblique to the snipers' position. Tom called out the range to Harry who acknowledged it: 425 metres and moving away. Nisbet told them to take him. The rest was up to Harry.

The patrol was holding its position, waiting on Nisbet to tell them to move. Nisbet had no time to pass on what he saw; they'd just have to wait. Harry fired and the machine-gun-toting Taliban slumped forward. Others scattered, unsure where the fire was coming from. They knew where the patrol was, and it was only a matter of time before they put it all together. Harry chambered another 338 round and quickly got back on target. The FAM machine-gunner started to drag himself back up—Harry had only clipped him in his left shoulder. Another round cracked off and struck him square between the shoulder blades, ripping right through his heart. This time he stayed down for good.

The remaining Taliban now turned their attention to the ghar, some even pointing up. It was inevitable, but 66A had done what it had set out to do. Nisbet radioed the latest contact to the patrol and the CP. The snipers scanned the area for further targets, but nobody dared move. The patrol stepped off again and had an uneventful walk back into the camp. The trap had worked, the bait had returned home, and the enemy had lost two fighters and suffered a loss in morale.

Nisbet now had a decision to make. The original plan had them staying in position until dark and then moving back to the RCDs' OP Khyber. Nisbet looked at his watch. It was well before noon. The thought of staying up there for several more hours did not sit well with them. They knew they had been burnt. The enemy did not know exactly where the snipers were, but they knew the general vicinity and could move fast when they wanted to. Sometimes they sent kids to find their enemy, other times RPGs or 82mm recoilless rifle rounds. The det didn't feel like dealing with any of those scenarios. If they were going to leave, they had to do it ASAP. The four-man team was packed and ready to roll. Sergeant Nisbet made the call to the CP. Shoot, communicate and now it was time to move. They pulled out.

Down was easier than up and daylight helped. They walked down and across the flats and into the Khyber without incident.

Their ride showed up minutes later and they were whisked away to PB Folad, homeless. They pulled into the patrol base and were greeted by a few of the guys from the patrol. There was no fanfare, no high fives, just nods and comments about getting a couple of them. It was a tour, a marathon, they would have good days and plenty of bad. It was just another day, a good day. All came back this time, none worse for wear.

But images were etched into their minds forever. *What runs through your mind as you stare through the scope? Crosshairs moving with your breath, a face magnified on the other end. It's personal, almost intimate. What is it I am about to do and what makes it right? My rules of engagement allow me to take a life, to kill. Legality vs Morality. Your life for mine, for my comrades. It just becomes you and you become it. It never goes away—it's just in you. You will identify with it no matter what you do in life. It is unparalleled.*

The debrief was quick, the OC was happy. The joke around that camp was that the patrol had been the bait, but it wasn't like that. Everybody had their role in the operation including the enemy and, on this day, death came to the enemy. Nisbet walked back to the tent; they cleaned guns and equipment, they rehydrated. It was mid-afternoon, lots of day left. After finishing up with the gear Nisbet laid back on his cot. He pulled his sweat-soaked, sweat-stained ball cap over his face. He never washed it. He closed his eyes and drifted off. The silence of Afghanistan had a way of lulling him to sleep and at the same time the ability to wake him from a nightmare into something altogether worse. There would be good days and bad. Take a life to save a life.

11

It Was a Mission Not an Occupation

Sergeant Gordon Cullen, Unit Master Sniper
Detachment 66, Task Force 1-10
Panjwai District, Kandahar Province, Afghanistan

A few days after Operation *Medusa* and the A-10 strafing of C Company, my det and I were still occupying our position on the northern side of Masum Ghar. By this time, we had the terrain around us memorized, much like the enemy we had been engaged with for the past two weeks. Looking out across the Arghandab River into the maze of mud huts and walls, I asked the boys, "What do you think is going to happen to this place when we leave?" I chuckled at the time, and still do to some degree, but the answer that came from behind the rifle was, "What the fuck can anyone do to this place that hasn't been done already." The Panjwai valley was stalled in time. I would only be guessing about whose thumb the locals were held down by or what ideology kept them from moving forward but these people had been through multiple occupations, warlord flexing and countless bouts of instability. We were just another intruder on their land and one day we would leave and someone else would take our place.

Fast forward to 2010. I am standing on the same ghar looking across the same river into the very familiar maze of mud huts and walls. The only things that had changed were the scars we'd left on the ground, more fortified positions for us to operate out of and improved roads for us to access their lives with. The little red generator on the north side of the river next to a half-destroyed grape hut that we had used for confirming zero during *Medusa* was still sitting in the tall grass. I know this sounds cold and perhaps a bit unsympathetic, but I never thought we were there to launch Afghanistan into the 21st century. I was there to ensure that radical and terrorist groups did not have a haven to train in and launch missions from. Even more important, my number one priority was to make sure that we, snipers, provided our brothers and partners the safest possible environment for conducting counterinsurgency missions through the prosecution of the enemy. During my three deployments to Afghanistan, I never once thought that anything we were doing was going to bring western society and beliefs to it.

So, recently I was asked how I felt about the U.S. departure from Afghanistan. My initial "military" response was, "Who cares, we left years ago." But the answer isn't that simple—as soon as the words left my lips, I felt ashamed and disloyal. I will leave the way they decided to exit the theatre and subsequent actions to try and ensure the safety of the local nationals employed by us to another author. My emotions came from another place.

Most of the missions that we were tasked with—based on intelligence over multiple deployments—involved conducting overwatch, hunting IED emplacement teams and actively pursuing areas of interest or increased insurgent activity. We would deploy forward of our friendly forces or in support of them to ensure we could interdict anyone looking to do them harm. We were very good at this. We understood the terrain and pattern of life throughout the area of operations and could vector in on oddities or peculiarities in the pattern of life. On a number of occasions, we were able to kill the enemy before he was able to cause harm to our friends, sometimes just moments before it would have been too late.

But we were just nine snipers trying to cover an expansive area of operations. I made recommendations to the chain of command where we should be focusing and followed orders to ensure the best possible support to operations. There was no way we could be everywhere. Snipers, in my opinion, are the sheepdogs. We take pride in watching over the flock, making sure our blanket of protection is spread as wide as possible. We would take unmentionable risks to ensure we were in a position to provide the best cover or drive as deep as possible into the enemy's happy place to protect our friends. So yes, friends, the friendly forces. Canada is a small military, and we are that group that when asked, probably does know the Mark you are talking about. When out providing that security, we saw who was on the ground. We knew by their walk or animated hand gestures exactly who was in the patrol we were providing support for. Often, we would comment on their antics as we passed real-time commentary on their next corner or the people in a compound they couldn't see—we didn't dehumanize the locals like the enemy we prosecuted.

The one thing that truly upset us was when one of our friends was killed or injured. We often thought that if we had been there, we could have stopped it. Of course, this was impossible to rationalize and, like many of our brothers, we compartmentalized the event in our brains with hopes to revisit later. As a rule, we always tried to ensure we talked about what had happened and how we felt. Ya, a little wish washy but having that brief moment of expression and understanding allowed us to stay focused. It also ensured that we continued to make solid decisions when identifying the enemy and not get emotional about what we were doing.

Unfortunately, during my tours in 2006 and 2010, we lost several friends, heroes every one of them. They volunteered, like all of us, and sacrificed their lives while fighting with their brothers. Again, I am not going to comment on the why. We all volunteered for our own reasons and deployed to fulfil what we thought was right. I do not and will not accept comments that Canadian soldiers died for no good reason—you just didn't have the honour of knowing what motivated them. I am fortunate to have fond and lasting memories of every one of my friends who didn't make it back alive. I hold them close and deep in my very compartmentalized brain. Periodically I will visit them and remember our times together, being diligent to coral them back up and secure them safely back in place.

How do I feel about the U.S. departure from Afghanistan and all the souls we left behind? I am indifferent. The question has so many layers that my previously mentioned compartmentalized brain needs to process. In the news the focus was on the local nationals we employed who were being hunted and persecuted for their duty to us. Hordes of people rushing to the airport and borders for evacuation: is this the question being asked, "How do I feel about leaving them there to fend for themselves?" During my deployments to Afghanistan, I did not have the need to interact with interpreters or locals. We relied on our abilities to develop and predict the locals' habits and what it looked like when bad guys came around.

However, there was one instance when this did not hold true. It was shortly after we had moved to Sperwan Ghar with the ODA and elements of C Company. There was still a good amount of bad guy activity in the area, but they had become sloppy. The fighters that we'd faced during the push on Objective Rugby had been replaced by what we referred to as the B Team. They were able fighters with decent equipment but lacked the experience of the A Team.

One afternoon we had an interpreter come up with his ICOM radio. As the bad guy transmissions were usually in plain, we used the same radios to listen in, and in the case of some very spicy ANA commanders, taunt the bad guys. On this day, we were listening to several bad guys who were trying to effect a link-up as one of them had a sackful of explosives that he was looking to get to his cell. We literally could not believe the, well, the naivety of these guys. Bad guy 1 comes on and says he is in the western end of the village with the explosives and wants to meet up with bad guy 2. Okay, let's start scanning the ground: a few fighting age males wandering around, one has a sack, the other a sack in a wheelbarrow. Bad guy 2 then says, "Hey my friend, let's meet at the small bridge on the edge of town." Cool. Wheelbarrow guy is off the hook: he's heading towards the river and there are no bridges in his path. Sack guy, if he turned left down the wadi, he would be right on target for lining up with a small footbridge. Confirmed, sack guy is bad guy 1. He has turned left and is metres away from the bridge. I should mention that this is all happening west of Sperwan, approximately three kilometres away from us. When all this had started, I got on the radio to see if there were any air assets on station that could provide PID (positive ID) and/or interdict. Luckily there was a Predator with about ten hours of loiter time still available. We had vectored the pilot on to the sack guy and through a couple of reference checks had ensured we were looking at the same guy. Now bad guy 1 is standing on the bridge and out of an adjacent compound comes bad guy 2 sporting an AK-47 across his back—that's PID. The Predator launches a Hellfire onto the bridge, kills bad guy 2. Now bad guy 1 is back on the radio looking for safe haven as the skies are raining death upon him. Bad guy 3 comes on the radio. We really can't believe this is happening.

"Come to my location my friend. I am in the compound with the blue door."

Scan the ground in the area: yup, one very distinct double blue door at a small compound in the vicinity of the bridge. Still need to confirm though. We send the grid of the possible insurgent location to higher to ensure a timely response. The interpreter, with his face in his hands, explains to us that the two are arguing about who is coming out or going in. He is in as much disbelief as us. The solution is that bad guy 1 will meet bad guy 3 at the door and give him the sack. The door opens and the sack is transferred, but at the exact second that custody of the sack is exchanged, the second Hellfire kills them both. Absolutely crazy; however, this was our only real interaction with an interpreter in Afghanistan.

I did later have the opportunity to work with a source handler to help identify a rat line (a safe path the bad guys used to move between positions), but this was the most intimate we were with a ventriloquist, as we often referred to them. So, the fact that these souls put themselves out there at our request to help shape and attrit the enemy is clear. The bad guys, as foolish as they sometimes were, also know that it was because of these local nationals that they lost comrades and ground. Was there a plan for them? I don't know. The young man on top of Sper with us had one. He was going to save his money and move his family to Pakistan where he had an uncle who would take them in. Did they all have a plan? I don't know. Was it our job to give them a plan or way ahead? Again, I don't know. So, when I say I am indifferent, I just mean that I would like to believe that the locals employed by NATO understood the risks and had the ability to plan ahead. Fool me once, shame on you; fool me twice, shame on me—this wasn't their first rodeo.

In retrospect I believe the question being asked of me was, was it all in vain? Did we just spend ten years fighting and dying in a foreign land for no good reason? Absolutely not. We were soldiers, this was our profession. What a cliché, but true. I joined the military to be part of something bigger and make a difference. It would be ridiculous to think that I was going to make a difference in the world, but I could make a contribution to my country and my brothers and sisters. We did what was asked of us regardless of political views or personal perceptions. We all wanted to do what we had been training to do for so many years. How accomplished would a teacher feel if he or she never had a pupil to teach? How successful would a lawyer be without a case to work on? It's no different for us. How are we supposed to gauge ourselves as soldiers without a war? It sounds callous but that's what the truth looks like sometimes. So, did my brothers get injured or die in vain? Absolutely not—my opinion. Am I saddened by the memories that were brought to the surface when asked about the departure from Afghanistan? Absolutely. I left a lot of me over there as many of us did and initially reacting to the question the way I did gave me a rush of confused feelings. We did what was asked of us to the best of our abilities. I will always remember our times over there and I will always honour my friends who didn't make it back. Afghanistan will find its way, whether leading or led.

To be fair, where haven't we left from before? These emotions and feelings aren't new to us. There will always be an inclination to place blame and say that lives have been wasted. We deploy on missions and conduct operations. What part of that makes anyone believe that we are staying? I have been to Bosnia twice, Kosovo once and Afghanistan three times. I believe the name of the game was stabilize not occupy.

12

Years Gone By

Barry Nisbet, Retired
Canada
2025

All things, all people change. I retired from the army in 2012. My life is not defined by Afghanistan, it was enriched by it and although my memories fade over time, how it has shaped my character will never fade. Pain, exuberance, loss, triumph, life, death, laughter, hate. These are just a sliver of the emotions I have felt. One does not trump another; they do not depreciate over time. I appreciate what Afghanistan taught me about me, and I hate Afghanistan for who and what it took from me.

I did not expect to win the war on terrorism. I was one soldier sent to do a job. Each and every time I went back, I asked myself if I did my job. I could change things I did, do better, different, smarter but that was inherent with experience. I could not change Afghanistan, a culture, a society, a way of life. I had no such ideas of grandeur. I am one soldier in an army, not an army of one.

As Afghanistan fell again to the Taliban in 2021, I felt indifferent. There was so much talk of what we had fought for, people complaining it was for nothing, lives lost for nothing. We all volunteered ... a soldier's profession is a perilous one, as old as time. People always fight, wars are always waged, and I did not and will not diminish those who lost their lives in Afghanistan by saying it was all for nothing.

There are moments of pure terror fused in my head, of the smell of death, the salty taste of my tears. What I saw and learned over five tours, three in Afghanistan, guides me now and every day, not always in a positive way. The flag-draped coffins I saluted and laid in the earth remind me of the fragility of life. I don't live my life for those who lost theirs. I live my life remembering those we lost. War is a cruel cold word to me; it is and will always be synonymous with death. That is how we gauge war, by the body count. My count is the bodies of my friends laid to rest and that was not for nothing. I only know why I fought, why I returned to fight. In those brief moments, now history, as we fought in a country thousands of miles away from our own, it was for something for each of us, dead, alive, or wounded.

Afghanistan did not define me, it refined me.

PART FOUR

The Future Looks Bright

13

The Future of Sniping

Gordon Cullen, Retired Master Sniper
Canada
2025

Meritorious Service Decorations (Military Division)
Warrant Officer Gordon Percy Cullen, M.S.M., C.D.
Meritorious Service Medal (Military Division)
Decoration awarded on June 22, 2012
Sergeant Gordon Percy Cullen, M.S.M., C.D.
St. James, Manitoba
Meritorious Service Medal (Military Division)
From April to November 2010, Sergeant Cullen served as
battle group master sniper. His frontline leadership
enabled his two sniper detachments to provide exceptional
support to ground forces operating in Afghanistan. In addition
to facilitating the conduct of numerous counter-insurgency
operations, he expanded the battle group's sniper capability
by personally mentoring soldiers from other units.

Regularly exposing himself to enemy fire in order to draw the enemy out, Sergeant Cullen was critical to the success of many operations.

In the early months of 2020, I had the opportunity to attend a five-eyes conference in Washington D.C. to look at addressing some of the equipment shortfalls facing us all. This weeklong meeting would look at everything from vehicles, weapons, communications equipment and cyber tools. After a very in-depth World brief by an intelligence officer, we started discussing the shortfalls in the extended long range sniper capability. This was a hot topic due to the changing landscape of the future battle space. Most of the participating countries special forces were expressing a requirement to extend the precision fire engagement band past three kilometers. This was mostly due to the technology that was being developed that would detect and engage their sniper teams. While discussing what the platform should look like, weight, barrel length etc., a UK representative piped up from the back row, "if I am going to engage anything at that range, I am going to send drones." The room literally fell silent as some very accomplished five-eyes SOF reps gazed in bewilderment at the two UK reps. Some in disgust as one of the reasons the new capability was being looked at was to defeat drones and some because their sniper souls had been slightly crushed by the thought of some joystick ranger replacing the capability of well trained and battle-hardened warriors. After the initial shock of the statement had worn off, and additional discussion about the employment of drones in addition to the increased precision rifle fire capability had been digested, more interest started swinging towards drone employment. Was this the writing on the wall for the future of snipers "just send drones"? The low cost, fire and forget, autonomous system that would never need to see a repatriation or ramp ceremony for its loss had piqued the interest of the leading nations in modern warfare. As we look to the future, the landscape of military operations and sniping is poised to undergo significant transformations. These changes will be driven by technological advancements, strategic innovations, and evolving geopolitical dynamics.

Prior to the war in Ukraine, as part of Operation *Unifier*, Canadian snipers were assigned a number of tasks to support Ukrainian sniper units. These included:

1. Instruct and qualify snipers in Desna;
2. Instruct and qualify sniper instructors in Desna;
3. Mentor sniper instructors in Zhytomyr;
4. Assist and mentor snipers in Berdychiv;
5. Assist AFU (Armed Forces of Ukraine) with the development of sniper courseware;
6. Assist in maintaining standards at each schoolhouse; and
7. Ensure the training of AFU sniper is inter-operable with NATO.

An example of the force laydown sees Canadian snipers located in Desna, Zhytomyr, Berdychiv and at the International Peacekeeping and Security Center (IPSC) near Lviv. Desna focused on the land forces, Zhytomyr the airborne/airmobile forces and Berdychiv the special forces.

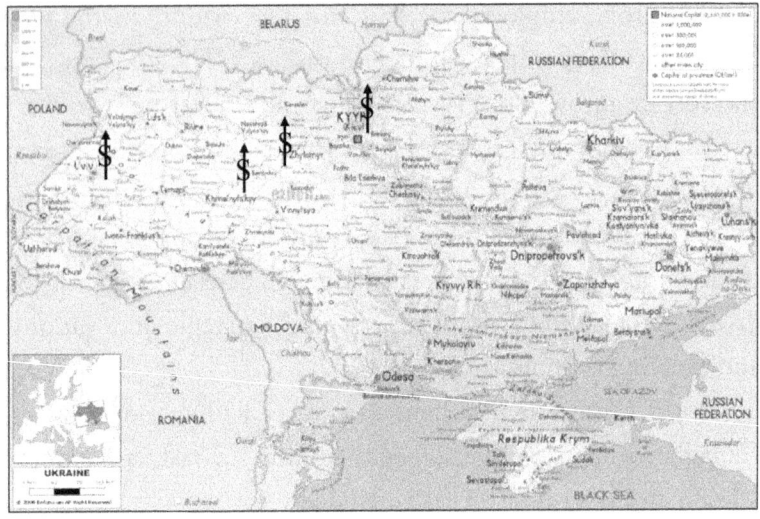

The situation in the ATO (Anti-Terrorist Operation Zone/ Donetsk and Luhansk regions) was continually evolving, forcing the AFU to push hard for sniper training and equipment to counter the pro-Russian insurgents. Many of the sniper teams were still employing SVDs (Dragunov sniper rifles), donated Remington 700s, and a small number of Desert Tech rifles against the insurgents.

February 24th 2022, the world watched Russia invade its neighbour, Ukraine. This ongoing action has seen the world unite in some respects and divide in others. Many nations have tried to come to the aid of the Ukraine financially and through sales and donations of military arms. This massive dumping of arms and more importantly, look behind the Russian curtain at its equipment and capability, has been the catalyst for military innovation. We now see what a conflict with a world power can look like and what tactics and weapons they are employing. For the Ukraine snipers this has been a massive learning curve, taking them from the basics of sniping into fighting against all the things we had been discussing in that conference in 2020. Operating in both rural and urban environments against a formidable and technologically advanced enemy, we have watched from the sidelines diligently taking notes, developing new tactics and conceptualizing new technology to aid us in a fight, should it come knocking on our door. From a military perspective, the war in the Ukraine is forcing the world to rapidly adapt to an overwhelming situation.

One of the most notable trends in the future of military operations is the increasing integration of autonomous systems and robotics. Unmanned aerial vehicles (UAVs), autonomous ground vehicles (AGVs), and robotic soldiers are set to play a pivotal role in enhancing battlefield efficiency and reducing human casualties. These systems will be equipped with advanced artificial intelligence (AI) capabilities, enabling them to perform complex tasks, such as reconnaissance, surveillance, and combat operations, with minimal human intervention.

Warrant Officer Curtis Allaby, former UMS, writes:

"Another hurdle for Snipers are Unmanned Aerial Systems (UAS) or 'Drones' as they are commonly referred to as. Drone Warfare has become prevalent in modern war fighting and proof of its effectiveness can be found in the current Russia-Ukraine war. Some of these drones come with long range thermal capabilities that can compromise a patrol not versed in counter UAS methods. Snipers have taken the initiative in compiling lessons learned from other nation's TTPs on how to both employ and avoid detection of drones. Employing UAS is nothing new as we had them

in Afghanistan. They were an asset for having eyes forward on enemy locations. Locating enemy positions down to the grid they were meant that indirect fire could be brought down on them with effective results. UAS would remain 'on station' for limited periods relaying real time data to patrols observing enemy behavior and posture."

AI and machine learning will revolutionize military decision-making and operational efficiency. Predictive analytics, real-time data processing, and autonomous decision-making systems will empower military commanders to make informed decisions swiftly. AI-driven algorithms will analyze vast amounts of data from various sources, including satellites, drones, and sensors, to provide actionable insights and optimize mission outcomes.

As digital infrastructure becomes increasingly integral to military operations, the threat of cyber warfare will escalate. Future conflicts will see an intensified focus on cybersecurity measures to protect critical systems and data from cyberattacks. Offensive cyber capabilities will be developed to disrupt enemy communications, disable infrastructure, and gather intelligence. The integration of quantum computing and encryption technologies will further enhance the resilience and security of military networks.

Directed energy weapons, such as lasers and microwave systems, are expected to revolutionize modern warfare. These weapons offer unparalleled precision and speed, capable of neutralizing threats with minimal collateral damage. Directed energy weapons will be deployed on various platforms, including aircraft, ships, and ground vehicles, providing a versatile and effective means of defense against enemy projectiles and drones.

So where does this leave the fate of Snipers and our mantra to be experts at Shoot-Move-Communicate? How will we fight in the technologically overmatched battle space as mere human beings? We will have to adapt like everyone else. The future of sniping will be characterized by unprecedented levels of precision and accuracy. Advances in optics, ballistics, and targeting systems will enable snipers to engage targets at greater distances with pinpoint accuracy. Smart scopes equipped with AI-powered targeting assistance will compensate for environmental factors such as wind, humidity, and temperature, ensuring precise shots even in challenging conditions. Snipers will employ drones to overwatch their movement, provide deception or assist in their strike capability. These are the obvious and easiest advancements to be made through research and development, partnering with our five-eye friends and leaning even harder on industry to push the envelope we are seeing develop. The hard part is transforming our already small numbers into the modern warriors they need to become. The basics will always be the basics, and they will always need to be mastered, but now the expectation of the follow-on training needs to have as much weight as the core training.

WO Curtis Allaby writes:

"In 23 years, I've been a rifleman, LMG/GPMG gunner, LAV driver and LAV gunner. I also served in Mortar Platoon with the 81mm and Anti-Armour Platoon operating the TOW system. With these weapons I've shot at a lot of things, farther than anything I've ever hit with a bolt gun. That said, nothing is ever as satisfying. Maybe it's the fact that to get the rifle into an effective position to shoot, you must get yourself there. A vehicle or aircraft might

assist in getting you partially there but at some point, you're walking or crawling in. This is most likely done navigating shit terrain with a ruck that feels like it's trying to pull you down into the earth. Once at your destination your reward for all that hard work you've done so far is a day or two spent lying in god knows what type of weather until it's time for you to engage. The stress of making a successful shot and the exhilaration you feel when you do, comes from analyzing the terrain relative to the distance of the target, studying the environmental conditions and determining the proper sight settings on your optics."

Currencies and qualifications will need to maintained, cross training with other arms to ensure interoperability with loitering munitions and higher ISR are practiced and efficient.

Arpad Kavanaugh, sniper, writes:

"Thinking shooters bridging old ideas, skills and SOPs with new technology and threat models to evolve ahead of the curve and stay lethal and relevant. Especially in the peace time army that is the CAF, never becoming complacent and never settling for good enough, as the skills, drills, SOPs and mindset we fuel and embed into the new generation, even if we never see war ourselves need to be of the highest standard as the generations we pass on will eventually have to use them. Just as the generations that went to war and learned lessons in blood, passed that on to who they taught."

The really hard part will be keeping the units interested in their snipers and the maintenance of the program. Historically snipers are a "break glass in case of war" asset. When we are needed, all of the light and support is on us. We are amazing force multipliers who operate at the very tip of the pointy end. But, when there is no conflict or interest, we are prima donnas pulling at the purse strings of the Battalions. We are sidelined and forced to eke out our existence scrounging for range time and training. This cycle of self-destruction has been the norm for the last 30 years. Breaking this cycle will be the only way to achieve success and create a sniper program that will survive the conflicts waiting at our door. In the early 2000's the re-org of the Sniper Group was discussed in order to make it into a Platoon, this needs to happen.

WO Curtis Allaby writes:

"Over the past couple of decades, the Sniper Group was detached from Recce Platoon. Previously, snipers were a part of Recce but at some point during our involvement in Afghanistan, that changed. The group is run by only sniper-qualified personnel and that means no officer. This leaves all training and mission planning to snipers in the group at the NCO level. As such we rely on the soldiers to maintain a certain level of professionalism and fitness that is higher than that throughout the unit."

Snipers need to be properly equipped, properly led and properly employed. This may need to look a little different than the traditional grouping and higher commands like the Brigade that they belong to may need to play a larger role in their success. The line between the green army and the special forces needs to be greyed out a little to ensure lesson learned and enhancements to capability are shared, allowing both groups to benefit from the collaboration. The cause needs to be championed by people who can implement change and guarantee sustainability, or we will forever be eating our tail...preach over. Snipers will evolve with conflicts and meet the technological requirements to bring the fight to the bad guys. It's only a question of what we are willing to lose in order to achieve it.

14

Where we've been, Where they're going

This project was a long time coming. We have Mir Bahmanyar to thank, his passion and persistence convinced us to put pen to paper. To him we will always be grateful for the opportunity and confidence he had in us.

Looking back at our stories on the page, it was difficult to impart our experiences as snipers in training and combat. Can words accurately depict our experiences that elicited so many primal feelings and emotion's? We hope we did some service to the reader and the sniper community in these pages. These stories are but a few, our fellow snipers from the Princess Patricia's Canadian Light Infantry (PPCLI), Royal 22e Regiment (Van Doo's), U.S. Green Berets (ODA), and JTF 2 (Joint Task Force 2) all shared time and battlespace with us. Their contributions in Afghanistan are certainly not lost on us. We thank them for the knowledge they passed on and time spent together as we rotated in and out of Afghanistan.

JTF 2, and their snipers, always welcomed us when we arrived in country. Their facilities, food, and most importantly time spent conversing on the range was invaluable technically and in confidence gained, we thank you. We understand that their testing and training with large caliber weapons took a significant mental and physical toll on their shooters, contributing to many cases of TBI (Traumatic Brain Injuries). They did this so that we didn't have to, but sometimes you need deeds, not words.

We all became snipers for different reasons and it is something we all hold near and dear to our heart. It is a brotherhood, with its own language, traditions, and standards. It's much more than shooting. It's not for everyone but for those who have successfully completed the training, and been called a sniper, it is something we identify as. For those of us who have deployed as snipers in combat, and came back, it becomes part of your DNA. We will forever be snipers.

Others have come and taken our place, as they should. We don't want to hump up a mountain with 100lbs of gear in blistering heat, although we would all still try if needed. We stepped into Afghanistan with no combat experience, green. We left battle hardened, experienced, and all with a sense of loss on different levels. Many soldiers felt that when Afghanistan fell back to the Taliban that everything we fought for was for nothing. Combat experience is not nothing. Combat experience is invaluable, it is how we learn, how we get better, and if that knowledge can save just one life in the next mission, then how could anyone say it was for nothing. We pass that knowledge on when we train, teach, from lessons learned, to the stories we share.

Train like you fight, it will help when RPG's scream by, when bullets ricochet and buzz around you, when an IED blows you off your feet and you're calling in a medivac for your comrade who lost his. We train and train and train until one day our boots are hitting the ground in a foreign country some of us couldn't find on a map. *Am I ready for this? Can I actually do this?* We all had doubt, but the confidence in our training and abilities helped to silence it. We start to put all that training to the test, embedded in that training is combat experience gained by our predecessors. We walk, fly, and crawl into combat. We shoot, strafe, and bomb the enemy as they shoot and detonate IED's from above and below. We experience the highs and lows of combat. We learn to fight, we evolve, we adapt.

We deployed to Afghanistan as snipers, but we did not know how to *be* snipers in Afghanistan. We had to learn on the ground, listening to those who had gone before us, step by step, shot by shot, mission by mission. Through our successes and failures, we got better, but it always came at a great cost.

This book is a snippet of what a handful of Canadian Snipers experienced and learned in Afghanistan. We had to adapt from green to tan, from the boreal forests to red deserts and rock. If we didn't, we would die.

Our experiences are rare, between 2001 and 2014 more than 40,000 Canadian Armed Forces members served in Afghanistan. Of those, we would estimate less than 160 deployed as snipers, less than thirty deployed as a sniper a second time.

The next theatre of operations, where ever it may be, will present new challenges to snipers who, like us, will begin with no combat experience. Simply put they will have to adapt, as we did, and gain experience by listening to those who have gone before them, step by step, shot by shot, mission by mission. Then come home and pass on those experiences, lessons learned, and stories.

158 members lost their lives in Afghanistan. Could this number have been less with more of us? This is a question few of

us may actually know the answer to. We will always remember Afghanistan by the lives we lost, not the lives we took.

Without Warning, Without Remorse.

Pro Patria

APPENDIX A

Army Lessons Learned Centre
Land Force Doctrine and Training System
PO Box 17000, Station Forces
Kingston ON K7K 7B4

3333-1 (ALLC)

6 October 2009

Distribution list

LESSON SYNOPSIS REPORT
(09-013) EMPLOYMENT OF SNIPERS

Ref: A. 3350-1 (ALLO JTF-Afg), Topic Lessons Report (TLR) 09/013, Employment of Snipers Update, Dated 26 Aug 09 (SECRET not enclosed)
B. 3350-1 (TFK Tech LO ROTO 7) Theatre Lessons Report (TLR) 010/09 Requirement for Effective Cooling in Armoured Vehicles - dated 17 August 09 (UNCLASSIFIED, not enclosed)

(U)   GENERAL

1.   The purpose of this report is to review the employment of snipers and highlight the major observations and lessons stemming from the employment of snipers in ops within COE Afghanistan. Observations were reported by the sniper teams, the master sniper, key Battle Group (BG) personnel deployed and the Army Lessons Liaison Officer (ALLO) during the past summer months within Afghanistan. This summary report covers the following topics on the Army Critical Topics List (CTL): Force Protection, Train as You Fight and Equip as

You Fight. The classified reference documents must be consulted in order to obtain additional information.

(U) KEY THEATRE ACTIONS/OBSERVATIONS

2.   Background. Snipers have been recognized as some of the best soldiers in the Army. Indeed, snipers represent a significant asset for the BG CO to influence the mission. Snipers have proven to be very useful in Counter-Insurgency environments and especially within the Contemporary Operational Environment (COE) of Afghanistan.

3.   Operating Environment. A sniper detachment is often required to work in adverse conditions. They must be mentally ready, conscious of their duties and the environment to successfully complete the mission while frequently deployed in a hostile area. Operating in very difficult and complex terrain, most times in extreme weather conditions averaging 40°C, and at times 50°C during the warm months; having to carry the heaviest amount of mission and survival equipment, it is very demanding for snipers to move between positions of engagements. As such, they will occasionally have to rely on ground or aviation assets to cover their initial movement.

For the planers, there is a requirement to consider and coordinate numerous logistical and security aspect.

4.   Situational Awareness (SA) Structure. In order for the sniper group to prepare for their missions, they must have access to the most up to date Intelligence, Imaging and situation reports concerning the battle space. Doctrinally snipers are integrated and complement the BG ISTAR plan and provide a significant amount of vital information.

5.   Force Protection. In the COE of Afghanistan, a sniper detachment is the minimum entity of manning to operate safely and efficiently. This small grouping does not provide them the possibility to use vehicles. Therefore, they are required to use other resources within TFK to move closer to their objectives. See Ref A. 8. a, e, j, n and 9. a. (1).

(U) KEY LESSONS

6.   The following lessons identified and recommendations are from the perspective of the soldiers and HQ personnel deployed on

operations. Key lessons from Ref A. are categorized in the DOTMP format in order to focus SME review of issues:

a. Doctrine/ITP.

(1) Imagery/Intelligence Priority. The BG established a series of priorities to identify their key positions and sub-organisations who can gain access to imagery/geo products from BG and TFK Intelligence assets. See Ref A., para 8. b.;

(2) Insertion and Extraction. As a best practice, snipers in COE Afg adapted their TTP to fit the situation and the resources avail. See Ref A., para 8., e.;

(3) Snipers and the ISTAR plan. Because of their specific capabilities, equipment and modus operandi in BG ops, snipers represent a very significant asset to be employed to support the BG ISTAR plan; and

(4) Op Tempo versus Rest. Commanders and Planners at all level should be aware of the factors that may impact the snipers capacity to perform their duties. The harsh environment (long exposure to heat, complex terrain, weight of the equipment, limitations, etc.) conspire to limit sniper ops. The sniper battle rhythm and modus operandi must be adjusted accordingly.

b. Organization.

(1) TO&E. TO&E issues pertaining to BG sniper assets in Afghanistan are described in Ref A 8.a. and n. Consideration to increase their numbers should be considered; and

(2) Force Protection. In order to preserve a minimum force protection level for the snipers deployed forward, there is a requirement to use integral sniper detachments. When possible, local

protection for snipers should be provided by other troops.

C.   <u>Training</u>.

    (1)   <u>Pre-Deployment Training (PDT)</u>. It is essential to conduct thorough screening throughout PDT and to select only the most suitable soldiers for the job. In Addition, when planning to include snipers on a collective exercise, a plan should be in place to provide specific sniper training, such as challenging ranges where they can maintain and improve their shooting skill using different sniper weapons through a variety of scenarios; and

    (2)   <u>Use of Mentors</u>. It is recommended that mentors and veterans from past rotations assist in the planning and execution of pre-deployment training for the BG sniper group.

D.   <u>Material and Equipment</u>.

    (1)   Sniper Equipment. Since accuracy is a critical aspect of sniping, there should be enough rifles and eqpt purchased to allow the snipers to train and deploy the same weapons and equipment used during RTHR as operations; and

    (2)   Liaison with DLR 5. Direct liaison between the Master Snipers in units and DLR 5 is very successful and has resulted in improved sniper equipment and keeping snipers informed of the new technologies relating to them. It is recommended that this liaison be maintained.

E.   <u>Policy</u>

    (1)   Security Clearance. Due to the sensitivity Op SEC nature of their work, snipers must receive the necessary level of classification access prior to deployment; and

(2)   Rules of Engagement. There are some considerations to maintain the delegation level of ROE 421 and 422. See Ref A., para 8, c. and d.

SUMMARY

7.   Snipers have been recognized as a key asset within the BG operating in Afghanistan. They play a crucial part in planning and conducting high risk COIN operations, and they are considered a substantial force multiplier. Snipers operating in Afghanistan must operate in a most challenging and extreme environment, one that impacts' on their mission success. It is essential that commanders and planners at all levels have a thorough understanding of Sniper capacities and limitations to exploit their full potential. Snipers should continue to be provided with the best training, equipment and support available.

Maj
SO Ops ALLC

Distribution List Action
LFDTS Kingston//COS/DAT/DAD/PSTC/IA TF
CMTC Wainwright//Comd/COS CMTC/CMTC LL Cell OIC
CTC Gagetown//COS AITA/AITA TDO Coord

Information
NDHQ Ottawa//LF COS STRAT/DG /DLR /DLFD/C-IED TF
NDHQ Ottawa CEFCOM HQ//Comd/COS/J7 LL LFDTS Kingston//ATA
NDHQ Ottawa//LF COS OP/G3 NDHQ Ottawa//SJS DSR
NDHQ Ottawa CANCOM HQ//COS/17
NDHQ Ottawa CANSOFCOM HQ//COS/17 LL NDHQ Ottawa CANOSCOM HQ//COS/J7
LFDTS Kingston//DAT Plans/OTS/G3/CFLCSC/PSTC/DLSE
LFWA HQ Edmonton//G3/COS
LFCA HQ Toronto//G3//TF 1-10 LFAA HQ Halifax//G3
LFQA HQ Monteal//COS/G3 TF 6-09/COS TF 3-10
DLCD Kingston//COS/DLSC

ABOVE: 63C's OP during Op Medusa, 2006.
BELOW: A side view of 63C's OP during Op Medusa, 2006.

ABOVE: The terrain in front of 63C's OP during Op Medusa, 2006.
BELOW: Gord Cullen resting behind 63A's position, Op Medusa 2006.

ABOVE: *Houlihan preparing to fire with Gord Cullenas his spotter, Op Medusa, 2006.*
BELOW: *63C on the move near Zangabad Ghar. In the distance is a "grape hut," a thickwalled building often used by insurgents.*

ABOVE: *A sniper waiting in ambush, Afghanistan, 2006.*
BELOW: *The tools of the trade. From left to right, a C-15, C-14 and AR-10 rifle.*

ABOVE: Cullen and Nisbet in position at Sperwan Ghar, 2006.
BELOW: Gord Cullen takes a break on patrol, 2006.

ABOVE: *Group photo of battlegroup's snipers, 2006.*
BELOW: *Barry Nisbet resting in a rooftop position, 2006.*

ABOVE: Snipers on patrol, Afghanistan 2006.
BELOW: Air support striking a target near Sperwan Ghar, 2006.

ABOVE: *The sniper position at Sperwan Ghar, 2006.*
BELOW: *66A in COP Ballpeen, 2010.*

ABOVE: Barry Nisbet stalking on basic sniper course, 2005.

About the Authors

GORD CULLEN, a 28-year veteran of the Canadian Armed Forces, was born in St James Assiniboia, Manitoba, but spent much of his childhood in Whitehorse Yukon. He began his career as a soldier with the 1st Battalion the Royal Canadian Regiment with postings to the Lake Superior Scottish Regiment, 3rd Battalion the Royal Canadian Regiment and CANSOFCOM. His deployments include two tours to Bosnia, a tour in Kosovo, three tours in Afghanistan and a short deployment to Poland. Gords employment with Snipers started as a part of the Sniper Group deployed with 1 RCR in Kosovo but culminated as the Battle Group Master Sniper for Task Force 3-06 and Task Force 1-10 in Afghanistan.

He concluded his military career as Sniper Program Manager for one of the CANSOFCOM units, where he helped shape their Sniper program and enhance their capability. Gord has been awarded the Meritorious Service Medal for action during combat, the Commander CEFCOM Commendation for action during combat in Kandahar and the Commander in Chief Commendation as part of the 1 RCR Battle Group during Operation MEDUSA.

Following his retirement from the Canadian Forces, Gord continues to serve the Canadian Armed Forces from the private sector. Gord remains passionate about Canadian Snipers and supporting their continued success as a board member with the Canadian Sniper Association. He continues to reside in the Ottawa Valley with his family.

BARRY NISBET joined the Canadian Forces in 1997. He completed RCR battle school graduating at the top of his class and was posted to the 1 Royal Canadian Regiment in Petawawa. He completed numerous courses including Airborne School, mortars, machine gunner, communications, Light Armoured Vehicle Gunner, reconnaissance, Basic Sniper, Sniper Detachment Commander, and Advanced Sniper. In 2003 he completed U.S. Army Ranger School, the first at the rank of Corporal in the Canadian Forces. He deployed to Kosovo in 1999 and Bosnia in 2003 as a rifleman. His first tour to Afghanistan was to Kabul in 2005. In 2006 he deployed to Kandahar as a sniper, call sign 63C, taking part in Operation *Medusa*. He received the Chief of Defence Staff Commendation for professionalism and leadership while rendering first aid to a severely injured soldier, 1 RCR Battle Group, Joint Task Force Afghanistan, 11 January 2007. Barry taught on multiple basic sniper courses in Petawawa training soldiers from the 1st and 3rd RCR Battalions and Canadian Special Operations Regiment. He returned to Afghanistan in 2010 as a Sniper Detachment Commander, call sign 66A, this was his 5th and final deployment before retiring as a Sergeant in 2012.

MIR M. BAHMANYAR brings a unique perspective to military history having lived in four countries across three continents. He holds a BA in History from UC Berkeley, then enlisted in the

Second Battalion, 75th Ranger Regiment, and earned an MA in War Studies from King's College London. His jobs have included library clerk, janitor, bookstore owner, security services, military technical advisor, German language coach, producer and writer in Hollywood. He also writes thrillers.

DOUBLE✝DAGGER
— www.doubledagger.ca —

Double Dagger Books is Canada's only military-focused publisher. Conflict and warfare have shaped human history since before we began to record it. The earliest stories that we know of, passed on as oral tradition, speak of war, and more importantly, the essential elements of the human condition that are revealed under its pressure.

We are dedicated to publishing material that, while rooted in conflict, transcend the idea of "war" as merely a genre. Fiction, non-fiction, and stuff that defies categorization, we want to read it all.

Because if you want peace, study war.

Index

www.ingramcontent.com/pod-product-compliance
Lightning Source LLC
Chambersburg PA
CBHW061557120626
46550CB00004B/1521